WHAT SIZE BALLS DO I NEED?

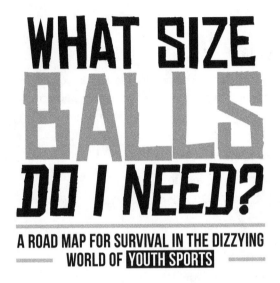

WHAT SIZE BALLS DO I NEED?

A ROAD MAP FOR SURVIVAL IN THE DIZZYING WORLD OF **YOUTH SPORTS**

STEVE MORRIS

Printed in the United States of America

Hardcover ISBN: 978-1-7352033-0-0
Paperback ISBN: 978-1-7352033-2-4
E-book ISBN: 978-1-7352033-1-7

Cover Design: Alan Morris
Cover Illustration: The Imagists
Author's Photograph: Mary Beth DeLucia
Interior Design: Creative Publishing Book Design

For Marcy, Evan, Dori and Griffie

Table of Contents

Foreword

The word "genius" gets tossed around pretty lightly. People hear a piece by Mozart or a Beatles tune and think: *Genius.*

Oh, please. Music. Big deal.

The word genius is so overused that some people – not me – but some people even use it to describe a perfectly ordinary guy like Isaac Newton.

Gravity. That's what Isaac Newton discovered. You know the story. An apple fell on his head and Sir Isaac realized . . . what? That things fall down? Seriously. What did people think before that happened? That apples fell *up*?

No. I do not use the word genius lightly. Other people may, but not me.

Steve Morris is a genius. Of that I am sure.

You want proof? Fine. Let me tell you about my son Clay. Great kid. Well, now he's a great twenty-four-year-old man. But not that long ago, a great kid. Sweet. A bit anxious. Well, more than a bit. But so sweet. You know the kind of kid. Maybe you were like that. Maybe your kid is.

Clay was not a natural athlete. When he got his first hit playing T-ball, he watched the ball for a bit and then started running. Unfortunately, he got confused and ran straight to third base, which most umpires discourage. Worse (worse for me, his pretty anxious dad), Clay sometimes didn't play. Sometimes he'd just watch, because that was less scary for him than playing.

First day of a summer camp called Coach Steve's Summer of Fun, Clay was nervous. I hung around with him for a while, assured him that he'd have a great time, told him everything was going to be fine, that he'd make lots of new friends. Then I went home and cried like a baby. Because I knew that Clay wasn't going to have a great time, that everything wasn't going to be fine, and that he wasn't going to make lots of new friends – because he was going to spend the whole day just watching other kids have fun.

I know. You're waiting for the part where Steve is a genius. Here it comes.

The next morning when I took Clay to camp, Steve, standing in the middle of a pack of about 537 kids, looked up and shouted, "All right! We can get started. The General is here!" The kids cheered. Clay instantly grew about a foot and a half and ran off to join his new friends.

Steve had seen Clay that first day when I wasn't around, but more than that, he'd seen something inside of Clay. I had told Clay that everything would be all right, but Steve found a way to *make* it all right by giving Clay chances to lead, and by helping the bravest, happiest, boldest version of my son leap to the front. He hadn't just given Clay a cool nickname that first day; he'd found a way to let my son actually be that guy, The General, leader of kids. Something changed for Clay that summer. He was still the sweet, thoughtful little guy I'd always known, but he also stayed The General.

Steve Morris did that. For real.

Steve knows that joy and play can be the best possible ways for kids to grow into their best selves. He knows that scared kids can become leaders and that fun should never be a four-letter word. Fun is important. Fun, Steve figured out, is the way you find out who you want to be and how to become that person.

So if Steve Morris is talking about anything to do with kids, fun, or sports, I'm listening. You can keep your Isaac Newton. Steve Morris turned my scared five-year-old into a bold leader. The man is truly a genius.

Claude Knobler
Dad and Author of *More Love, Less Panic:*
7 Lessons I Learned About Life, Love, and
Parenting After We Adopted Our Son from Ethiopia

First Touch: Why Are We Here?

Mᵧ son Evan's first word was "ball." I was pretty sure that in the history of first words, it wasn't the first time that one was uttered, but for me it was Columbus sighting land, Isaac Newton plunked by the apple, and Roger Maris hitting that sixty-first home run to break Babe Ruth's record, all rolled into one. I hit the local Big 5 and loaded up the cart with Nerf balls, beach balls, golf balls, baseballs, whiffle balls, footballs, tennis balls, playground balls, basketballs and soccer balls. Evan was just nine months old, but I had to be ready.

Over the next couple of years he bounced from ball to ball, throwing this one, shooting that one, hitting or kicking another one, and tumbling over most of the others. Like every other parent in sports-crazy America, I only wanted the best for my son, and if that meant a baseball card with his picture on it or a Nike endorsement deal, I was good with that. In my saner moments, I just hoped that sports would provide him with health and happiness, enduring friendships, and memories to relish when his knees gave out.

One morning a few years later, Evan leaped onto the bed with the declaration, "Dad, it's time to play soccer."

"Sure, Ev, in a little while." I rolled over. "Isn't *Rocket Power* on?" Then I was just about sleeping again . . .

"*Da-aad!* Not you and me in the backyard. *Real* soccer. With a coach."

Evan was still in preschool, and organized sports was already invading my sleep. I did some research and found out from Tony, the other dad who regularly showed up to croak along to "Wheels on the Bus," that there was a thriving class of three- and four-year-old budding superstars taking soccer lessons over in Westwood. Like many parents of firstborns entering sports, I jumped in, only to find the water deeper and the current more perilous than I expected. Welcome to youth sports.

Ball + Kid = Fun. That was the foolproof equation my friends and I got to prove every afternoon, riding our bikes to the field, choosing up sides and playing till homework or dinner beckoned us home. We shaved bases in the dirt with the heels of our Keds. We argued "out" or "safe," then settled it with a do-over. And we kept score but forgot it by morning. Since the waning days of the last century, though, an upheaval in the youth sports universe, rocket-fueled by changes in technology and the culture at large, has relegated our recreational formula to the realm of ancient history (but with a caveat we'll get to later).

Some changes have ushered in tangible benefits – increased opportunities for personal growth, social development, and community building. Others invite us to the edge of the abyss, where negative coaches, predatory programs, and destructive agendas are waiting to swallow up our children and families. The decisions we make as parents trigger ramifications that can reach far beyond what we may be aware of in the moment. Now, Ball + Kid = Confusion.

* * *

It's been a blur of years since I stepped onto that first soccer field with Evan. During that time, I went from parent to coach to Coach Administrator (essentially, head coach) of our AYSO (American Youth Soccer Organization) region. I've spent fourteen years on the board of local soccer club LA Breakers FC (formerly FC Los Angeles, formerly Galaxy Alliance SC, formerly Real Madrid . . . back to the beginning of time), serving as chairman and field coordinator. And I've coached or managed a few squads shy of fifty teams. Thousands of kids have cascaded through my sports programs and camps, including Evan's younger siblings, Dori and Griffie. What I've learned from my time in the trenches fills the pages of this book.

What Size Balls Do I Need? is meant to be a perspective injection for parents, a road map for navigating the bumpy stretches and blind curves in the ever-changing landscape of youth sports. As our kids frolic on the field and in the gym, developing athletic and social skills that they will call upon for the rest of their lives, it is we, the parents, who hold the power to make these wonder years truly wonderful. Riffing on the advice of a former mentor, "If it were easy, someone else would be doing it," we parents need to be tireless in resisting the drift toward specialization and professionalization. There's a reason the two dirtiest words in the lexicon of youth sports are "potential" and "expectation."

The push to maximize potential and exceed expectations feeds into one of the most insidious narratives driving today's culture: that children need to be rigorously prepared to excel from their earliest years. We're told that intense focus and specialization will help them to compete in high school, in college, and ultimately, in life. Youth sports, as a microcosm of society, has morphed into an extension of that worldview. Kids in competitive sports programs confront higher expectations, increased demands on their time and energy, and fewer opportunities to discover life at their own pace.

Being your child's champion in this arena means exercising a healthy skepticism in the face of relentless pressure and persuasive mission statements that promise college glory in exchange for three practices a week and three grand a year. It's also important to stand up for the old-school concept of recreational play in multiple sports as the optimal way to meet a child's need for emotional, mental and physical growth. Oh, yeah, and happiness.

"*What size balls do I need?*" is asked by almost all rookie coaches or those moving into higher divisions, as each age group utilizes different equipment. But the humorously anatomical question invites a deeper probing. It's really asking: "How courageous do I need to be to enter this universe with my kid? What am I in for? What's it going to cost me? Are the other parents going to drive me crazy? What am I going to get out of it?" This road map should point you in the right direction by demystifying the process and sifting the helpful from the hype. We'll consider the agonies, the ecstasies, and the epiphanies that will increase your understanding of what the ten-year window of youth sports is all about.

Youth sports aren't just a means to an end, or a box to be checked on a college application. They have the power of a life-affirming, transformative force. But to make sure that force is with you, we must ask the tough questions and push back against the professionalization of today's children.

To that end, I offer specific strategies to help avoid destructive coaches and programs while reconnecting with the lessons of youth sports that are most valuable to our kids: commitment, cooperation, empathy, sportsmanship, and civic responsibility, among others. These values can help rebalance a culture of entitlement where all too often we expect more, but give less.

In my experience, "youth sports" is life felt to the fullest. There are no higher highs or lower lows. We thrill to the goals scored, the balls caught, the races won, and feel the sharp sting of a missed shot, a ball dropped or a close game lost. The good news is that the slump of those tiny shoulders slinking back to the car will be gone by the time you get to the front of the In-N-Out drive-thru line. For children, youth sports exist exclusively in the present tense. Ten minutes ago is ancient history; ten minutes from now – who can contemplate such a distant future?

Most kids couldn't care less about getting onto the "right" club team to "maximize" their college prospects. They just want to have fun. The sooner we acknowledge this, the better we'll be able to appreciate the experience for what it is: kids playing games.

As Griffie, my younger son, was nearing the end of his high school soccer career, his team made a thrilling run in the playoffs. The semifinals were on deck, followed by a post-game Senior Day ceremony to highlight the careers of the graduating class. But as the day loomed, I found myself anxious and antsy. I wanted the boys to do well as a reward for their years-long commitment to the game, their love for each other, and the lifetime of sweet memories a victory would provide. I confessed my agitation to Gary, a similarly passionate dad, who put everything in perspective. "Relax. This is kids' sports. It's all good."

And it was "all good" – until a stunning golden goal in overtime sent the boys crashing out of the playoffs. As the other team celebrated across the field, our sideline was consumed by a silence that screamed of heartbreak and dashed dreams. Through tears and pain, the boys hugged and consoled each other, while the coaches stood to the side wading through their own grief. The last thing anyone wanted was to proceed with the Senior Day observance. And yet, the show must go on, and after a rocky start, with emotional gears grinding, slowly a few smiles broke through the gloom. As each senior was toasted – and roasted – the mood brightened. No amount of Listerine could rinse away the bitter taste shared by all, but the humorous "war" stories and the embrace of community initiated the healing. The boys and their parents were reminded of the distance they had traveled, from fledglings to skilled practitioners of an artful game, pursuing their passion and growing into young adults through the experience. Evident was a joy that even the disaster of a career-closing defeat couldn't extinguish.

Before you know it, your child's ten-year window will close and his or her time in the world of youth sports will be over. What you make of it between now and then will be determined by the goals you set as a family and your level of preparedness, patience and stamina in striving to reach them. I hope this book will be a useful guide to help you make wise decisions, protect and empower your kids, and get the most from this wonderful adventure. The stories you'll find throughout the book are all true, although I changed some names to avoid unintentionally embarrassing anyone.

Today, the baker's dozen of knee-high knuckleheads that greeted me on the first day of Coach Steve's soccer class tower over me as they proceed into adulthood. What at the outset felt like an endless highway filled with long weekends and marathon car rides bookending countless games proved to be just a brief pit stop in the much longer journey of these kids' lives.

I've come to realize that sports are but a slim chapter, not the whole book. I've also learned to appreciate the sage wisdom in this advice: Close your mouth and open your heart. Count your blessings that the little person who has your name, your face, and the purity of who you once were, wants to get out on that field and do it again. Celebrate your kid. Savor every moment. And for as long as it lasts, have a ball.

CHAPTER ONE

Coach Ray and the Big Bang

Coach Ray was an imposingly sculpted figure of bravado and charm who offered soccer classes for three- to five-year-olds in our area. Evan was a few months into four and bored with kicking a ball in the backyard. So when I heard from my friend Tony that his irrepressible, Samson-curled son Jacob was taking a soccer class, I hounded him for details. With an air of proprietary mystery, he said he'd contact Coach Ray first to make sure it was OK for me to call him. After all, this was Los Angeles, where everyone has layers of social insulation. Why not a soccer coach?

A few nights later, the phone rang at ten o'clock. Friends with little kids certainly wouldn't be calling that late and who else did we really know anymore? Though I was tempted to let it go to the answering machine, something made me pick it up.

"Is this Steve?" The voice on the other end was DJ-worthy, deep and smooth. "It's Ray."

Ray, Ray . . . Ray, who the hell was . . . *oh!*

"Coach Ray?"

"Hey man. Tony told me you're a writer. Movies or TV?"

Wow, so much for easing into a conversation. Coach Ray peppered me with questions about my latest projects. Who was my agent? What was I working on? Was I an action guy or could I write comedy? Did I know so-and-so from CAA, whose kid was in his program? *Isn't this supposed to be about soccer? About the kids?* I wondered uneasily. But Tony (who'd never read anything I had written) must have praised me as if I had a trophy case overflowing with Academy Awards and I didn't want to disappoint.

Leaning up against the kitchen counter, curling and un-curling the phone cord around my finger, I was initially amused and then weirded out, as I realized I was being vetted to make sure I was cool enough to have my kid play four-year-old soccer. After a half an hour of industry-based banter, Ray abruptly ended the conversation: "I'll see you on Tuesday. Bring a check." Phew. I made it.

Tuesday came and I couldn't tell who was more excited, Evan or me. Actually I do know. It was me. No writing got done that day as all my energy was directed toward the 4:00 class. I had no idea what to expect. Tony wasn't much help. He volunteered that the kids played a lot of soccer, then they sat on miniature chairs for a drink and at the end, Coach Ray would toss candy on the ground and they'd dive for it as if it were kiddie crack. Tony nailed it, sort of. The class consisted of that, a whole lot more, which he had judiciously kept to himself.

That afternoon, twenty four-year-olds descended on the soccer field, raucously rebounding off each other as if in an invisible bounce house, while their moms sat on blankets arrayed around the periphery.

No one seemed to be in charge. No Coach Ray. Nothing was set up. So we all just waited. Jacob hadn't arrived either so Evan stood close by, intrigued by the chaos but unready to commit.

After a few minutes, a gleaming black Dodge Ram 1500 roared into the lot. Ray, flashing a swashbuckling smile, jumped out, grabbed a bulging duffel from the truck bed and bounded toward the kids. Their demolition derby halted and they froze, waiting . . . Ray tossed his bag to the side. The thud as it hit the ground split open the zipper and I was able to see the goodies stuffed inside: boxes of soccer shoes, shin guards, T-shirts, water bottles and kid-sized backpacks to carry it all in.

"Everybody get a ball. Let's go."

The kids snapped to attention like mini cadets, collected the balls and dribbled to the edge of the field. I nudged Evan ahead of me as we ventured toward the coach. Ray spotted us without turning his head.

"You Steve? That Evan? Grab a pair of cleats from the bag." He tossed a glance toward Evan's feet.

"Looks like a size 4. Also shin guards and a shirt. Make it quick."

I never saw Evan move so fast for anything other than a spot on the couch in front of the TV. We found the shoes, rolled the blue shirt down over his camouflage tee, and sent him out into the great soccer unknown.

Looming over the band of pee wees, Coach Ray had them dribbling in precise lines up and down the field. Evan caught on quickly, the athletic gene we'd seen expressed from nine months revving into high gear. I saw Jacob dash onto the field and take his place behind Evan. Tony joined me on the sideline.

"Pretty cool, huh?"

I nodded, totally impressed. The kids moved to a line of cones and I marveled, watching them slalom in and out, the balls pinging back and forth from foot to foot. With less than half an hour in the sport, Evan was one of the stronger players, which at the time I was too excited – and green – to realize meant . . . absolutely nothing.

After a few more dribbling drills, Coach Ray barked, "Drink break."

The kids all rushed for a row of tiny plastic chairs lined up on the far side of the field. Evan followed the crowd and flung himself down next to Jacob. Ray's assistant, Coach Julian, who would remain a beloved fixture in the Los Angeles soccer world for years, passed out Mott's Apple Juice boxes. At home, Evan would hold his out beseechingly – "Will you open it?" – and adult fingers would peel the wrapper off the straw and aim it into the foil-sealed hole. Here, Evan managed the process like a pro. I turned to Tony in disbelief. He was a beat ahead of me.

"He gets them to eat vegetables, too."

There was a rustling of half-hushed voices from a nearby blanket and I turned to see a few moms in heated discussion.

"Go ahead. Just give it to him."

"I don't want to make a big deal . . ."

"Susie, Justin's your kid. Just go . . . *go!*"

Susie, smartly dressed in a suit and low heels, probably an attorney with a successful practice in one of the nearby Century City towers, stood up and grabbed a bottle of water. I followed her eyes across the field. All the kids were contentedly slurping away, except one, a little boy whose chin was nestled in his chest, the juice box balanced on his knee. He wasn't making a fuss or calling attention to himself, but his face was a mask of misery. Susie circled around the end of the field and warily approached the row of players.

She came up behind Justin and with a magician's sleight of hand, she palmed the apple juice while leaving behind the water bottle. Coach Ray was down at the other end of the row, teasing one of the little boys while sucking on his own apple juice box, tiny in his giant's grip. His Spidey sense tingled and, wheeling around, spied Justin gulping down water and Susie skittering away.

"Hey, what's going on?"

Susie ignored the bark from behind and turned the corner at the end of the field.

"Yo, Justin's mom. I'm talking to you."

Susie froze. Ray strutted down the row, every little head turning as he passed. His bark grew louder and more insistent as it chased Susie.

"You know how this works. Kids here. Parents over there."

"I know, Coach Ray . . ."

This was crazy – a grown woman, who obviously made a living dishing it out to others, cowering beneath the withering gaze of the soccer coach.

". . . But we're trying to cut down the amount of sugar Justin gets . . ."

"You think I'm giving Justin too much sugar?"

"No, no. It's just that the doctor said . . ."

"The doctor said?" Ray scoffed. "These kids are running around. They need energy. What sugar there is in this darn juice box speeds up the metabolism so that they'll burn even more sugar and fat when they get back on the field."

While I was shocked by the scene playing out before me, and unconvinced by Ray's grasp of the science, I have to admit that I was impressed that he had taken a "damn" and PG'd it to "darn." I looked over to the kids, Justin in particular, and all were hollow-cheeked, sucking vigorously on their straws, bug eyes witnessing the humiliation of their teammate's mom.

"Who's the one constantly telling the kids to eat their broccoli?" Now wheeling on the parent gallery, "Me, right?"

Heads bobbed in browbeaten assent. Wilting under the weight of a hundred eyes, Susie fought back tears as she stammered an apology and hurried back to the parent zone. She blew past the blanket where her friends offered sympathetic looks, and vanished into the parking lot.

Storm passed, mood sunny again, Ray smiled at the kids. "All right, drinks in the trash. Everybody get a ball."

The kids moved from dribbling to passing, then shooting and a small-sided scrimmage, where Evan managed to bang a couple of goals into the tiny nets. He was having the best time. I was still in shock. I looked to Tony, who had conveniently wandered away to take a phone call. Susie returned, makeup repaired, and took her spot next to her friends. She waved off their good intentions and turned her forced smile toward the field where Justin wasn't moving fast enough to burn anything.

The hour wound down, and Ray convened the kids in the middle of the field for what I assumed would be a pep talk and a high five. Instead, he pulled a backpack from the gear-stuffed duffel, reached in, and, like Johnny Appleseed pollinating the earth, began sprinkling something at the feet of the kids. The boys fell to the ground in delight, greedily gathering the candy that Ray was tossing. The girls, smarter and more patient, stood back and picked up the more far-flung treats.

In their excitement, two boys dove onto the same spot and bonked heads, which normally would have caused a torrent of tears and parents swooping in to sweep them up. But, with candy calling, the boys blinked back the pain and continued to scurry for Ray's offerings. Evan came running over, holding out his hands, which were overflowing with Jolly Rancher hard candies and a few clods of grass and dirt.

"I love soccer!" he cheered.

After that class I wasn't so sure. But what did I know? My last brush with soccer had been PA'ing an American Express commercial featuring Pele (*Nao saia de casa sem ele* – Don't leave home without it) and returning home with an autographed ball, long since shredded on the streets of New York. (I didn't have the prescience to predict the rise of today's collectibles-crazed culture. Out the window may have gone enough to cover a year of college for my kids.)

The only soccer coaches I had known, back at Baldwin High School, were well-meaning science and Driver's Ed teachers, whose go-to coaching tip was "take a lap."

But Coach Ray was a pro, right? He'd played college ball at UCLA, he was chiseled and commanding, and everyone scrambled to get their kids into his class. He obviously knew what he was doing. Evan was a kid with enough energy to power a small city, who, at that moment, was channeling it into soccer. He loved it so much that his between-class behavior was easily manipulated by threats of "no Coach Ray this week."

Being a quick study, Evan escaped the sarcasm, ridicule or outright bullying Ray directed toward a weepy kid or a succoring parent. His magisterial manner either worked for you or it didn't. Wandering the parent corner, I'd overhear snippets of conversation . . .

"I love how he doesn't take any crap from the kids. He really gets them to focus."

"Jackson is tired for days after this class. It's the best."

"Scotty says that Coach Ray knows when he eats his broccoli…"

A coach with a Broccoli-cam? I found all of this distasteful, bordering on perverse, but I hated to take the soccer away from Evan.

"Hey Ev," I asked him one day on the ride home. He was busy tallying his haul of Jolly Ranchers so I had to ask again. Finally he looked over. "What if I put together a soccer class for you and your friends?"

"With Coach Ray?"

"No, with Coach Dad."

He laughed. "Funny, Dad. What do you know about soccer?"

When I look back, after coaching scores of teams and thousands of kids, I have to admit that an honest answer to Evan's question might have stopped me before I got started. Truth is, I knew very little. My high school career could most charitably be characterized as . . . undistinguished. I was blessed with the ability to use both feet with equal mediocrity, and the only thing exceptional about my game was my marked lack of speed.

I arrived for that first class at Barrington Park with a set of clunky PVC-pipe goals, a bag of the wrong-sized soccer balls (I had no one to ask) and enough energy to overwhelm even the most frenetic ADHD kid. I grabbed whatever soccer books Barnes and Noble had – this was before the internet became the one-stop-shopping mecca for everything soccer – and boned up on a few drills. While Evan contented himself by scattering all the balls as far afield as he could, I waited, having no idea how many of his pre-school chums, if any, would even show up. And then in true *Field of Dreams* fashion, cars streamed into the parking lot discharging Jacob (pried loose from Coach Ray), and Jake, Ben One and Ben Two, Ian, Augie (and his Uncle Steve – one less name to remember – to help me), Adam, Hayden, and mascot Dori. That's when the nerves kicked in, and I realized I really didn't have the answer to Evan's question. What the hell *did* I know about soccer?

Enthusiasm and ignorance got me through those first few practices. I was louder and sillier than the boys, but if I wanted to keep them around, I had to actually teach them something. I quickly learned that if I could stay five minutes ahead of them, in terms of knowledge and skill, I could keep this going. Coach Ray, through his self-important bullying and scientifically dubious behavior, had provided me with a template for what *not* to do. Discovering the qualities of a positive and productive coach was the challenge, and each week The Team (an admittedly weak and generic moniker I imposed, vetoing the more popular Stinky Poopooheads) and I worked it out together. I was able to distill the experience to a few key questions, which I now encourage all my parents to ask themselves as well: *What are my goals* (not to be confused with "expectations") *for my child and our family? How do we make sure youth sports will be a healthy and productive vehicle for achieving all of these goals? How do we help our kids get the most from youth sports?* Yet the most important question, the one that we must revisit again and again at different intervals throughout this process is: *Who are we doing this for?*

CHAPTER TWO

Keep Your Eyes on Your Own Paper

Life bombards us with a dizzying series of questions. From such cosmic mindbenders as "Why am I here?" and "Is there a God?", to the frivolous, brain-tickling, "Why can't I have ice cream for breakfast?", we chart our growth through the answers we discover. When we're young and still in the thrall of our parents, most replies take some form of "Because I said so," usually intoned with an impatient finality. We learn when we flip roles and become the parents ourselves that the ramifications of questions such as "Who is this tiny creature I'm now responsible for?" and "How am I going to keep him in one piece?" and "Why *can't* I feed him ice cream for breakfast?" will drain our patience and shoehorn us into the knee-jerk "Because I said so." It's the circle of life.

As our children leave toddler-dom for a sturdier mobility, the realm of youth sports beckons. We register in a rush of excitement, and from that moment we're on a freeway with few exits. Because once soccer classes begin, here comes basketball, then baseball, flag football, swimming, tennis . . . and we're barely out of preschool. Before we know it, we're neck deep in gear, fields, schedules, laundry, playoffs . . . with little time for breathing, even less for reflection.

But who are we doing this for?

It's a question with an answer that's screamingly obvious, yet so many of us get it so damn wrong. Of course, we're doing this for our kids, hoping that they will reap the benefits of a lifelong love of sports: fitness and well-being, personal growth and development, friendship and community. Studies abound that confirm the advantages of getting our kids off the couch. The Aspen Institute's Project Play[1] reported that organized sports activity helps children develop and improve cognitive skills, while positively affecting academic performance and classroom behavior by enhancing concentration and attention. High school athletes are more likely than non-athletes to attend college and get degrees. The value extends to the workplace, where active children grow into adults with higher earning prospects.

The formula I stumbled upon was surprisingly simple: Recreation + Perspiration = Exhilaration. Keep them moving and laughing and they'll come back for more. This is what our little band at Barrington practiced. We stretched and laughed, then dribbled and laughed, then played a few games, like Star Wars or Rugrats, and laughed, had a drink and a snack – Evan whined in vain for Jolly Ranchers – and went home, still laughing. Even the inevitable pushing and shoving

---

1 "Sport for All, Play for Life: A Playbook to Get Every Kid in the Game," Sports & Society Program, The Aspen Institute's Project Play (January 25, 2015)

and fighting over one ball (when there were another dozen perfectly acceptable ones lying around) were brushed off as the stirrings of the competitive spirit, or the catchall vindication: "They're boys." We met once a week for six glorious months, then all answered the call to join AYSO Region 69, the soccer league servicing Brentwood, Pacific Palisades, and Topanga, on the Westside of Los Angeles.

If there were any *Danger* or *Do Not Enter* signs, none of us saw them. There was no John Williams' theme from *Jaws* to scare us off. And no Magic 8 Ball to help divine the future. Would the answer "Better not tell you now" have set off an alarm? No way. It was impossible to know at the time that for many, youth sports would become a battleground of family friction and disappointment, littered with the dashed dreams of eight- and ten- and twelve-year-olds. How could it not be? Youth sports is a competitive $17 billion a year indus-try.[2] From gear and equipment to leagues, private lessons, training programs, showcase camps, recruiting services, and medical support, the machinery of youth sports grinds in one unforgiving direction.

As the stakes get higher, the competition stiffens and the expecta-tions mount. It's no wonder that some parents begin to lose sight of what motivated them, and their kids, to get involved in the first place. Somewhere along the way, our central question, "Who are we doing this for?", mutates into more insidious queries such as, "How come Joey gets more playing time than my kid?" or "Why can't my kid do what Lauren is doing?" Around seven or eight, the stakes escalate. "How do I get my kid on a better team?" and "If my kid doesn't go

---

2 Christina Corbin and Lydia Culp, "The human cost of raising youth sports to a '$17 billion' industry," Fox News, https://www.foxnews.com/sports/youth-sports-17-billion-industry-human-cost (April 30, 2019)

to another team/league/program now, will she fall behind?" Around nine or ten, we catapult into the future. "What do I have to do to prepare my kid for a high school career?" and "Will this program help get him a college scholarship?"

Social media relentlessly reinforces our paranoia; not only is everyone prettier, happier, more interesting, more successful and having way more fun than we are, but their kids are perfect and destined for greatness. In this context, the college admissions scandal, with parents paying bribes to secure their kids' placement into prestigious institutions, becomes not only comprehensible but also inevitable.

We confront a world that seems more precarious for our kids than it was for us. Countless studies conclude that today's generation won't enjoy the same opportunities and advantages that we took for granted. The number of thirty-year-olds who find it economically imperative to live at home testifies to a rupture in the natural social order.

This fear that kids' options are dwindling leads parents to grasp at anything they perceive will keep their children competitive. Now, when parents consider introducing their kids to a new sport or activity, there is an agenda beyond the enjoyment of a new experience. It's not enough for the child to simply have fun for an hour. "Where will this lead?" we ask.

A nine-year-old whacks a ball over the centerfielder's head and our overheated brains leap into action: "If he's this good now, how great will he be at fifteen? What if I post this online and it goes viral? Will a college coach, or even better, a sports agent see our video? Will my son then get a scholarship to Arizona or Ohio State or Harvard?"

Crazy, right? Totally over the top. But these flights of fancy are inching closer to the norm. It's no longer good enough for a kid to be good; he has to be the best, or at least headed in that direction. Anything less is unacceptable, a waste of time, energy and dollars. Witness this conversation I overheard at the gym as one of my coaching cohorts was cornered by a parent:

Parent: *I'm thinking of finding a private coach for Josh.*

Coach: *Really? Josh is doing great. He works hard, his shot is coming along and he plays the best defense on the team.*

Parent: *I agree, he's getting so much better. And, please don't think I'm one of those parents, but I just think if Josh had some one-on-one coaching, it could take his game to the next level.*

Josh was six.

Here's another one:

From: •••••
Sent: Sunday, October 13, 2019 5:53 PM
To: info@coastsports.com
Subject: Website Inquiry

Would you please refer me to a few soccer personal trainers for private lessons for my almost 3 year old boy? He loves to play and I don't want him to fall behind the other kids. Thank you in advance,

•••••

It would be easy to laugh at the cluelessness of these parents – but don't they only want the best for their kids? What they don't realize when their kids declare, "When I grow up I want to be a professional athlete . . . or a hedge fund manager," is that it's not serious; there's no comprehension of next steps or long-term process. A kid's world is binary: I'm having/not having fun, which is true north on their experiential compass. Fun is both the vehicle and the destination, and anything that can provide them with smiles and laughter will be something that they want to come back to. Sports for kids can be that "something," an avenue for getting in touch with their physicality, a point of connection to a community, a means for making memories and a way to have a blast while it's all happening.

When I quizzed my own kids – all of whom played sports from the age of four through the end of high school – about their memories of that period, they had some very telling answers. Dori remembered the bitter loss to Culver City in the Area P championships and the sweet redemption of beating them three weeks later in Sectionals. Griffie chimed in with the amazing run of ten tournament victories with his U10[3] Palaxy All-Star team. And Evan pointed to the disappointing CIF semifinal loss his senior year of high school (same round the Griffies crashed out).

---

3 The term U10 stands for under 10. From the late 1990s through the mid-2010s, the age groupings in AYSO were U5 (under 5), U6 (under 6), U8 (under 8), U10, U12 (under 12), U14 (under 14), U16 (under 16) and U19 (under 19). In the two-year configurations of AYSO, the calendar for a division commenced on August 1 and ended July 31 two years later. So if a player turned 10 in August and another blew out his birthday candles in late July two years down the road, they would both compete in that season's U10 division. Within the same August-July calendar calculation, club soccer fielded teams in single-year formulations, e.g., U9, U10, U11, on up through U19.

In 2015, U.S. Soccer announced that to conform to international standards, all leagues would convert to a January through December birth year schedule. U10 teams would henceforth be designated as 10U (10 and under). Same with 5U, 6U, 8U, all the way up to 19U. Many club programs dropped the "U's" altogether, in favor of birth years, e.g., 2002, 2003, 2004 . . . 2010, 2011, etc.

The transition proved frustrating for administrators, who had to revamp their systems, and coaches, who saw their rosters reconfigured. Parents lamented that classmates born on either side of the New Year's divide could no longer be teammates. The players themselves were mostly sanguine about the change. They just wanted to play.

Yet, they all chipped in that their most vibrant memories revolved around their interactions with teammates, the car rides and the overnights, and the meals and the celebrations. The trip to Disney World where the soccer was forgettable but the time in the Magic Kingdom was . . . magical. The waterslides and French fries at the Arizona Grand Hotel. Going to John's Incredible Pizza, the culinary epicenter of Victorville, plugging quarters into the arcade games and exchanging five hundred tickets for a pencil eraser. The field in Walnut that was too soggy for soccer but just right for sliding in the mud. (Griffie stressed that his all-time favorite experience was the Paul Revere Mud Bowl, played in pounding rain and ankle-deep puddles, where kicking the ball would send up a wall of water while the ball wouldn't budge.) Seriously, what could be better?

When I run into the kids I coached, many of whom are now towering adults, there's an instant and palpable connection. The years melt away in the glow of reminiscence, followed by some variation of, "Those days were really fun, just playing ball, before it became a job or an expectation. Those were some of the highlights of my childhood."

Blink and it's over. From diapers to diplomas to adulthood, the march of time takes no prisoners. We live in a world that puts very little premium on childhood innocence, and anything that we can do to preserve it should be fostered. Professionalization, specialization, and any —"ation" that encourages children to work for the future rather than play in the present needs to be resisted. Worrying about what our kids will become rather than celebrating who they are now shortchanges both them and us. So how do we do this? How do we dial back the natural human impulse to strive for a better future while navigating a milieu whose demands are antithetical to a healthy experience? How do we strike a balance and achieve a sense of peace and fulfillment in our home lives?

Maybe we have to take a step back to make that leap forward. Encourage our seven-year-olds to play as many sports as possible. Don't throw our nine-year-olds into a program that trains three and four times a week. Recapture the joy of play unencumbered by the pressure of results.

Having a road map to help you navigate the process and provide a broader understanding of the programs and people you will encounter along the way could be invaluable. Get in the car and let's go . . .

CHAPTER THREE

You Gotta Run
Before You Can Walk

The moment the ball left Kevin's hands everyone knew it was going in. He turned and started back up the court even before the telltale whoosh of ball kissing net. He wasn't being cocky, though he rarely missed from anywhere on the court. Rather, it was his "condition" that impelled him to head back on defense without tracking his shot. Kevin was velocity-challenged. A snail in ankle weights could have beaten him down the court. Kevin ran on his heels, scraping across the blacktop instead of gliding gracefully on the balls of his feet. Over time, as everyone he played against grew taller and faster, his game began to wilt. His parents, wanting to help, plied him with every pro-endorsed shoe on the market. None of them worked, and at the advanced age of twelve, Kevin was a has-been. The problem wasn't the shoes; Kevin had to learn to run before he could walk.

It might sound counterintuitive – in life we walk, then run – but in sports the reverse is true. Before we can achieve any mastery on the court or the field, we have to know how to properly propel ourselves. It's not something most parents or coaches of young kids think about, but set them loose and just watch. You'll see arms flapping and flailing, heads lolling as if loosely attached, and legs skipping and stabbing at the ground. There are those who bat wildly at the air as if fighting through a swarm of mosquitoes.

Dani ran like a baby Tyrannosaurus, her arms raised in front of her chest, hands flopping like bobble-head dolls as she charged down the field. Head cocked, Byron would stare down at his right leg admiring himself as he motored about.

And then there are the kids like our friend Kevin who lurch forward flat-footed or on their heels. Less frequently you'll see the precocious ones that already resemble budding Usain Bolts, sailing effortlessly as if carried along on the wind.

No athlete will survive the physical and hormonal carnage of adolescence unless he can run correctly. Yet most programs skip over this critical fundamental in the interests of getting to the good stuff – dribbling, shooting, hitting, scoring. So, Kevin with his velvet touch blows into middle school ready to lead the basketball team to glory and finds himself a sloth on a team of gazelles. His concrete gait strands him in first gear, and his butt finds itself permanently pinned to the bench. (As we'll discover with most of the athletes discussed in these pages, an early exit from sports does not automatically consign one to a lifetime of misery. Kevin found his voice, literally, and thrived in the choral and theater world through high school and college. There is life after sports, usually.)

Basic running technique is easy to teach; all of our little-kid sessions begin with a quick lesson. Ask the kids to walk. They begin to laugh because, of course, everyone knows how to do that. Have them slightly lean forward so that their weight is over the balls of their feet. Not their toes and certainly not their heels. Then show them how to piston their arms, back and forth, both arms parallel to the ground. If they want to curl their fists for added emphasis, that's fine. Add the arm motions to the walk, making sure that the opposite arm moves with the opposite leg. Left arm, right leg. Right arm, left leg. Tell them to keep their heads facing straight ahead, eyes focused on the horizon. Cue the sound effects – have them all *chugga-chugga-chugga-chugga* like a train. (The coaches add the *whoooo-whooo* of the whistle.) The kids are laughing again, because this is silly, and silly is good.

Once they've nailed the walk, leaning forward, pushing off with the balls of their feet, with the proper accompanying arm motions, speed it up . . . slowly. The arms should accelerate at the same rate. Let them break into a slow trot, checking that all the parts are still in sync. Finally, say the word and let 'em go! And they will, with bursts of glee and zero technique, which will have been left back at the starting line. Heads rolling, dinosaur arms flapping, bodies bouncing, a total mess but appropriate for a first attempt . . . or a second . . . or a tenth . . . Sooner than later it will all click, and a smooth, efficient, though not necessarily cheetah-speed gait will emerge from the herky-jerky chaos of those early efforts.

The importance of proper form can't be overstressed. Not only will it facilitate an athlete's growth and development, down the road it could diminish the risk of injury.

It's unclear whether Kevin's departure from basketball was driven by the plateau his flawed technique stranded him on, whether he gravitated toward other interests like theater and singing, or whether he developed foot, knee, hip or back problems from his heel-heavy stride. As young athletes age, injuries enter their lives. Poor technique can hasten and exacerbate them.

Across the spectrum of youth sports, injuries are on the rise. The *Wall Street Journal* reported that in 2013 there were 3.5 million sports-related injuries sustained by kids eighteen and under. According to the Centers for Disease Control and Prevention (CDC), high school athletes alone account for an estimated 2 million of those injuries, resulting in 500,000 doctor visits, and 30,000 hospitalizations every year. These are jaw-dropping statistics.

When thirteen-year-olds are tearing ACLs and sixteen-year-olds are undergoing Tommy John reconstructive elbow surgery so they can continue pitching, you've got to start questioning where we went wrong. One doesn't have to look far for the answer. When programs and coaches – and even parents – focus on competition, getting to the next level, and winning, which can translate into playing a hundred games a year, an increase in injuries is inevitable.

Enlightened minds in U.S. Soccer and other athletic organizations have devised new guidelines for numbers of practices vs. games per week for kids up through a certain age that provide optimal results (usually one practice and one game). But even with intervention from on high, far too many reject a "less is more" approach and watch young athletes overuse the same body parts in a system of overtraining. The rush to early specialization may produce short-term, ego-inflating benefits. But the long-term costs are what parents need to be aware of.

Reacting to the furor over the death of a fifteen-year-old basketball player, whose father blamed exhaustion from year-round play as a prime cause, Puerto Rico's Olympic committee began instituting rules to limit the number of games, practices, and tournaments for young athletes. In 2018 it enacted a regulation that "called for age-appropriate play, drawn from the best practices endorsed by sports governing bodies in other countries. No tournament play or keeping score before age 9 and no more than three games a week through age 16."[1]

In a perfect world kids would play multiple sports year-round. A sport in the fall, one in the winter, and another in the spring. Summer could be a time for rest or general, noncompetitive recreation. It's an old-school model that is by far the healthiest for young players whose bodies are just beginning to develop. Unfortunately, in today's hyper-competitive, results-oriented culture, the three-sport varsity athlete is an increasingly endangered species.

The ball is in our court, as it were. We parents should lead the way in deciding how we want these programs to service our children's development. So we need to know how the best of them operate and how to replicate the good teachings and successes that they provide.

The Developmental Phases
of Youth Sports Programs

As a kid growing up on Long Island, I couldn't wait to be old enough to play Little League. There was no soccer or basketball, certainly no flag football. Little League was king and everyone signed up when they hit their eighth birthday. There was something mystical about seeing the older kids parading around town in their dirt-streaked uniforms, their metal cleats clicking across the sidewalk. What I wanted more than anything, though, was a pair of pro-style

---

1 Tom Farrey, "The Government is Reining in Youth Sports. The Adults are Worried," *New York Times*, January 7, 2020

flip-up sunglasses to help spot fly balls in a blazing sky. (I got them and sat on them the first day. So much for glare prevention.)

This desert of athletic opportunity persisted into the 1980s. Daycare programs in many communities evolved, often aided by local YMCAs, into Mommy and Me classes, which begat toddler gyms and beginning sports classes for two- and three-year-olds. Still, into the mid '90s, when I took Evan to Coach Ray, the options for little kids to play and learn sports were few.

Evan and his chums were just turning five when they stormed the plains of Barrington. Over the next few years, parents in my program pushed to lower the entry age to three, and crowd-pleasers that we were, we acquiesced. We drew a non-negotiable line at two-year-olds and the squish of their diapers, but a concerted parental assault overwhelmed us and soon even those uncontrollable hellions began to toddle up and down the field.

Whatever the age, our focus was firmly on fun. Skills acquisition took a back seat, though it ineluctably came along for the ride. As Hamlet so presciently put it, "The play's the thing." And play we did, with games such as Star Wars, Rugrats, The Blob, Bumper Cars, Volcano Island, even Bumper Cars *on* Volcano Island. We had hundreds of them. All employed fundamental soccer skills – dribbling and ball control, with some passing and shooting. All were variations on childhood classics: Red Light-Green Light, Capture the Flag, Red Rover, Keep-Away . . . Yet we'd festoon them in characters and plot lines from popular cartoons, movies and video games, and bury skills instruction in narratives of adventure and whimsy. Dribble through the asteroid field to free Luke and Leia. Drive on the freeway, but don't let your cars crash. Dribble from Tommy to Chuckie's house making sure the evil Anjelica doesn't steal your ball.

We were guided by our imagination and a few simple rules: no lines, everyone had a ball at all times, and instructions were kept to a minimum. We moved fast and furiously, dealing with an age group with a non-existent attention span. We made sure that fun superseded challenge to keep the kids engaged and successful. If they kicked the ball, great. If they rolled on the ground, great. If they ran into a tackling dummy (always handy to have around), fantastic. We saw no upside to frustrating the kids, triggering tantrums, and possibly jeopardizing their future enthusiasm for sports.

By mixing into each session a healthy helping of silliness, the kids connected the use of their bodies with the use of their imagination. And they loved it! Repetition week to week was key, so the kids grew accustomed to playing their favorite games. They'd scream, "Let's play Rugrats" or "Let's play Star Wars." By the end of an eight-week session, their confidence and skill levels had risen dramatically.

As they careened past four-and-a-half and slid into five, our kids were ready for the brave new world of organized soccer. AYSO. The American Youth Soccer Organization. Real teams wearing real uniforms playing real games. This was the big time.

While each community has its own region, parents are free to register wherever they'd like their kids to play. Living in Santa Monica it made sense to sign up there. But one Saturday morning, tooling down Sunset Boulevard, in Brentwood, I came around the bend and saw a long line of parents and kids stretching across the field at Paul Revere Charter Middle School. I figured I should jump on the end of it.

That line changed my life. An hour later Evan was registered to play and I was signed up to coach. Didn't matter that we were now tethered to Region 69, Brentwood-Pacific Palisades, and not Santa

Monica. Region 69 became my home, my community, the source of my kids' friends – and mine. Soccer became my life.

For the youngest, U5 and U6, it's a cavalcade of cuteness. Kids in their billowing polyester jerseys and baggy shorts that droop below the knee. Team names consisting of a color and a kid-friendly noun – like the Red Dragons, Pink Princesses or Green Geckos. Game time is swarm ball, a mobile mosh pit. The stronger athletes, who are often but not always the ones with older siblings whose games they've been dragged to for years, lead the pack around the field chasing the ball from goal to goal. Those at the rear may never even see the ball, but they're content to be part of the posse. And then there are the kids obliviously rooted to one spot as the game swirls around them.

In Griffie's inaugural AYSO year, as a member of the black-and-gold-striped Yellowjackets, he spent his first practice hunched on the ground in the fetal position. One of his teammates thought that looked cool, so he crouched down beside him, while the rest of the boys pinged around inside the grid, kicking and chasing their balls. At game time, Griffie projected himself into the action. If the ball was near him, he would leap, like a wrestler off the turnbuckle, crashing to the ground, taking a bunch of teammates and opponents with him. Everybody would bounce back up and stage the action again farther up the field.

Dori's two seasons in U6, as a member of the Bluejays and then the Wicked Strawberries, followed a similar pack pattern, though if two girls found themselves charging the ball at the same time, they would throw on the brakes to avoid a collision. After a moment's pause, the dominant girl would break free with the prize and head to goal. For Dori and her friends, U6 revolved around fashion. Pink and purple were the coveted colors, with hair ties and ribbons to match their kits. For both the boys and the girls, though, the common denominator was having a good time.

Glimmers of actual soccer emerge as the kids turn six and seven. Basic tactics – when we have the ball, everyone attacks; when they have the ball, everyone defends – can be taught. As kids begin to age out of their "me me me" stage and become aware of space beyond their own, positional play materializes. With the additional room to maneuver, there is greater likelihood of others getting to touch the ball. Yet the strongest athletes still succeed with Darwinian regularity, racking up goals and monopolizing field time. Years back, a lad named Virgil had ball skills that were light years ahead of his peers. He could dribble the field, undisturbed, as if hypnotizing those in his path, then casually dink the ball past the mesmerized tender. In U8, Virgil was a god. By thirteen, he was a has-been.

Nine- and ten-year-olds can replace the ego-based myopia of their younger selves with the patience necessary to acquire mandatory skills such as first touch, ball control, accurate passing, 1 vs. 1 defense, and more. Teamwork becomes intentional and not a random, pinball-like accident. There's a recalibration of the fun-to-work ratio, with the latter rising in prominence. Still, the "work" must be enjoyable or the rush for the exits will be unstoppable. At this age, athletes will either continue to play multiple sports or make the decision to specialize. Research endorses greater variety while society tilts toward playing one sport year-round, the consequences of which we'll discuss further on.

And then comes puberty, the great un-equalizer. Growth spurts and lack thereof define this stage for the eleven- through thirteen-year-olds. From squeaky-clean faces to groomed goatees, a jagged skyline of players will greet the referee at check-in. The early bloomers may be able to exploit their physical advantage, while those on a slower timetable have to rely on guts and guile. Alas, bigger isn't automatically better, as the greater distance it now takes a signal to travel from the brain to the extremities can affect the balance and coordination of these newly-minted giants. Sudden growth may also stretch connective sinews too quickly, causing knee and foot pain.

But the brain at this age, with hormones spiking synaptic activity, can process more sophisticated information. Skills and tactics become more readily replicable on the field. For some, this division showcases the stirrings of athletic prowess; others are cresting the peak of their powers, with decline imminent as the rest catch up.

For those who have survived boredom, burnout, injury, distraction and the lure of other activities, playing sports from the ages of fourteen and up is what it's all about. Young men and women have replaced little boys and girls, and their strength, speed, and agility allow them to perform at a high level. With increased size and greater intensity, however, comes an amplified opportunity for injury and damage.

When Griffie flattened everyone in U6, they all popped up and kept going. In U14, when Evan launched a left-footed shot and an opponent ran through the arc of his follow-through, his strained hip flexor took months to heal.

If one were to distill the myriad forces and influences that affect the progression of kids through sports, three primary phases would emerge: the fun, the technical, and the tactical.

Up through the age of eight, fun dominates. These are the years of discovery. Enjoyment is its own reward. From nine through fourteen, mastering skills while still keeping it fun is the key to development. Those fifteen and older need a diet of strategy in order to prosper and thrive.

As parents and coaches, we risk a rebellion if, even at these upper stages, it's all work and no play. It's not about Jack becoming a dull boy; it's about Jack deciding that the hard work, the setbacks, the potential injuries and subsequent rehabilitations just aren't worth it anymore. Easier to drop out and move on to something else.

Unfortunately, an unhealthy number of programs today are ignorant of the *fun, technical, tactical* model. Too many are running three-year-olds through cone courses, promising hopeful parents that their kids will gain an edge, a palpably ridiculous statement. Even worse, you'll see kids sitting on soccer balls while the coach pontificates from above. The coach may be the Hans Christian Andersen of youth sports, but kids need to run, jump, and stay physically involved. No lingering on lines; kids have neither patience nor attention span. In fact, if you want your three-year-old pee wees to line up you'll have to physically place them in a spot and say, "Stay!" And just like the puppies they are, they'll find a way to wriggle away.

And that's OK. In fact, it's not just OK, it's normal kid behavior. Too many programs treat children as pint-sized adults. Ascribing to kids the abilities and motivations of adults is doing them – and you – a disservice. Our rush to make miniaturized adults out of our children comes from a fundamental misunderstanding of what childhood is all about.

Since the era when we first started recognizing children as children – not workhorses groomed for supporting a large family – researchers have detailed the stages of development from birth to adulthood. If you look closely enough and work with enough kids, certain truths become self-evident: all children are different and they develop at different rates and ages. Psychologically, socially and physically, their development cannot be rushed and still achieve positive and consistent results.

In terms of sports development, for example, a young child in the "Me me me" phase can't possibly appreciate the concept of teamwork. If a four-year-old passes the soccer ball, it's likely an accident. But a few years later, that same child will comprehend that *it's not all about me*. He's organically reached the stage where sharing doesn't repudiate who he is. And since sharing the ball is the same as passing the ball, it becomes another tool in his toolbox. You won't have to cajole or force the shift to happen. It happens naturally as a result of an increasing social-emotional awareness, technical proficiency, and good coaching.

Whenever parents assess a program, it's critical to determine whether the coaches engage and challenge the kids at age-appropriate levels. The best way to know: show up and observe a class in progress.

Upon arriving, check out the children. Are they smiling, laughing, and bouncing around? Or are they serious, regimented, and in work mode? Are the kids active for most of the lesson or is there an abundance of sitting around while the coach talks? Are the games geared toward the age of the kids or are they struggling to succeed at what they're doing? Do the coaches relate to each child one-on-one, having an "eye-level" experience with them, or are they strutting around barking instructions they expect the kids to execute?

The answers to all of these questions will be obvious and once you have them, there's one last question to ask: "What do I want for my kid and my family?"

If you're looking for a decade of excitement, memories and magic, you might consider this path: general classes at a young age, with fun and energy disguising instruction. Play a different sport each season up through ages twelve or thirteen. If your child falls in love with one sport, maybe then join a club team. If not, there's no stigma playing recreationally in less competitive outlets. It doesn't need to be more complicated than that. Granted, there will be voices telling you that your child needs "more." And who among us is secure enough to ignore those voices?

The parents of Sam Darnold, that's who. Sam Darnold was a gifted young athlete. Soccer, basketball, baseball, football and taekwondo were his early favorites,[2] and when quizzed it was difficult for him to choose one to the exclusion of the others. So his parents resisted the loud and persistent calls to specialize, and he continued to play all of them as long as he could. Finally, football won out, and as the quarterback for USC, he was able to access the skills he learned in all of the other sports to become one of the top QBs in the country. Obviously not everyone is Sam Darnold; not everyone will go on to quarterback the New York Jets. And not every parent has the courage to stand strong when everyone else is rushing in the other direction.

If the answer to the core question is that you'd like to board the high school express, and possibly even the intercollegiate express, your route may look a little different. The first few steps, however, remain the same. Recreational classes to introduce physicality and sports for the very young. Introductory leagues in multiple sports would be the next step. Again, competition should be downplayed; enjoyment is key. Come middle school, given interest and promise, your kid could specialize in one discipline and possibly move into a high-caliber club or travel program. An enlightened approach to downtime during summer and school breaks will minimize the risk of overuse injuries. Hard work and skill will earn your kid a spot on

---

2 Jeff Pearlman, "Sam Darnold Is The Realest," Bleacherreport.com (August 2, 2017)

her high school team or possibly a well-respected club team. After high school graduation, she'd either bid a fond farewell to her golden years in youth sports or, if she was lucky and determined enough, move on to play in college.

That's the dream many parents have for their kids. But only a fraction of the four-year-olds who start out in youth sports make it onto a college roster. There are so many ways that this journey can be derailed. In addition to the kid-centric pitfalls of injury, growth rates and burnout, there are obstacles for parents as well.

False promises and misleading information about a player's prospects can distract a parent from what is inappropriate or even pernicious about a program. Laziness, gullibility or lack of awareness can blind them to what their child may be going through. Pushing too hard too early or putting a child in a program that poorly fits his demeanor or skill set can send a child reeling down the wrong path. If you're pushing at six, seven, and eight, your kid won't be playing at fourteen, fifteen, and sixteen when it can be more important to his future and healthier for his present.

Even the most vigilant parents can stumble during their child's ten-year window. Stay open minded and supportive, let go of expectations and allow the kids to make some of the important decisions, too. Try not to get personally invested in the successes or failures of the moment.

It all comes back to the fundamental question, "What do I want for my kid?" I believe that the enlightened answer is some version of, "I want my kid to love sports and play them at whatever level for as long as he or she can." Participation doesn't – and shouldn't – end in high school or even after college. Sports can be enjoyed throughout one's life because playing is as fulfilling, therapeutic and beneficial for adults as it is for children. *Besides, why should kids have all the fun?*

Moderating our adult expectations and the desire to see our children "maximize their potential" is no small feat. In fact, one of the great challenges that we face as parents is learning to set aside our attachments to specific outcomes. We all want to see our children blossom, but when we allow them to set their own pace, it gives them the opportunity to grow into the best versions of themselves.

CHAPTER FOUR

The Two Dirtiest Words in Youth Sports

"What makes you qualified to coach our kids?"

A perfectly appropriate question; we should all want to know who we are trusting to lead, teach, and be close to our children. But the skeptical tone and the context of this query, posed on a warm-for-January evening in the oak-paneled confines of Mort's Deli's Tap Room, hung in the air, a challenge that set me back in my seat.

Ken's skepticism was echoed by Gary. "Yeah, why should we entrust our kids to you?" These were two high-powered professionals whose sons, Henry and Jordan, were members of this newly-formed U10 All-Star team. It was a team not originally slated to exist.

Historically, Region 69 had fielded two teams per division, an "A" team of the strongest second-year players, and a "B" team comprised of the next tier of talent, mostly second-years, with a few deserving firsts sprinkled in. These teams competed throughout the winter and spring against similarly-skilled teams from other regions across

Southern California. It was a prestigious program and it drew almost seventy nine- and ten-year-olds to two weekends of tryouts.

Evan was eight, a first-year in U10 boys, and a sparkplug who, when firing, could instantly turn the tide in games. Throughout the season, I kept mental tabs on the top players we'd encounter each week, and I felt that Evan was capable of competing with that bunch. Standing on the sidelines at All-Star tryouts, sweating nonchalance among all the other anxious parents, I recalibrated my calculations, counting all the standout second-years, while trying to rank Evan among his first-year peers. The older boys, graduates of the previous year's B team, were a confident clique whose been-there-done-that attitude all but confirmed their soon-to-be A-team status. Where would Evan fall in the next cut of fifteen or sixteen boys who would comprise the B's?

As it turned out, nowhere. He missed the cut. Thirteen of the slots went to second-years deemed just a notch below the A's. Three youngers, Michael, Patrick and Johnny, compelling candidates all, rounded out the B-team roster. I found this out a few hours before the annual coaches' meeting, where we convened to rate our players for the following year's teams.

I arrived at the meeting, spirits dampened by the news about Evan, when I was cornered by Coach Chuck, the robustly enthusiastic A-team helmer. He shook his head in commiseration.

"Shame about Evan. Just too many boys trying out. We had twenty-four who didn't make a team. Lotta great kids."

If that was supposed to make me feel better. . . But Chuck wasn't finished.

"How would you like to coach a third team? Evan would be on it, of course. You could co-coach with Hadi. His son Nicky would be on it, too . . ." He had me at "like to coach."

44

And that put me at the table six weeks later in the same Tap Room. This was our introductory meeting with the parents of the "consolation" team. Hadi, who had grown up in Iran playing soccer, and I sat across the room from the rest of the parents, as if we were testifying at a Congressional hearing. The more experienced of our duo, Hadi spoke about teaching skills, fostering teamwork, and the equitable distribution of tournament participation and playing time. With a skimpier resume, only four years of coaching under my belt, I focused on building an esprit de corps, ensuring that the experience would be fun for all. Smiles and nodding heads told us that our rap was pretty good.

And then Ken threw down the gauntlet.

"What makes you qualified to coach our kids?"

As I acknowledged, it was a fair question. What in our experience would we draw upon to run this team? The deeper and more pointed meaning of Ken's question was how were we going to meet these parents' expectations and develop their kids to their full potential?

Potential and expectation. The two dirtiest words in youth sports. Many a budding sports career, or just a love of the game, has been derailed by the identifying of the former and the pressure of the latter. It's insidious, but as accepted as breathing.

When a child exhibits a hint of potential or aptitude, a parent's pulse quickens. *Hey*, Dad thinks, *my kid is pretty good at this!* And in that moment of innocent wonder, "expectation" rears its ugly head and the downward spiral begins. It can appear as early as the womb, with the swipe of a tiny limb across a distended belly. *"Did you see that?"* Mom says. Dad jumps. *"Look at that kick! We've got an athlete!"* Both laugh at the absurdity, and yet, even in jest lies a ripple of hope.

As a new parent, I was as guilty of this as anyone. Evan's early agility led me to think the same thought: *Could there be something there?* I didn't make the mistake of defining what that "something" might be. But I did wonder if sports would feature in his future, even if, in my core, I knew that with his genetic composition it would most likely be as a spectator.

It's natural for parents to value athleticism and its accompanying benefits. But nowadays, too many infer a future of glory from a glimmer of talent. Our all-day-every-day exposure to news and social media, which presents a never-ending comparison of our lives to everyone else's, fuels an obsession to not only "keep up" with the Joneses but to do them one better. Normal, goofy, nose-leaking kids no longer exist; they've gone the way of the Game Boy. Today, every kid is exceptional! Every kid is amazing! Twenty-first century kids exude genius, whether in computers or academics or theater or sports. Each and every one will conquer the world or at least amass millions of "likes." Since all of our kids are universally spectacular, having heightened expectations for them is as natural as a Band-Aid on a boo-boo.

But "expectation" is as subversive a noun as "potential." Few things in life turn out to be as wonderful as we've dreamed them to be. A handful may exceed our hopes – the first blush of love, the excitement of getting engaged, holding your newborn for the first time. But across the experiential spectrum, anticipation eclipses its realization nearly every time. When we allow our dreams and fantasies free rein, or when we define ourselves by their attainment, one of two things will happen: the outcome won't materialize in the way we imagined, or we get precisely what we want and it's a letdown.

If we stay open-minded, though, reality can exceed our dreams. We know this, but do we accept it? Every parent wants his child to thrive; the danger comes in trying to shoehorn that child into our preconceived definition of success.

Marcus came into U10 bearing the unofficial mantle of Most Valuable Player. Part earned and part hype, no one could deny the strength of his game and the impact he had on his team's success. The squad's deep run in the playoffs reflected his combination of power and finesse. On the sideline of the semifinal game, his father came over excitedly to tell me that a sports agent friend was there to watch Marcus play. "No way," I laughed, then realized he was serious. Really, a sports agent to scout a ten-year-old? Unfortunately for Marcus, his superpowers abandoned him that day and he played his age, where the only thing that's consistent is inconsistency. His father sheepishly bundled Marcus off the field after the game.

The family's disappointment was short-lived, though, as Marcus's parents pulled him from the league the next season and set him up in club. Here his talents would surely flourish. Somehow, though, they didn't. He bounced around on marginal teams for a few years, never quite living up to his reputation, until finally, washed up at thirteen, he dropped out of soccer to focus on basketball.

I'm sure that Marcus's parents thought they were helping him by pushing him to do the thing that he loved. But bringing a sports agent to watch him play at ten? Trying to project Marcus's soccer future at that age would be like trying to see the California coastline from Colorado. Life is unknowable, and adolescence is especially opaque. With years of tectonic changes on the horizon, there was little guarantee Marcus would still be playing soccer that far down the road.

What was Marcus's dad's aim in corralling a scout to watch his ten-year-old son play? That day on the sideline he didn't tell me, but it had to be more than helping Marcus get into middle school or even play ball in high school. Likely, it was to begin to pave a pathway to college for his superstar son. If that was the goal, well, the move was premature. College coaches can't even initiate contact with players until their junior year of high school. While Marcus probably thought it was cool to have the notoriety and attention, one has to wonder if it didn't heap more pressure on his 4-foot-10, ten-year-old shoulders.

The Marcus story does have a happy ending. In high school, he returned to AYSO with his friends, and played two more seasons, finally free to enjoy the game he loved.

And then there are kids like Jacob. He was the five-year-old phenom, who used to fly down the basketball court, dribbling through his legs and chucking up three-point prayers that grazed nothing but net. Most of the other kids on the team were content to carry the ball between dribbles and play defense as if they were a blanket smothering a fire. The rest wandered cluelessly around the court counting the minutes till the post-game pizza. The parents, sitting on the stage of the shoebox-sized gym, carried on as if it were the final seconds of the Final Four. "Come on! You can do it! Look at Jacob!"

Such comparisons are never productive. Watching Jacob dominate reinforced the other kids' feelings of inadequacy, which were exacerbated by the realization that their parents felt the same way. And the parents walked away questioning their kids' future and even their own competence. *"Why can't my kid play like Jacob? What am I doing wrong?"*

Every child treads a different developmental path. And guess what? If Jacob doesn't grow when he hits puberty, then Brady, who's four inches taller but doesn't catch the spark until he's ten, may be the better player by the time they both hit fifteen. A child's athletic trajectory hinges on many factors, almost all beyond anyone's control. Most young phenoms plateau and wind up watching other kids blow past them.

As parents, we must maintain perspective to prevent outsized expectations from taking root. We need to exercise restraint, patience, and faith that things will work out as they are meant to in the end. Jacob might be able to knock down a three-pointer while everyone else is still sucking his thumb, but does that ensure he'll go on to a career in sports, a happy marriage or a fulfilling life?

We parents invest a considerable amount of time, energy and money in our children's athletic endeavors. The more involved we are, the more we let ourselves dream. In fact, 26 percent of parents with high school kids on sports teams hope their child will become a professional athlete.[1]

Yet NCAA-published statistics[2] detailing the likelihood of a high school player continuing on to a professional career paint a sober, if not depressing, picture.

In 2017-18, only .009% of males who played high school then college basketball (52 out of 551,373) and .008% of women who played high school then college basketball (32 out of 412,307) advanced to the NBA or the WNBA. In the NFL, only .025% of high school players are eventually drafted by a pro team (255 out of an original high school pool of 1,036,842). (We'll go into greater depth in Chapter Seventeen.)

"Well," you say, "I know my kid probably won't play for the U.S. Women's Soccer team. But what if she can get a scholarship to college? Wouldn't that justify all the sacrifices we've made as a family?"

---

1 NPR/Robert Wood Johnson Foundation/Harvard T.H. Chan School of Public Health, "Sports and Health in America," in Public Opinion Poll Series (June 1, 2015)
2 "Probability of Competing Beyond High School," NCAA Research (2017-18)

Don't kill the messenger, but even the hope for scholarship money isn't as straightforward, or feasible, as it may seem. Fewer than 2 percent of high school athletes receive athletic scholarships to college, with an average scholarship carrying a value of $10,409[3]. And except for marquee, money-minting programs like football and basketball, most college sports have to carve up the lesser sums they receive from their athletic departments to stretch across entire rosters.

Factor in the staggering sums parents spend over the years on league fees, travel teams, private coaching, equipment, recruiting services, doctors and more, and you could arrive at the lopsided expenditure of hundreds of thousands of dollars in return for a $2,000-a-year partial scholarship that barely covers the yearly $50,000-plus costs of college. Math has definitely changed since I was in school, but even I know these numbers don't add up.

Armed with the facts, ask yourself again: *What do I want for my kid? Would I want him to be a professional basketball player, even if it were in the realm of possibility? Is it the healthiest of disciplines?* Weigh the upside of money and shoe contracts against the drawbacks of injury and abbreviated career span. For every player who makes it into the NBA, there are ten million who leave their dreams on the schoolyard. Even for those with passion, talent, and a diehard work ethic, the possibility of heartbreak looms large.

Growing up, Grant was a gold-standard baseball player. He excelled on every team, hitting titanic home runs and winning the endorsement of every coach. Seeming to fulfill his destiny, he was drafted right out of high school by the Philadelphia Phillies. Yet over the past nine years he has bounced around the minor league system of the Phillies, Cubs,

---

3 "Scholarships: Slicing the Pie," *New York Times* (March 10, 2008)

and Diamondbacks. He has battled injuries and pinballed from team to team, still clinging to that dream of making it to the major leagues.

Should Grant ever make it to the "show," staying there will be a whole different ballgame. The pressure to perform is unrelenting. There's always someone else battling for your spot. And a crippling, career-ending injury could be just around the next base. From the outside the fun appears undeniable, but the reality of 162 baseball games (or eighty-two basketball games, sixteen football games, dozens of soccer games), plus preseason training, additional games and year-round conditioning, can be a grind. As adult professionals, playing solely for fun is no longer an option.

"Show me the money" was Rod Tidwell's battle cry in *Jerry Maguire*, and the cash doled out in many sports is jaw-dropping. But 16 percent of NFL players, or 1 in 6, have declared bankruptcy within twelve years of retirement, according to the National Bureau of Economic Research.[4] A 2009 *Sports Illustrated* exposé revealed that 78 percent of NFL players are under financial stress within two years of retirement.[5] Sixty percent of NBA players go bankrupt within five years of hanging up their athletic shoes.

This is a frightening trend that cuts across disciplines, a direct result of giving outrageous amounts of money to young adults with limited financial literacy. These days the leagues are working hard to teach their players about money management. It's a start.

---

4 Kyle Carlson, Joshua Kim, Annamaria Lusardi, Colin F. Camerer, "Bankruptcy Rates Among NFL Players With Short-Lived Income Spikes," Working Paper 21085, National Bureau of Economic Research (April 2015)

5 Pablo S. Torre, "How (And Why) Athletes Go Broke," *Sports Illustrated* (March 23, 2009)

But we're getting ahead of ourselves.

All young athletes, from the recreational to the competitive, need guidance and limits to help them make good choices. Parents can be a positive force in this arena; they can just as easily be part of the problem. Downplaying their own expectations while keeping lines of communication open and actively listening to their young athletes will help create a healthy environment. It's harder than it sounds.

When Griffie was eight, a group of parents decided that their kids needed "more." More intensive coaching, more serious competition, more everything than AYSO, as a recreational organization, could provide. Club soccer gleamed bright and shiny, so off these boys went. What did the boys themselves think? Club for this age group was not yet a "thing," so it's doubtful they really knew much about it. This was a decision driven by the parents.

Luca didn't say much, so his mom, Pam, had to frequently translate his looks and moods for the outside world. His feet were more communicative, and their sharp, quick cuts could eloquently slice and dice an opponent. After leaving AYSO, Luca spent the next six seasons wandering from club to club. Whether it was the coaching or the level of competition or the chemistry with the other the kids, none of the teams felt "right." He adored the game, even considered playing in college, but he just couldn't find the perfect situation in which to – here it is again – maximize his potential. He finally landed back at the beginning, on a team composed of kids he had played with – and who had stayed – in AYSO several more years before graduating to club. While it may not have been as competitive a squad as he and his family were initially seeking, the emphasis on enjoyment and camaraderie proved a compelling blend. He remained with this group through high school.

After two years on his post-AYSO club team, ten-year-old Ryan complained that soccer had begun to feel like a job. Gone was the fun, and with three practices a week, all that remained was the work. As Ryan's passion waned, his work rate flagged and his development slowed. Better players joining the team pushed Ryan to the bench, which further smothered his enthusiasm. By thirteen, Ryan was finished with soccer.

Alejandro lasted two years in club, then, voicing the same complaint as Ryan, found his way back to the more recreational AYSO. Bryce lasted a year in club before dropping out of sports altogether.

In the years since this group headed off to find fame and glory as eight-year-olds, club soccer has begun to snatch an ever younger set of players. Six-year-olds now routinely populate teams.

Michael shot out of the womb with the hand-eye coordination of a seasoned professional. A preschool superstar, the uncrowned king of the kinder yard, he excelled in every sport. After his first year in AYSO, his mom, Donna, a college athlete herself, told me that everyone who saw Michael play urged her to put him in club. He was six. I recited the litany of reasons he should wait, but Donna shrugged. "It seems to be what he wants to do." Bye-bye, Michael.

One day two years later I got a phone call from Donna who reported that Michael was having a great time, loved the other kids, and she enjoyed most of the other families. I could hear the hitch in her voice. "But our coach wants to go from two to three practices per week and with one, sometimes two games each weekend, we think it's extreme. Michael's only eight, and he also wants to play basketball. He's even starting to like baseball. What do you think we should do?" I wasn't surprised that the mesmerizing spell of club, capable of beclouding all reason, was wearing off.

I rattled off the steps of Michael's repatriation. "He can come back to AYSO and we'll make sure that he has a good coach. In the spring he can play All-Stars to get a bit more of a competitive experience. He can be a leader on the team, while still having the time and space to play basketball, baseball and anything else he comes to fancy. How's that sound?"

When Donna hung up, her relief lingered on the line. We enacted the plan, found the right coach for Michael, and he made an All-Star team at the end of the league season. An email followed:

> I just wanted to take a moment to thank you again for helping me jump off the club merry-go-round last year and re-join AYSO. We had the most wonderful families on our team and Craig is truly one of the best coaches we have ever had (apart from being likable and wonderful in every way).
>
> I truly appreciate you looking out for Michael and putting him on the perfect team so he would have the right experience with soccer again. He regained his love of the game and we regained having our family back again over the last year. It was a win/win for all. Michael is now greatly looking forward to All-Stars, Extras and the like.

Here was an example of an enlightened parent who went off not quite knowing what to expect while hoping for the best for her child. Ultimately, she was flexible enough – and knew her child well enough – to slam on the brakes when she realized that the environment wasn't right for her family.

It's difficult to know. These days the culture is screaming that kids, even the very young, need to fulfill their amorphous, poorly-defined potential, or risk falling behind. Behind what? What can a six-year-old who's not playing in the top tier of a travel team lose out on? A college scholarship? A pro contract? A happy life?

Hadi and I survived the Inquisition in the Tap Room, and a month later we headed to our first tournament: The Riverside Locomotion. Hundreds of teams, thousands of kids, parents, siblings, lawn chairs and coolers. The gathering of the tribes. A giant red and white tent rose above the venue, projecting a grand party vibe. Twenty-four fields of round-the-clock action, with each team playing four, and if advancing to the Medal Round, five or six games.

On Saturday, the Pali Xtreme (a name crafted to elevate our "C"-team roots) won both games. The boys knocked the ball around with the easy assurance of long-time teammates out for a day at the park. Their performance far surpassed any hopes we may have quietly harbored. Hadi and I rubbed our hands raw from all our high-fiving. The parents slapped us on the back – "Great work!" – as they huddled behind us. Even the skeptical Ken and Gary betrayed approving nods when they caught our eye from down the sideline. Maybe we'd been selling our team – and ourselves – short in that parent meeting. Perhaps we actually were pretty good. Two more wins or even a win and a tie on Sunday and we'd be playing in Monday's semifinals. Heady stuff. Traffic was brutal on the ride home that night, but our wheels never touched the road.

Sunday the sun retreated behind the clouds and for the most part, so did we. Both games were a humbling tumble back to Earth. The precision play of the previous day must have gotten a better offer because it sure wasn't around for us. Every pass that was completed on Saturday was a ball that sailed out of play on Sunday. Every heads-up defensive adjustment we made in the first two games became a backdoor goal for the other teams. The games lasted only forty minutes but they seemed to unfold in slow motion. The drive home felt as if we were riding on rims.

Sunday proved to be a snapshot of the rest of the season. We'd come out firing but gift our opponents goals on counterattacks. By halftime the wheels would come off and we'd lose by unconscionable 11-0 or 12-1 scores. Keeping a beating to seven or eight goals felt like a minor victory. Still, we kept practices fun, the kids laughed and slowly acquired skills, and the season rolled on.

We entered a tournament in Palmdale, a desert community on the outskirts of the commute into LA. The fields sat just below the freeway, and the gusts that swept through the canyon could drop the temperature twenty degrees in an instant. The boys performed true to form through the first three games, losing on silly mistakes – over dribbling, lax marking, ball watching – but we scored goals and remained competitive. We won the coin toss before the final game and opted to take the wind at our backs for the second half, figuring that if we could keep the score close until halftime, perhaps we could eke out a win with the aid of the wind.

As the game got underway, we quickly realized that we had underestimated the bias of Mother Nature. Going against the wind, our goalie's punts would sail back in our face. The other team's crosses, which on a normal day would have landed harmlessly outside the box, suddenly soared into the upper reaches of our goal. Quartz Hill breezed to a 6-0 lead at the half. Still, as the boys gulped down their water and Gatorade, Hadi and I were confident we could stage a comeback. Except for one thing.

When the referee blew his whistle for the kickoff, it was much louder and carried farther than it had in the first half. The wind, deafening earlier, could now barely manage a whisper. Neither could we. Quartz Hill steamrolled us to a season-high 15-0 defeat. The funnel cake each kid carried to the car for the ride home provided slim consolation.

Hadi and I managed to keep the parents, even Ken and Gary, reined in for the remainder of the season, squeaking out a few wins, a numbing number of losses, and a ton of laughs. The kids bonded and became a family, the core of which continued to play together through high school and the later years of club, forming a support system that thrives to this day.

* * *

As adults, we have expectations of things progressing in a somewhat predictable direction. But rarely in life do we get from Point A to Point B without twists and turns. If we remain open and receptive to the detours, it's possible to be pleasantly surprised instead of brutally crushed. Because Hadi and I were flexible, we were able to navigate our squad through the gauntlet. The next year this team, more experienced and more mature, if one can use that word when referring to ten-year-olds, won nearly every game. The seeds of success had been sown in the lessons of failure. And by putting the needs of the kids above the expectations of their parents, we enhanced the experience for everybody.

Expectation, while a dirty word, comes in shades of grime. Overwhelming anticipation layered thick with pressure will certainly wreak palpable damage. But apathy, the lack of any expectation at all, will also take its toll on the aspiring sportsman. I've seen kids who exhibit a fair amount of skill and desire whose parents were distracted or disinterested altogether. Not surprisingly, these kids failed to launch or washed out early as they lacked the support that would have encouraged their growth. The daisy picker may reveal no initial interest in the game, but that doesn't mean the spark may not ignite in the future. I've seen kids who, with subtle support, wake up and excel years later.

Then there are those who never shake off their initial reluctance but whose parents keep pining for change so sign their kids up well into their teens. It's difficult to watch a peach-fuzzed giant still bending down to study the foliage. Can't be good for his back.

No one escapes childhood unscathed. Freighting kids with our expectations, or trying to live vicariously through their experiences, is neither productive nor profitable. Holding fast to expectations for your kid as an athlete will inevitably result in clashes that both of you will look back on and regret.

But if you cultivate a wider, more accepting perspective, this can be a happy and exciting time. Winning is fantastic. But connection, sportsmanship, dedication, sacrifice, unselfishness – these are qualities that will enhance your child's life, long after his knees have given out.

If we must have expectations for our children, let them be that they grow up to be curious, kind and diligent. Let's teach them to show grace in their victories and seek wisdom from their defeats. Let us invest in their potential as happy, productive human beings. Let them win in life, not just in games.

CHAPTER FIVE

Power to the Peeps

It's been said that the best place to score on a young goalkeeper is on the ground . . . or in the air. Basically anywhere. As such, it's not a position for those with easily bruised feelings.

Evan's Pali Xtreme All-Star team, notable for the magnitude of its defeats, nevertheless greeted each opportunity to play with enthusiasm. Over the course of its years-long evolution from doormat to dominator, the team had two boys who eagerly trotted out to play in the goal, Chuck and Doug. Both were heroic, staring down attackers and making impossible, acrobatic saves. And both were achingly mortal, getting caught off their line or watching balls tapped in from the unprotected back post.

Chuck's Waterloo occurred in year two, during the finals of the Chino Milk Can, so named for the dairy farms that gave the community its flavor . . . and scent. The nose-wrinkling fragrance of freshly fertilized fields wafted over the event as an added bonus.

Our opponents were a year-older team from Chino Hills, and from the whistle it was obvious how big a difference that year made. In a flurry of one-touch passes, the Chino players eviscerated our defense and slipped a shot past a diving Chuck. Moments later, they did it again. And then, only a few ticks deeper into the game, another ball rattled the net. Before the first quarter had ended, we were squinting up out of a 5-0 hole. Chuck took it personally. My senior partner that year, Coach Bill, dashed onto the field to keep Chuck from damaging himself as he pummeled the goal into submission.

When Doug took his turn in the box, his willing spirit exacted a toll on his all-too-mortal flesh. He sustained knocks and bruises and fractured a finger stopping a shot during a round of penalty kicks. He stayed in, blocked the final shot to win the tournament, and then the swelling began. He walked through the high-five line with his right hand in a bucket of ice.

Both boys also enjoyed playing on the field – Chuck frequently sacrificed his Gumby-malleable body, flopping to garner many a penalty for the team – so we sprinkled the joys and burdens of goalkeeping onto other members of the squad.

There was Julian, a soft little guy with a brush cut, who used to suffer a sympathy injury every time he'd let in a goal. He'd writhe on the ground or clutch his shoulder, disguising tears of embarrassment in sobs of pain. Chris usually took a fourth-quarter shift, and either saved a few with the game already out of reach, or watched a few more sail past him. As the last man standing, though, the referees frequently singled him out for a sportsmanship medallion, meaning he took the punishment without complaint. By the end of the season he'd amassed a collection rivaling the number of goals he'd surrendered.

In the opener of year one's Thousand Oaks Pot O'Gold tournament, it was Evan's turn in the box. He had a history with the position. Coming out of the keeper-less U6, Evan couldn't wait to don the gloves for the upcoming U8 season. He spoke about it incessantly, and all summer long he had me kick him balls in the backyard and toss them in the den, where he'd leap across the couch to make the save.

On the eve of the Red Dragons' first game, Evan refused to close his eyes until I assured him for the umpteenth time that he would be our starting goalie. When I looked in on him later, he was sprawled across the bed, his goalie gloves securely on his hands making saves in Dreamland.

The next morning we couldn't get to the field fast enough. I'd never seen Evan this revved up and focused at the same time. I was feeling the same way. Right before kickoff it was time to don the goalie jersey, a polyester smock of green, black, teal, purple and gold. This nightmarish mash-up, issued by AYSO to distinguish the keeper from the field players, hung to his calves, the sleeves dangling beyond his hands. He stood there stiff and stilted, like Boris Karloff's Frankenstein. We managed to roll up his sleeves and push him out to the goal.

As the game began, I watched the ball bounce around in the attacking end of the field with our forwards chasing after it. Barely discernible from behind me came this tiny, high-pitched whine that slowly insinuated itself into my consciousness. It took a few seconds to resolve itself into a voice.

"I . . . hate . . . goal. Goalie sucks. I don't wanna play . . ."

Suddenly, one of the other parents spun me around to see Evan storming toward the sideline.

"Goalie sucks! I'm done!"

Luckily he was small and the field was big and it took him a while to cross it. "Whoa, wait, Ev, what are you doing?"

"Quitting!!!"

While the game swirled around me, I grasped for a solution, any solution, which would keep Evan on the field, at least until the end of the quarter, when I could throw the more compliant Simon into the net. I cycled from "Evan, the team needs you" to "Evan, get back there, this isn't OK" to the last-ditch, "Evan, after the game we can go to Toys R Us." Nearly at the sideline, he paused. I could see his little brain weighing the options. Walk off and probably get punished later . . . or hang in and get some Hot Wheels or a Mario video game?

"You promise?"

The tide had turned and the other team was now racing toward our goal.

"Evan, quick, get back!"

"Dad, you promise?"

He had the leverage. "Ev, yes, I promise. Toys R Us!"

"Awright!!! Thanks, Dad."

Evan sped back toward the goal and arrived just in time to deflect the first shot of the season. As it turned out, that was the only shot he repelled, as the saves of summer dissolved before the onslaught of fall.

Later I realized that it was the suffocating polyester jersey that had soured his mood. (As I gained game savvy, I substituted training "pinnies" for the confining jerseys. Made of lightweight mesh, and able to slip unobtrusively over one's game jersey, the pinnies became a preferable alternative. If I'd only known about them that first day.)

By the time Evan stood on the goal line two years later at the Pot O'Gold tournament, he had lengthened sufficiently so that the jersey, now a red and white striped number, bottomed out just below his knees. Still, a ridiculous look. For much of the first half, the other team matched our level of futility and there was little for Evan to do. At one point, though, the ball skipped behind our defense and rolled in his direction. He trotted out to get it, and for a moment the breath caught in my throat. The ball was outside the penalty area, beyond the zone permissible for a goalie to pick it up. I was about to warn Evan when I saw him collect it with his foot. I relaxed. Good boy!

I wondered if he realized that he could dribble it back into the penalty area, then pick it up and punt it down the field. I couldn't remember if Hadi and I had gotten that far in our coaching. But instead of corralling it, or passing it to another player, or just kicking it down the field from where he was, he took off on the dribble. A perfectly legal, if imprudent, maneuver.

"Evan, get back! Get in the goal!" But he couldn't hear me. Or he chose not to. He just kept rumbling forward. Perplexed, players from both teams slowed to watch. Both sidelines fell silent. Even I finally gave up . . . and watched. Evan showed no signs of slowing down.

He passed one player, than blew by another, his silly, oversize jersey flaring out like a sail. He reached the halfway line . . . and kept going! At this point, our parents began to cheer – "Go Evan, go!" – urging him onward. He juked one player, shouldered past another. When he penetrated the other team's penalty area, a member of the opposition finally woke up. He swooped in and booted the ball into the next time zone.

Suddenly deprived of the oxygen of excitement the field fell silent. Evan stood for a moment, taking stock of what he'd done, and then, unruffled, he casually trotted back toward his goal. Both sidelines exploded, bathing him in a chorus of whoops and applause. Even the referee acknowledged him as he passed: "Nice work, young man." Evan jogged back to his line, a sly smirk the only hint anything had happened.

For whatever reason, at that moment on that morning, Evan felt the impulse to improvise. It might have been a synaptic misfire, or more nobly, a desire to do something to spark his team. Either could have boomeranged back in his face. Any semi-sentient attacker could have stripped away the ball and scored on our empty net. But it didn't happen, and the lesson I learned is reinforced every time I'm out on the field.

It's OK to occasionally let the kids run the show. Let them experiment, push the envelope. Kids in general, and athletes in particular, sometimes need to work things out for themselves. Win or lose, good or bad; perhaps there will be a teachable moment. Or maybe it will just be fun.

With parents and coaches looming, the kid decision-making process constricts. *Will dad approve of what I do? Will coach get mad?* Certainly as our kids get older we want them to consider the consequences and ramifications of their actions. But while they're developing their athletic IQ, they need to enjoy the freedom to make mistakes and grow. Let their voices be heard. Allow them the validation. What better milieu than the playing field where the consequences are no greater than a win or a loss that may be forgotten down the road . . . or even by lunch.

This can be a tough concept for adults to swallow. From their perspective, players, by virtue of their youth and inexperience, are dependent figures. They need us. And to a certain extent they do. But when coaches and parents overpower them and drown them out, players lose independence and ultimately, interest. At a certain point, they will just drop out of the game, or tragically, the sport.

In response to this dispiriting trend, the president of a girls' soccer league concocted a plan to neutralize the sideline.[1] His aim was to dedicate one day during the season on which the kids had total control. He named it Silent Sunday, and since its inception in 1999, leagues across the country have been adopting it. (Sometimes it's Silent Saturday, in accordance with game schedules.)

Whether Sunday or Saturday, the rules are the same. The kids play. The coaches watch. The parents applaud. Adult vocalizing of any kind is forbidden. Without their coaches and parents in their ear, the players communicate with each other. Their voices are supportive, enthusiastic and creative. It's an eerie sensation. Fields normally thrumming with oral adrenaline are becalmed; only the chirping of little voices and occasional fits of clapping disturb the peace. It's like watching a game on television with the volume dialed down to a whisper.

Silent Saturday has been a yearly fixture in Region 69 for almost two decades. At the end of the game, we canvass the kids and every year the response is overwhelmingly the same: "It was so much fun." "We loved it." "Why can't we have Silent Saturday every week?" Good question. It's the closest our overly-organized, hyper-regimented sports universe comes to old-school recreation, which, sans adult interference, fosters fun, growth and innovation. A kid, a ball, a team and a goal, with the decision making and problem solving left to the players. What could be more empowering than that?

---

1 Mike Wendling, "Soccer league muzzles parents, coaches," *The (Racine, WI) Journal Times* (October 2, 1999)

Adult reactions, however, range from anxiety to disgust. One aggrieved dad whined that it was his constitutional right to yell at his kid. Another lodged his protest by facing his lawn chair toward the parking lot. Some coaches worried that their players would be lost without a constant barrage of instruction.

Our response: Get over it. *It's about the kids, not about you.* It's one game, a single hour out of the entire season. What's the worst that can happen? Perhaps the kids will play badly . . . and lose. So what? One rabidly antagonistic Silent Saturday coach grudgingly admitted, "I hated every minute of it. But my kids never played better."

And yet, adding silence to the already volatile concoction of sports, competition, and kids can be a risky proposition.

Coach Alex took his coaching seriously. As a native of Britain he was genetically endowed with a love of the game. He desperately wanted his players to share his passion while executing the skills he worked so hard to teach them. To that end, he not only coached every moment in practice, he also kept up a running patter during games. For him, Silent Saturday was an abomination, a torture to be resisted. Thus, he maintained his characteristic yammering and badgering throughout the match.

On the opposite sideline, Coach Sam, who helped import Silent Saturday into Region 69, took exception to his friend Alex's flouting of the rules. Pushed to the brink, he finally shouted across the field,

"Hey, Alex! It's Silent Saturday. *Sssshhhh.*"

Nobody likes to be shushed, certainly not in public, and Alex bellowed back, "I'm talking to my players, Sam. Mind your business."

"It's not my business," enjoined Sam. "It's the kids' business, so why don't you just SHUT UP!"

An already quiet day turned deafeningly so. Alex felt the weight of his sideline's stares. But he refused to back down. "The kids need my help!"

The scene deteriorated from there. Voices from both sides rose to hush the two men. The referees came over to admonish them. But the spell had already been broken. The sidelines, now fully engaged, supportively echoed their coaches. The kids, whose attention was pingponging from coach to coach, stood by confused. This was not the way they expected the day to go. Unable to control the coaches and their raging minions, the referees summarily ended the game. The jeering and sniping bled all the way into the parking lot. Only a hearing in front of the regional board finally cooled tempers, but Sam and Alex never spoke civilly to one another again.

The Battle of the Coaches was regrettably not an isolated incident. Sideline craziness flares all year, every year. Nightmares about parents attacking coaches and coaches threatening referees fill the sports sections every day. As parents, and as a culture, we need to dial down the heat and realize that we are the beneficiaries of a blessing: sharing sports with our children.

It's unfortunate that Silent Saturday comes around so infrequently. Enabling kids on the field to make their own decisions, recognize their strengths and weaknesses, and experiment with modes of communication and conflict resolution, imbues them with confidence in dealing with their life at home, in school and in the world.

The best way to empower our children is to let them play the game. Practices are the coach's opportunity to teach and motivate, and game time is for the kids. It's said that soccer is a player's game, whereas football, basketball and baseball are more coach-driven. In football, a battery of coaches calls a new play every forty seconds. In basketball, the coach strides up and down the court, barking instructions at his troops. And in baseball, signals are relayed from the bench to the catcher and finally to the pitcher in a well-choreographed ritual. Yet in soccer, there are no timeouts, the players traverse a wide expanse, and the game moves quickly. For the most part, the players are on their own.

The inexperienced coach may balk at leaving the game to the players. He may not understand the difference between practice and games, and what the objective should be in each circumstance. He may even believe that the most important goal is winning. And to achieve that end, the kids require constant comment and reassurance.

Parents also may be ignorant of the most productive ways to show support for their children. Our culture has redefined the nature of good parenting, and attending one's kids' sporting events is a key requirement. But the line between support and distraction is easy to cross. Shouting, singling out their kids by name (as opposed to more generic cheers like, "Go team!") or criticizing referees can disturb a player's concentration and focus. Some parents believe that ramping up their volume will have a proportional effect on their kid's performance. The louder they cheer, the better their child will play. In my experience, it doesn't work that way.

Younger players present a unique challenge because they're bursting with energy while lacking in structure. Parents often feel it's their role to provide that structure until the kids achieve a level of comfort and competence. Unfortunately, this can lead to parents overstepping their bounds, and rendering the coach superfluous. This is why parents of younger kids are often the hardest group to wrangle. As kids emerge from the fumblingly cute flailing of their five- and six-year-old selves and experience the stirrings of competition as seven- and eight-year-olds, a parent's ability to negatively influence the situation hits its stride. Here's a universally recognizable scenario:

The game seesawed back and forth but a last-minute goal by the other team clinched the contest. Joey sat on the bench for the last quarter fighting the vestiges of a cold that had kept him out of school all week. He had given it his best but after a few sprints down the field, he was winded, bent over, his hands on his knees. He slumped through the high-five line, waved off the cookies on the snack plate, and trudged to the car. His dad, frustrated for Joey, mumbled a few quick goodbyes and hurried after him.

"What the hell was Coach thinking," Dad growled as he tried to back out of the space. Disappointed, Joey stared out the side window. "How could he sit you in the last quarter? For *Derek?* No wonder you guys lost."

What was Joey supposed to say? What *could* he say? Could he have felt any worse? Did he need Dad to hammer home the misery of the morning? Was questioning the coach's competence productive for Joey in the moment or for the season going forward?

Parents can be oblivious of the negative impact they can have on their young athletes. Most assume they're commiserating with their kids in these trying moments. Some are just venting their own frustrations. From a coaching standpoint, these words can undermine a child's experience. The child second-guesses the actions of his coach as well as his own performance on the field.

What Dad should have said was, "Tough game. I loved watching you play. What do you want to eat?" Joey may lament his team's loss, but Dad's more positive reaction will facilitate a faster, healthier recovery. Timing is everything, and in the moment, it's important to be restrained and discreet. Bedtime, when kids are more open and receptive, might offer a propitious opportunity to reprise the conversation, with open-ended questions, such as, "What was it like playing against that no. 7?" or "Did you learn anything you didn't know before?"

Parents, like kids, also need time to decompress after a game. Otherwise, that post-game conversation can have an edge that only makes things worse. Questions like "what did you do that for?" or "what were you thinking?" are harsh and accusatory. Given time to process and heal, the conversation on both sides will be more productive.

Sports can bring families together, but they can also be flash points in the parent-child relationship. It's not easy but it is our responsibility as parents to defuse tension and maintain balance and realistic optimism. On too many occasions I've been guilty of tossing tone-deaf comments toward my three kids and their response has usually been some version of, "Dad, you're way too close to this. You want this too much. This is too important to you." I found that one of their siblings, or my wife or a family friend or one of their other coaches could deliver the message in a less fraught manner. It's a strategy that might not work for everybody, but it's certainly worth a shot.

Kids are powerful and perceptive creatures. They can tell by the way we enter their room that we've got an agenda. They'll know that the discussion is not really about them – their wins or losses, their growth, their process. It's about us and our expectations. And that's when we may as well turn out the light and close the door. The conversation is over.

But if we give them the time and the space to work through their challenges, they'll feel safe, and actually appreciate our support. And maybe, just maybe, they'll open up and allow us a deeper and privileged access into their world.

Kids will feel the most alive, energized and carefree when we adults acknowledge what this is all about: kids playing games. When we accept that the fate of the world, or our child's value, success and happiness, doesn't hinge on the outcome of any game, team or season, we can relax and enjoy the ride.

CHAPTER SIX

Kids Just Wanna Have Fun

Dori didn't stand a chance. All the tutus in the world, a good portion of which hung in her closet, couldn't get Dori to resist the call of the pitch. Once Evan began his classes with the boys at Barrington, Dori's fate was sealed. She paraded around in a smaller version of Evan's red soccer shirt, sprawled across the bag of black-and-white soccer balls residing in the den (while Evan claimed the beanbag), and attended every one of his practices. In a photo hanging in my office, a soccer ball looms in the foreground with curly-haired Dori standing against the fence thirty feet behind. The ball and Dori are the same size, their connection indelible.

But it was anybody's guess what kind of soccer player Dori would be once she took the field in her own right. Absent her (tor)mentor's formidable presence, would she be the energetic bunny always up for a kick-around when he summoned her to the backyard? Or would she reveal a more reserved persona, respectful or maybe a little fearful of the ball's unpredictable bounces? Based on Dori's full-tilt effervescence, my money was on the former. I figured she'd bolt onto the field, grab a ball and never look back.

Every parent wonders whether his kid will take to sports. Will she be a game-changer or a scrub? Will she be hyper-competitive or just happy to be there? Will she sweep blissfully from one end of the field to the other or crouch down to watch a bee dive bomb a clump of clover while the game churns around her?

Here's a simple truth: kids are smarter than we are. Certainly less complicated. They understand that sports are games. Games are meant to be played. And play is fun. Kids' desire to have fun colors everything they do, and for budding athletes it is what keeps them going and growing in their game. When sports are no longer enjoyable, they'll be stampeding toward the exit.

AYSO gets it. The organization elevates "Everyone Plays" to the top of its list of basic principles. Not just a call to universal participation, it's an acknowledgment that fun needs to be baked into every part of the program, from the first practice to the final team party. Because if it's not fun, why do it?

For parents new to sports, though, the big question is, what kind of athlete will my kid be? A glance at the individual's personality – is she curious, outgoing, reserved, (fill in every other adjective imaginable) – will assist in formulating that answer. Also helpful, I hope, is the following roster of player archetypes I've come to recognize over the years.

Most kids belong to the **FUN BUNCH.** They thrill to the energy, the flow, the immersion in the moment. They relish being part of something bigger than themselves, of competing and testing their limits, and walking away with a cupcake at the close. Whether they contribute by scoring the goals or by swooping in for a high five, there are endorphins enough for all. Athletes in this group range from the "so-so" to the "so good." They work hard, they goof around, they get better, they plateau, they understand the game, they haven't a clue. In the end, their grandest aspiration is having a good time.

The social aspect of sports – playing with pals or the getting the chance to make new ones – serves as a key motivation to participate. It's also one of AYSO's principal successes. In a world where we don't know our neighbors and all the kids on the block attend different schools, AYSO strives to be a community built upon common interest, volunteerism, and shared values. When kids expand their circle of friends, so do parents. While Evan, Dori and Griffie were minting friends for life, so were Marcy and I. From every one of the kids' All-Star teams, we created new bonds and relationships that continue to flourish.

Some players are so passionate about their friends that it may color the dynamic of the team. Witness the **BEST FRIEND.** She lives for her time with her teammates, tumbling out of the car and into their arms, chattering and sharing, so happy to be there. She is loyal, and will sacrifice anything for those close to her. When Dori's best friend Jillian publicly announced the conclusion of her club soccer career, she pointed to Dori and said, "And she's done too." Unfortunately, this was news to Dori. But with all eyes now focused on her, Dori didn't disappoint. "Jillian's right," she said, backing up her pal. "I'm done too."

Beware, though. A Best Friend can mutate into a **BEAST FRIEND.** She will latch onto another teammate and try to wall her off from the others. This friendship can become insular, and then smothering, and if left unaddressed, it can be devastating to team chemistry. Beckett adored Frankie, couldn't get enough of her, and glued herself to her side at every opportunity. But Frankie was also tight with Amelia, Darby, Jolie, Veronica and the rest of the field hockey team, who resented Beckett's attempts to claim Frankie for herself. The situation festered over several months, finally exploding in tears of betrayal over a movie invitation. Then the parents got involved, one insisting the girls work out their issues in group therapy, which felt a bit extreme as the girls were twelve. In retrospect, perhaps the coach should have counseled the team about unity and sharing, switched up practice partners, and maintained a greater overall vigilance, which could have led to a less dramatic conclusion. Then again, we mess with hormonal teenagers at our peril.

Emotion is not a factor in the **PROFESSOR**'s calculus. He approaches the game cerebrally. While his teammates can look at a ball and know it just wants to be kicked, the Professor needs to understand each concept on a quantum level. His mode of mastery requires an endless litany of questions. "What," "why," "where" and especially "how come" greet every pronouncement by the coach.

The Professor who reads the flow of the game and predicts what's going to happen several moves before it does enters the realm of the **GRANDMASTER**. Vision, anticipation and leadership characterize this player's value. It's like having a coach right on the field.

The **LITIGATOR** is a Professor with an advanced degree in annoyance. Like the Professor, he will spout nonstop questions, but in the Litigator's case, the coach's answers are never enough. He has to argue and plead and correct, presenting his own opinions and solutions, whether he knows what he's talking about or not. Griffie reveled in his reputation as a Litigator, and over the years, generous teammates and forgiving coaches gave him that space, while at the same time having no problem shutting him down when their patience eroded. Tell it to the judge, Griffie.

Another legal eagle is the **VICTIM**. More often than not he's a player of considerable skill and even more attitude. You'll see him scurrying downfield, zigging and zagging past opponents before entering a punishing 50-50 tackle, where he'll crash to the ground and lose the ball. He'll jump to his feet, or more efficiently, remain on his knees, and cast his arms skyward in a gesture that screams, "Ref, you're not going to call that foul?!? Is there no justice??? CAN CIVILIZATION POSSIBLY SURVIVE???" Referees usually ignore these histrionics the first few times, but continued performances will assuredly merit a yellow card, or, for the truly obnoxious offender, a red.

Henry and Ari were maestros on the ball. Henry could seemingly unhook his hips from his spine to slip through a thicket of defenders unscathed, possession intact. But if a spasm of over-dribbling cost him the ball, or a shoulder-charge knocked him off balance, he'd go full-Victim. Ari was sturdier, not as slick as Henry. Where Henry could find holes, Ari's bullish momentum created them. But landing him on the ground activated the same "Hey Ref!" sequence. While Henry felt truly wronged, Ari would jog back with a little smirk belying his grievance.

The Victim, unchecked, can morph into the **VIGILANTE**. Aggressively frustrated that his pleas are gaining no traction, he lashes out in retribution. Pushing, tripping, targeting opponents off the ball, the Vigilante needs to be removed from the match before he hurts himself or somebody else.

Another of our player archetypes is the **CLASS CLOWN**, a character who lives for the laughs. The Class Clown comes in two varieties. He can be a super though lazy athlete, who uses humor to deflect from his anemic work ethic. The other is the insecure kid, anxious about his ability, who goofs around to garner attention. An unrestrained Class Clown can become a **TROUBLEMAKER**. Think Heath Ledger's Joker, committed to existential chaos. He's not angry. He doesn't hate sports. He doesn't *not* want to be there. But something in him says, in true Willy Loman fashion, "*Attention must be paid.*" From breaking goals to kicking cones to teasing other kids, the Troublemaker emits an energy that cries out to be re-directed.

Another easily identifiable genus and species, as its members tower over the competition, is **THE EXCELLENT.** It's not the height that counts, though it could be a bonus; it's the preternatural ability that captures the attention of anyone not wearing post-cataract surgery sunglasses. These are the kids who perform feats their peers can only drool over.

Among The Excellents, note the **PHENOM**, who glides down the field, effortlessly outmaneuvering the overmatched opposition, before pounding the ball into the net with authority. This is at four, maybe five, no more than six. His teammates recoil, intimidated. *I'll never be that good.* The parents of his teammates squirm as they silently puzzle, *why is that kid so good? How is he so much better than mine? What am I doing wrong?*

Truth is, the Phenom is an aberration. Kids need to simply say, "Wow, she is good. I hope she passes to me so I can have a chance too," rather than judging or comparing themselves. Parents should understand that her remarkable talents are not predictive of *their* child's capability or future prospects.

As discussed, life has a way of leveling the playing field. Growth spurts, both vertical and horizontal, or the lack of them, can be cruel to the aging Phenom. Puberty is the great equalizer, so parents of a young superstar should temper their dreams of shoe contracts and private jets. Phenoms can flame out faster than a match in the wind.

There are Phenoms who build their early promise into Hall of Fame careers. Though not as many as we like to think. Still, if you encounter one, enjoy the show.

The first thing that struck me about Jordin was her smile. It was a beacon that beamed across the Brentwood Magnet School blacktop, as winning as a new puppy under a Christmas tree. Jordin was a delightful seven-year-old whose mom ran the office at the school, which I leased for camp. It was a privilege to have Jordin in the fold and it was astonishing to watch her dominate everyone her age – and older – on the basketball court. Her competitive spirit was undeniable, but it was her love for the game that spoke the loudest. With a ball in her hand, she could climb mountains, compose symphonies and effect world peace.

Back on Planet Earth, she spotted me "H-O" in Horse, and I thought I had her. Then she hit me with that smile and I realized two things. I wasn't her first sucker. And I shouldn't expect any more gifts. She took me out in five straight shots.

It didn't take a crystal ball to see that Jordin's future would be bright. Before she was double figures in age, she was scoring double figures for her travel teams, collecting titles and growing her reputation. I next read about her as a freshman in high school, leading her team to honors and championships. By her senior year, as one of the top-rated point guards in the country, she carried them to the state championship. It was an obvious step onto the UCLA starting five, where four brilliant years catapulted her to the Seattle Storm of the WNBA. All the while still smiling.

Just as remarkable as the Phenom is the **NATURAL**. He's the kid who, picking up a ball for the first time, is already better than everybody else around him. Doesn't matter what sport; he's got the Midas touch in all of them.

Seven-year-old Matthew was a camp agnostic. His mom, Liz, brought him by the shipping container we were using for an office and he hid under her arm as she tried to guide his hand to shake mine. I gave him my best pitch about all the fun he'd have. Eyes down, he scowled, unconvinced. Yet, surrounded by balls, and kids kicking, throwing and shooting them, Matthew seemed to grow ten inches and age five years. He instantly morphed into a dominant force in every sport he tried.

In September, he debuted on my U10 AYSO team, the Gatorators. He took the league by storm, scoring a jaw-dropping number of goals, while exhibiting magical ball skills, wide-angle field awareness and the competitive moxie of someone with years, rather than months, in the game.

The Natural is a human highlight reel, accompanied by a soundtrack of "oohs" and "aahs." He is a born performer, feeding off the energy of the crowd while delighting himself with his unrehearsed feats of fancy. Where he differs from the Phenom, though, is in the bailiwicks of hard work, discipline and commitment. In my experience, the Phenom, whether born or made, is someone whose love for the game feeds an unquenchable desire to get ever better. The Natural, who came to greatness fully-formed, may stall or even switch off when the novelty fades or adversity strikes.

Matthew's soccer supremacy began to wane when defenders hit their growth spurts on a more accelerated schedule. Routinely matched against larger opponents who nullified his nimbleness with their physical play, Matthew's frustration soured him on soccer and into football – in fairness, a sport he'd always wanted to play.

Ultimately, he excelled and earned himself a walk-on slot with the USC Trojans. But he did return to the pitch for his high school senior season, managing to lead the league in scoring, and carrying the Brentwood squad to the brink of a championship.

The **DAREDEVIL** commits body and soul to the game. Absent too often is his judgment, which is soggy from the waves of adrenaline that propel this player. Acrobatic headers, divot-spraying slide tackles and wince-inducing collisions herald his crowd-pleasing presence, bringing everyone to their feet – except for his head-scratching coach and his anxiety-fatigued parents. The former is hoarse from counseling caution, while mom and dad are exhausted from trips to the ER amid worries about growth plate damage. At least these players are safe on the bench. Or are they?

For an already big kid, Cooper played as if he were fifty pounds heavier. He was Godzilla trampling Tokyo, bodies and destruction left in his wake. His monstrous exterior, though, couldn't protect the very human bones and sinew housed within, and in one cataclysmic crash, he fractured his foot and his opposite ankle, landing him in a wheelchair for a month. A few days in, however, sheathed in casts and braces, he was spotted doing wheelies over curbs, catching air. Nothing could slow this Daredevil down.

There was another daredevil Cooper (something about the name?) who fearlessly started doing headers at five. He thrived on the cranial contact and over the years he added banging heads, smashing into goal posts, and whiplashing against the turf to his repertoire. For thrill junkies like Cooper, one concussion is too many and five are not enough. The good news and bad news for parents of these kids? Many give up soccer (phew!) but segue to lacrosse, where they can add a stick to their arsenal of weapons. At least in lacrosse they wear helmets.

The **ALL-IN** is a distant cousin of the Daredevil. Related by their indifference to personal safety, the All-In at least considers the consequences of her hard-charging play. She recognizes that the result of every crunching tackle or pounding header could be pain, an ice pack, or worse. But it's heart over head with the All-In as she is animated by the highest calling of all in sports – doing whatever it takes to help her team. Fittingly, the Daredevil and the All-In tend to hold their family reunions at the same place – the doctor's office.

Carly was a senior, Natalie a freshman. Carly dominated the middle of the field; Natalie's strength was her speed down the touchline. Both could bring a crowd to its feet and their team back to life with a daring run, a whipped-in cross, or a laser finish. And before they graduated from high school, both had sustained a chilling number of concussions, which ultimately closed the book on their playing days. Could they have modulated their intensity and extended their careers? Sadly, as card-carrying All-Ins, full-tilt effort was all they knew.

The **GAMER** will drive you crazy. He's the sports version of Dr. Jekyll and Mr. Hyde. Distracted during practice, once the game whistle blows, he lights up like the sun and scorches the opposition. This was Evan, who exasperated more than a few coaches during his career. In training sessions, you'd find him sitting on a ball while his teammates were working on their skills. During games, he was energy incarnate, a cacophony of flailing limbs trying to bring a ball out of the air, capable of a long-range bomb or an in-your-face poke. He made things happen, and coaches couldn't take him off the field.

The Gamer's mirror image would be the **GHOST**, an athlete whose training persona conjures visions of victory, but who disappears, as if hiding in a hole, during the game. Off-field confidence building can help these kids diffuse the pressure of game time and allow them to perform to their capability.

At the top of the Excellents pyramid reigns the **WARRIOR KING** (or **QUEEN**). He may be blessed with outsized talent like the Phenom or the Natural, but athletic DNA is not a prerequisite for accomplishment. The Warrior King may actually arrive with little discernible aptitude and even less ability. But if you look closely, you will see his future success in the set of his eyes. He competes with himself, his pilot light always dialed up high as he does the little things, the extra work, embracing the hardship, all in an effort to excel.

David Michael came late to Griffie's club team. The boys were in ninth grade, with friendships and patterns already firmly established. Trying to crack this brotherhood seemed a daunting challenge, and in his first weeks at practice, David Michael didn't try. While the other boys would plop down in a gossipy group to gear up, David Michael stood on the side quietly honing his juggling skills. When the coach delivered instructions to a half-hearted team, David Michael hung on his every word.

In drills, he competed as if in a game. In games, he fought as if each contest were the championship. A total team player, affable, coachable, everything he did served the interests of the squad. Undersized and not particularly fast, he outworked everyone on the field, winning impossible headers, courageously throwing himself into crunching confrontations, and maintaining his poise and composure to put the ball where it needed to be. At first the other boys were content to simply marvel at David Michael's intensity. Soon, it began to inspire them.

None of this is to say that David Michael was all work and no play. Sharing the back line with Griffie, he would have had to be an automaton not to be amused by the character that prattled on through games with opponents about physics, the Simpsons, and Mario. It was symbiosis at its best. David Michael offered Griffie the security to play loose and Griffie kept a smile on David Michael's face.

Ultimately, as with all Warrior Kings, it was David Michael's enormous heart that made him the Hall of Fame kid and competitor that he was. Talent and commitment are essential ingredients but heart, which suffused everything that David Michael did, differentiates the "great" from "the greatest."

My friend Adrienne confided that her son Remi's fencing coach tapped Remi as "this close" to being great. Only three years since picking up an epee, fourteen-year-old Remi's hormone-inflected athleticism generated a steady rise up the rankings. "With just a little more effort," intoned the coach, "and a few more tournaments," Remi could be a top-flight fencer. Only problem was Remi didn't share the coach's vision. Training three times a week with occasional tournaments was swordplay aplenty, thank you very much.

The coach pinned his hopes on Remi's parents' ability to persuade, cajole or, if necessary, strong-arm their talent-latent son into, well, making his talent a little less latent. The story struck a chord with me. In the midst of his growth spurt Griffie transformed into a beast able to impose his will on the opposition. Coaches noticed, several venturing that with a little more time on the ball and a little less on the game controller, Griffie could be a contender.

Remi and Griffie were **THIS CLOSE** athletes. A modest additional application of time and industry could have put them over the top. But Remi wasn't ready and it's unclear if he ever would be. Griffie knew that come college, athletics would genuflect before academics. He loved soccer and all that it had meant to him through the years, but a clear-eyed calculation of his future meant stepping away from his past.

Parents of a This Close athlete have difficulty reconciling their kids being able to see the Promised Land but deciding, nah, not for me. More of a challenge is accepting that we can't influence, through reason or by fiat, their decision. If the hunger to be the best doesn't keep them up at night – if they're slumbering soundly, content with however good they are – then we need to stop tossing and turning and get a good night's sleep ourselves.

With all these ballers of various stripes and flavors, there's one important group we've yet to consider, the one that parents sprout gray hairs and grind teeth over: **THE RELUCTANTS**. They're prevalent at the early ages, when kids are taking their first sporting steps. By the time they roll into high school, it's a stage they've outgrown, conquered or surrendered to and drifted off to other pursuits.

But among the younger set, these are the kids who don't want to play – and they're keen to let you know it. Whether the protests are piercingly shrill or silently immutable, accompanied by tears or promises to do anything *else*, Reluctant kids make it a struggle to get out the door.

Sometimes their protests abate when they see their pals racing around on the field. Just as often, a Reluctant will straitjacket himself in his arms, burrow his chin in his chest and scowl so ferociously, early onset frown lines become a possibility. Bribery often helps. But once you're past ice cream, a later bedtime or an extra hour of YouTube, how far do you really want to go?

His unwillingness could be constitutional, a genetic indifference to sports. Chess, dance, painting, piano, or coding could be more interesting to this kid. Or it could be situational, a disinterest in the moment. Perhaps there's an issue at home or at school, with siblings or with friends. Divorce or an unavailable parent could explain the child's tantrums as a flailing exercise of power or a displaced cry for help.

Reluctant kids can be subdivided into the **IDONTWANNA** and the **IMNOTREADY**. The categories are not mutually exclusive, as one's resistance may stem from a premature introduction, whereas a lack of readiness could disguise disinterest. It's not an exact science.

Will was the Idontwanna poster child. He would arrive at class wearing a look of grim apprehension, his lips silently mouthing his mantra, "I don't wanna . . ." It didn't matter what we were playing – Red Rover, Red Light-Green Light, Super Secret Rocket Rangers, Star Wars – which all the other four-year-olds gobbled up greedily. Will remained unflinching in his resolve. "I don't wanna!" Unlike those who would root themselves to the spot or run from the field, Will would voice his objections and then grudgingly participate. An hour later, his mom would walk him back to the car, Will still mumbling, "I don't wanna . . ."

After a few weeks of this, Coach Cooper had an idea. "Who wants to play . . ."

"I don't wanna." Will didn't even let Cooper finish his question.

"Well, Will, what game would you WANT to play?"

"I don't . . ." Will stopped. He squinted up at Cooper.

"Will, we'll play whatever you like."

The rationale of his protest ripped away, this was almost too much for Will to handle. The other kids looked to him, waiting . . . and waiting. Will's eyes darted from them to Coach Cooper.

"I DON'T WANNA!" Will spun away and flew to his mom, wailing. A few minutes later, class over, Cooper was collecting the cones when he felt a tug on his Colts jersey. It was Will.

"Coach Cooper . . . next week . . . could we play . . . Cookie?"

It would be disingenuous to report that from that moment on, Will became an enthusiastic participant. But after a while even he was able to laugh at the refrain that had become more reflex than feeling.

Raleigh was another classic Idontwanna. She'd never met a horse she didn't like, but a soccer ball . . . she wasn't so sure. A member of Dori's U8 Stingers, before every game she would dig her fingernails into her mom's thigh and cling tenaciously as her mom, Jane, three-legged limped her onto the field. Raleigh pleaded the whole way. Once play began, though, Raleigh switched on, chasing for the ball, having a grand old time. Vegas would have offered long odds but Raleigh remained in soccer, playing on All-Star and club teams all the way through high school. Before she headed off to fulfill her equestrian destiny in college, she had become one of the most dynamic members of the squad. She just needed that loving push to jumpstart her engine.

There is a difference, though, between a push and a shove, which delineates the difference between the Idontwanna and the Imnotready. Imnotready kids are easy to spot. The parent has pressed the situation way too hard. You know it and the kid knows it. The only person in the dark is the parent. These kids have a wounded look that's unmistakable. It cries, *Why am I here and when can I leave?* We feel bad because we know that this is just the first of many uncomfortable situations the child will be thrust into. And we can foresee the unpleasant blowback down the road.

Sharon was thrilled that Jeremy, who just turned four, was finally old enough to start soccer. A preschool classmate of Dori, he was an enthusiastic little boy, a huge smile crinkling his eyes. Based on temperament alone, I figured he'd love kicking and racing around, so

I encouraged Sharon to bring him to Barrington. With all the kids convened, I shouted, "All right, everybody get a ball."

The sound that issued from Jeremy's lips was deafening, an alien rendering that melted faces and pulverized bone. Unable to calm him as the rest of the kids scattered to safety, Sharon yanked Jeremy and threw him in the car. They were halfway home before the sound faded from the field. Jeremy never appeared on a soccer field again, though years later I saw a *Palisadian-Post* article detailing his exploits on the volleyball court. Thankfully he outgrew the trauma, but in that moment Jeremy was an obvious Imnotready kid.

Drew Jr. was Jeremy's age but twice his size when he appeared on the roster for Evan's basketball team. His dad, multi-sport superstar and baseball legend Drew Sr., never admitted that Junior was two years junior to Evan and the rest of the squad, but it didn't take Sherlock Holmes to realize that a starstruck recreation director had acceded to Senior's wishes to have Junior play up. The years between four and six, however, are a dynamo of development, and Drew Jr.'s planting himself in the paint, waiting for the ball while everyone else ran the floor, illuminated the gulf those two years would shrink. As Drew Jr.'s exasperation began to stream down his face, Drew Sr. realized that maybe he'd pushed a little too hard a little too soon.

Many parents of Imnotreadys aren't as quick to send up the white flag as Sharon and Drew Sr. They dig in, rationalizing that their kids will "come around," that sports are "good for them," that this is what they did when they were kids. These parents, mistaking their child's resistance as a referendum on their parenting, plunge into a power struggle that neither party can win. It's an attitude capable of derailing a productive youthful career, as the damage can linger in a child's negative view of sports.

A patient parent, by investing the child with choice, can help turn an Idontwanna or an Imnotready into a willing participant.

Robbie was four, with long blond hair, pale to the point of translucent skin, and big eyes that took in everything. Mom Jamie signed him up for one of our after-camp soccer classes. While the other kids eagerly fetched a ball, Robbie would perch on one of the play structure's green, turtle-shaped seats. From there he would just watch. No matter how loud the laughter from his peers on the field, Robbie never blinked and never budged. It's not as if I didn't try to coax him out onto the field. His response – the subtle swishing of his hair side to side – was always the same.

During the break, I'd bring him a Capri Sun (this was before we were enlightened enough to switch to water), which he readily accepted, and each time I'd whisper the same question to Jamie.

"Is he OK?"

"He's fine," she'd answer, unconcerned. "This is what he does."

For eight straight weeks, Robbie observed from the play structure. He wouldn't talk or interact with his friends in the class. He just watched. Jamie was a paragon of patience, bringing him faithfully through the end of the summer. I mentioned that we planned a fall session to start after Labor Day.

"Robbie will be there," Jamie announced brightly. Robbie didn't react. I had my doubts.

Sure enough, the first kid to arrive for the first September class was Robbie. And rather than plop down on the blanket Jamie had laid out, he steered straight to the field, culled a soccer ball from the pack, and began shooting at the small goal. Once class began, he knew every game on the menu, and excelled at all of them, exhibiting skills the other kids had been struggling with all summer. I looked over to Jamie, who gave a shrug and a smile. Indeed, Robbie hadn't wasted his time sitting on the play structure. He just needed to feel comfortable – and capable – before joining in.

Now when parents show up with kids who don't want to participate I tell them to relax and let their children acclimate. I've never had a kid protest this arrangement; it's the parents who hyperventilate. They prod, "I didn't leave work to come out here and watch you sit!" The hard sell rarely works. But a retelling of the Robbie saga often earns the kid a reprieve.

It's true that the Reluctants may just be digging in against trying something new. Sports are their vegetables. After taking a taste, their resistance may crumble – eventually. But the root may lie deeper, in anxiety, insecurity, or peer issues that the child may not have the ability to articulate. As parents we must be able to "hear" our kids even in their silence. It's a difficult skill, but one well worth mastering.

Some stubbornly hard-of-hearing folks continue to register their Reluctant kids year after stressful year. Their guarded optimism – "this year everything will 'click in'" – long since abandoned, they now hold fast to the hope that keeping their child active will insulate him from the readily available dangers of adolescence – sex, drugs and social media. And yes, the correlation between breaking a sweat and leading a healthier lifestyle exists, but these are kids in palpable pain, or at best, dissociated indifference. Early on labeled as "daisy pickers," they're now defeated or disruptive, and their presence on a team constantly reminds that there are productive pastimes other than sports. Wouldn't it be great if their parents got that message?

So after all this, what kind of athlete did Dori become? Which category did she most embody? Well, fueled by a Starbucks Lemon-Loaf-and-foamy-Frappuccino breakfast of champions, over the course of her decade-plus of playing, she sampled nearly all of them. A member of the Fun Bunch, for sure, she was born to be a Best Friend, swung between Grandmaster and Litigator, and in consecutive matches, she could be a Gamer, then a Ghost.

Mostly, though, Dori played with the lion heart of a Warrior Queen. Her lack of speed, a casualty of puberty, as a central defender should have been disqualifying, yet she led with a Spidey sense alerting her to every threat, a deft touch to deliver the ball to the perfect spot, and an appetite for banging bodies that bordered on gluttony.

These qualities coalesced one rainy night in nearby Northridge when Dori played the game of her life, enabling her to shut down the league's most prolific scorer. Looking back, this was how she emerged from the womb, serious and focused, so there should have been no surprise she'd carry that determination onto the pitch. Maybe I'm extrapolating, maybe I'm imagining. Maybe we can predict our kids' athletic personalities based on their early days, or maybe it's the experience that reveals who they really are. What matters most is that they get the opportunity to be that person, no matter who that happens to be.

With this many varieties of players, you'd have to believe there would be a healthy number of coach types, too. You'd be correct.

CHAPTER SEVEN

Coaches 101

A tale of two coaches.

The game is over. Coach Randy's team won convincingly, 6-2. The kids are bouncing around the sideline, their elation heightened by a seemingly bottomless box of Krispy Kremes. Life is good. Across the way, the losing team, helmed by Coach Nelson, is a sea of slumping shoulders and tears, with parents swatting their kids' hands away from the donut box, "You don't need any more sugar right now!" Life sucks.

Both coaches summon their players.

"Great effort, boys," offers Coach Nelson, as he moves through the pack, shaking hands with his dejected troops. "We'll figure this out Tuesday at practice." The team, comforted by their families, heads out to the rest of their day.

"All right, boys, have a seat," Coach Randy says, gesturing to his team. The players drop to the turf before him. "Great effort today.

You should be really proud of yourselves." He then launches into a forty-five minute recitation, reliving the highlights and the miscues, singling out players for credit and others for constructive criticism. The kids are twitchy, they're getting cold, and the thrill of victory fades in the afternoon sun. The parents are antsy; they've got a dozen other stops on the weekend express. Coach Randy drones on, "Going into halftime with the lead was key . . ."

Two coaches, two different approaches. Despite losing, and probably having a legal pad full of notes and coaching points, Coach Nelson releases his team, perhaps missing the opportunity to correct mistakes while they're fresh. Coach Randy, whose team obviously outplayed Coach Nelson's squad, lingers at the field, essentially playing the game a second time.

Which approach is more productive? Who's the better coach? Some of us may gravitate toward Randy, others will prefer Nelson. Ultimately, it behooves us to first understand what the job of the coach is. And how do we tell if he's doing it right and doing it well?

Let's start with a list of qualities that the best coaches, whether volunteer or professional, should possess:

- Leadership – the ability to inspire and motivate players to achieve a common goal, while having the patience and creativity to see it through
- Vision – being able to project short-term and long-range goals; having perspective to understand that when development comes first, winning will follow
- Experience – should be knowledgeable in his discipline and be able to teach skills, strategy and awareness to his players
- Commitment – maintaining a balanced and unwavering loyalty to players and purpose

- Organization – being prepared for practices and games, punctual and disciplined, knowing when to delegate, remain flexible
- Communication – making sure that players and families are always informed, as well as being open and available to resolve issues
- Role Model – by example and word, living the positive values expected from your players and families: respect, honesty, good sportsmanship, confidence, empathy, humility, generosity, self-discipline
- Sense of Humor – an often overlooked and undervalued quality that can elevate effort, demonstrate understanding and make the journey fun

A truly excellent coach should also be a community leader, a teacher, a mentor, a confidante, a conscience, a cheerleader, a psychologist, a judge, a hypnotist, a rule follower, a rule breaker, a politician, a showman, a tour guide, a shlepper, an adult, a kid, a shoulder and a smile. He should be the first to arrive and the last to leave. He should know the questions, have the answers, and know that there's always much more to learn. He should be larger than life, yet comfortable blending in. He should be a steel umbrella when the sky is crashing down around his team. And he should be able to leap tall buildings in a single bound . . . though that requirement is optional.

How many coaches – how many humans? – can measure up to these lofty standards? Some can check off many of the boxes, but only a select few can lay claim to all of them. Find that person and follow him anywhere! The majority of coaches will more likely possess different combinations of these traits and it's important to seek out those who exhibit the ones that are critical to you and your child.

We'd all probably like to have Coach Eric Taylor from *Friday Night Lights* leading our kids. Tough but tender, pushing his players to excel, while always there for them at the first whiff of trouble. *Clear eyes, full hearts, CAN'T LOSE*, uh huh!

In the pantheon of real-life coaches, perhaps the most famous is John Wooden, who coached the UCLA men's basketball team for nearly thirty years, and still holds the record for number of NCAA championships, winning ten in a span of twelve years. He was a philosopher and a drill sergeant, a role model and a teacher, whose lessons ranged far beyond the basketball court. He devised the "Pyramid of Success,"[1] comprised of fifteen building blocks of character traits such as industriousness, friendship, cooperation, self-control, and initiative. At the very top stood competitive greatness.

John Wooden was determined to teach his players how to succeed in life, not just in sports. His definition of success was "peace of mind, which is a direct result of self-satisfaction in knowing you made the effort to become the best of which you are capable." For Coach Wooden, winning was a byproduct of hard work and character building. The journey was as important as the destination.

Today, the best youth coaches believe that while winning is important, development is the key to an athlete's success. (Many still hold out that winning beats everything else. We'll get to those guys.) Each of these coaches has his own method for actualizing this goal. And while each coach is unique, as with players, there are recognizable categories that most fall into. We parents need to evaluate the good, the bad, and the don't-go-there so that we can confidently decide which one will work best for our kids.

---

1 John Wooden and Jay Carty, *Coach Wooden's Pyramid of Success* (2009)

The John Woodens of this world are few and far between, so we have to set our sights at a more attainable height. How about a former high-level player, such as a professional of international repute, domestic in a pinch – **THE EX**. This person has a resume dripping with experience and accolades, a shoe contract, and surgical knees as proof. There is no question that the Ex knows the game, but playing it and teaching it to kids, often very young ones, are not necessarily compatible talents. Even if he has the patience and stamina to get eye-to-eye with a scrum of eight-year-olds, can he distill his years of sophisticated drill work for a squirmy, attention-challenged audience? With an Ex, the initial excitement of having a celebrity coach can wear off from his side or yours, with the players left dangling in the middle.

Former college players, more abundant than the ex-pros, fill the ranks of club and high school coaching. While not as prized as the upper echelon professionals, their youth buys them time to prove themselves as coaches.

The **INTERNATIONAL** is a subset of the Ex. These are the former pros that competed in leagues across Europe, Latin America, and Africa. Parents swoon from the accent, which, even if indecipherable, conveys legitimacy. As with the Ex, we have to sweep back the curtain and evaluate the entire package. Sometimes things get lost in translation.

There's **MR. KNOW-IT-ALL**. With the ramrod posture of Washington standing in the bow of the boat, confidence oozes from this character, and even without much wind, it can swell into arrogance. One of his introductory lines is, "I've been around this game for forty years," even if he's barely thirty. Because he knows everything, he's not shy about sharing his knowledge, which can test one's patience, and after a while, endurance. He likes to hear himself talk, so you'll often see his players sitting on their soccer balls or standing around, shifting from leg to leg.

A more enlightened coach knows to speak sparingly. Keeping the players active and engaged, learning by doing rather than by being lectured, is a more effective method. This coach is not a team player; why should he be? He's seen and done it all, thus he knows it better than anyone else. Suggestions or criticism will fall on deaf ears. Maybe not criticism. Mr. Know-It-All has a banana-skin ego, which when bruised, will send him into a pout or a grudge. The difference between Mr. Know-It-All and a coach who really *does* know his stuff, is that the **REAL DEAL** doesn't feel compelled to advertise it. Real Deals are generally a quieter breed, with a genuine smile instead of a superior smirk.

Beware the **NARRATOR**. This coach disgorges a nonstop drone, a verbal "Flight of the Bumblebee," directing each player's every action and movement. You'll hear him shout, "Chris, get your head up! Cameron's open in the middle. All right, Cameron, find Noah. Good. Noah, man on behind you! See, Max. Max, Archie's open for the cross." Screaming now, "Archie, make the run. Max, hit it! Archie, TAKE THE SHOT!"

His game-long urgency, which keeps his players at DEFCON 5, robs them of initiative, creativity, and the freedom to make mistakes. With his voice reverberating in their heads, how can they hear themselves think? Where is the space for them to learn to solve the problems that a fast-moving game will roll their way? Rather than teach his players necessary tools, he infantilizes them and keeps them dependent upon him. Should this coach be absent from a game, the sideline falls silent and the team goes to pieces. Unaccustomed to listening to, or trusting, themselves, the players run around like the proverbial headless chicken. With a coach like this, there is no joy in Mudville.

A hybrid of the Know-It-Alls and the Narrators is the **CRITIC**, though knowledge and chatter are hardly prerequisites for inclusion in this clan. These folks find fault with everything. If they're not sniping at their players, they're teeing off on the officials or grumbling about the parents. In their parboiled brains, their way is superior to everyone else's, and their criticism wrings excellence from their players.

There are long-time Critics who have generated considerable success, which doesn't absolve them from being unpleasant to deal with and unbearable to play for. No kid likes being picked apart, yet parents continue to flock to Critic-run teams because they get the wins.

If a child in a recreational program lands on one of these teams, the parent can take solace in the brief term of the team's existence, or try to convince the league to transfer their kid to another team. In a club setting, it becomes more challenging to disengage from the overly critical coach. The child may be stuck on this team for an entire year. At that point, the family faces an existential dilemma. Is it worth continuing to play when the pain-gain quotient is tenuous? It's not a question that suggests an easy answer.

And then there is the **EVANGELICAL** . . .

For Pierre, life was unimaginable without soccer. Back home in France, he played on farm teams for some of the major clubs. Coming to America, he latched onto adult teams, while honing his coaching chops with the YMCA and AYSO. He found his calling, though, as a coach and then director at one of the local clubs. For Pierre, soccer was more than a game. It was more than a passion. For Pierre, soccer was an all-consuming, lifelong journey that carried one from youthful ignorance to an exalted state of grace. All it took was commitment. Not the regular, run-of-the-mill, twenty-other-things-on-your-plate, half-assed, Westside of Los Angeles type of commitment. No, the kind of commitment Pierre believed in required a monastic dedication that eschewed all earthly distractions in favor of learning, training, competing, and repeating the same – again and again, year-round, forever and ever.

Only problem was that the Westside kids he was coaching came equipped with Westside parents, for whom soccer was just another one of their kids' activities. And it had to fit into a schedule overflowing with homework, tutors, school sports, religious school, saxophone lessons, recitals, fencing, doctors' appointments, community service projects, rec league basketball, visits from out-of-town relatives, family time, college counselors, and the most damning of all, vacations. Pierre hated vacations. They interrupted the flow of the season, which he painstakingly built to a crescendo tied to major tournaments. His code of commitment meant that players were his from August through June, two to three nights a week, and every weekend. Any deviation from this single-mindedness, short of major injury, was cause for benching or expulsion from the team.

Parents initially bought into his program, even if it competed with the rhythms of family life, as in winter break in Mammoth and spring break in Cabo. After a while, though, unwavering and resolute often turned into tired and over it. Parents faced the choice of all in or all out. Seeking a more balanced existence for their kids and their family, many opted for all out.

Despite their own love for the game, Evangelicals like Pierre lack perspective. They can't see that the majority of their players are looking for a pastime, not a be-all and end-all passion. And in his insistence on focus, commitment and specialization, the Evangelical coach can drain the life out of a wonderful experience.

One coach your kids will have fun with is the **BUDDY**. He's a blast to be around, and everyone – kids, parents, even the referees – flock to his sideline. He's comfortable and relaxed, and his charm puts everyone at ease. The **GOOD BUDDY** knows the game, is a strong teacher, and he promotes an atmosphere that's loose and light. Players look forward to practices, at the end of which they fall back into the car, exhausted, but happy. Then there's his "evil twin," the **BAD BUDDY**. He, too, is committed to fostering a fun environment. But where the Good Buddy understands the alchemy of recreation-infused learning, the Bad Buddy is flying blind. He may be an innocent bystander snared by a league desperate for volunteers, or a divorced dad looking to share quality time with his kid, but his pitch to the team runs like this:

"I need to apologize up front. I don't really know what's going on. I've never played _____ (fill in the sport) but my kid really really really wanted me to coach. So, I figured, why not? At the least, we'll have a great time."

The Bad Buddy knows his limitations but presumes that an honest effort should suffice. He'll be a booster and an entertainer, perhaps even a skillful party planner, but under his watch, most players will tread water, and many may lose interest. The parents with a short fuse certainly will. On the surface it can be difficult to distinguish between the two breeds of Buddies, as they both present as easygoing and fun. Experience and commitment are the qualities that set them apart. And while inexperience isn't a crime – everybody has to start somewhere – the commitment to improve can transform Bad to Good.

The Good Buddy can be a fantastic "starter" coach. His style will reassure parents seeking a gentle and pleasurable introduction for their kids. Absent will be the mind games and power trips inflicted by other coach types. But being everybody's best friend comes at a price. In the healthiest of scenarios, a well-delineated boundary exists between the coach and his players. He's the authority figure; they're his charges. He talks, they listen. He coaches, they play. When the lines blur, trouble may come knocking. Its genesis can be outwardly benign – the coach and some of the families share off-field meals, golf outings, and other social interactions. But those who haven't been included may perceive signs of favoritism – more playing time, less criticism – toward the kids of those in the social whirl. Or, the jocularity at practice can bleed over into games, where players may be unable or unwilling to execute the coach's game plan. Whispers, or an organized rebellion, can fray the team fabric, and whether it's a slow, agonizing dissolution as disgruntled families peel away, or a sudden roiling rupture, the team's demise is preordained. With the knowledge of these pitfalls, though, a smart Good Buddy can shape the team ethos and keep his ship afloat. For as long as it lasts, however, the Good Buddy coach is a worthwhile option for those for whom fun and enjoyment are primary goals.

"Winning isn't everything; it's the only thing," a quote widely attributed to Green Bay Packers' Hall of Fame coach Vince Lombardi, captures today's generation's memory of the iconic football figure. He also said, "Show me a good loser, and I'll show you a loser." Get the picture? This single-minded focus on winning motivates a litany of faux Lombardis, the **FLOMBARDIS**, whose numbers populate the pros on down to the youth ranks.

People tend to respect the "win at all costs" coach. Even as they balk at his methods, they relish the results. Parents who believe that winning on the field equates to winning in life are drawn to these teams. A Flombardi drills his players with military precision, either barking like a martinet or intimidating with a scowl. He is Scrooge-like in his approval, and players and parents dive for the few crumbs he drops. The genes for humor and warmth didn't crack his genetic code, so fun will be in short supply. But the team will win.

Before signing onto a team headed by a Flombardi, I would implore parents to revisit the goals that they've outlined for their child and the family. Where does winning rank on their priority list? What, if anything, ranks higher? Let your answers be your guide as to whether this is the right coach or team for your family.

The **WHINER** also wants to win, but he doesn't have the chops to develop his players, so he dons the mantle of the victim instead. *The game is rigged. My team is young. How will we score?* Five-year-olds are more mature than the Whiner. A few years ago, Coach Barry was an AYSO U8 volunteer. Like the rest of us, his teams were a smorgasbord of skill levels. There would be one or two players with energy and skill, another three or four with energy and no skill, and two or three more who, just starting out, didn't have much of either. Coach Barry sent the following email to his division commissioner:

> I have some questions about my team's roster. Let me preface this by saying my comments are using last year as a yardstick. Additionally, my wife and I know more kids than most coaches since we own a children's hair salon.
>
> Last year our U8 soccer team had five boys going into the second grade and six boys going into the first grade. How come this year I only have two boys going into second grade? Last year,

of the five boys going into second grade, two were upper echelon, two were in the middle, and one was below average.

How come this year neither boy going into second grade is in the upper echelon? I know this because one is my son, who is in the middle, and the other one I coached in baseball. I would be extremely surprised if he was in the upper level, based on the general athletic ability he showed in baseball. This leaves me with nine boys going into first grade, at least two of which have never played organized soccer.

My wife and I know at least five of the other boys fairly well and two of them I would consider below average. Another one is extremely small. Two others, the Twins, are pretty good athletes. As for the other four, one never played organized soccer and another is the youngest player on the team.

Now, I know you said that the teams are supposed to be close in ability. Also perhaps some of the nine kids new to U8 are great athletes. However, in general there's a big difference between boys going into second grade and boys going into first…

I guess what I'm saying is that I'm concerned that my team is so young. If I knew I had a couple of older boys who are above average soccer players I would not be as concerned. However, I know the two older boys and they are certainly not as good as the two older players on my team last year. I'm also concerned because my team last year was in the middle of the pack with those older players. I'm afraid that a young team such as mine might be overmatched against older teams.

The email went on and on . . . and on. Keep in mind, Coach Barry composed his analysis *three weeks before his first practice.* He hadn't yet seen any of these boys on the field, except his own, who he's ready to sacrifice to the wolves. Overriding all of this – he's talking about six- and seven-year-olds! He's consigned them to a season of failure based on registration forms that list their age, height and weight – and nothing else.

The Whiner starts early and never gives up. Through the season, he will continue to complain about his players, while groaning about game times, the unfairness of the competition, the unhinged demeanor of the opposing coaches, the bias of the officials, the uselessness of his team parents, the league's lack of responsiveness, and anything else that irks him in the moment. What he won't do is teach his players skills, strategy, sportsmanship, and everything else critical to their understanding of the game. And if the team happens to win all of its games, the Whiner will complain about the size of the trophies.

We see far too many **SCREAMERS** in youth sports. Actually, we hear them before we see them. Howard was a popular coach from Pasadena, a lovely, big-hearted man. After his AYSO days, he went on to create a foundation that built soccer fields and provided equipment and coaching to underserved kids. But on the field, coaching his U10 All-Stars, you had to stuff your ears with cotton or your head would explode. He was so loud you feared for his health. Another fellow from Lakewood sounded like that legendary radio DJ, Wolfman Jack, on steroids. His was a nasal twang that echoed inside your head as he shouted, "WILL SOMEONE MARK NO. 10! HE'S BEEN KILLING US ALL GAME LONNNNNNNNNNGGGGGGG!!!" Screamers tend to have a reputation for being mean; their volume can definitely frighten younger kids. I prefer to think of them as emphatic communicators who scream because they don't think their players are listening. In truth, their players have struggled to withstand their eardrum-blistering onslaught for so long that tuning them out became a survival mechanism . . . which caused the coaches to keep screaming.

A **MARTYR** wears his suffering in silence, albeit with great pride. Still, it doesn't hurt his reputation to have someone notice the effort he puts in while deeply aggrieved. Anyone can get caught in the trap of martyrdom.

When Dori was five years old, she expressed a mild interest in playing basketball. Older brother Evan had played at Barrington for a number of years and I'd coached his teams. Now it was Dori's turn. Let me repeat that her interest was tepid, sparked more by following in Evan's footsteps than by a gripping desire to blaze a trail of her own. Nevertheless, she was game to try. We signed her up; I volunteered to coach.

The season began inauspiciously. Not enough girls registered to create an all-girls division. So the few girls interested were parceled onto teams around the league. Dori's initial response surprised me. She was unfazed by the prospect of only one other girl on the team – until we got to the first practice. There were six boys and two girls. The other girl wouldn't even step into the gym. She peeked in, saw a gaggle of boys wrestling on the ground for a ball, then grabbed her mom's sleeve and bolted. That left Dori in an even more distinct minority.

During that first practice she kept staring at the door, trying to telepathically summon other girls. Yet, she participated. In the car on the drive home, I asked her how she liked her first practice. "It wasn't that much fun."

"It'll get better," I replied.

She eyed me dubiously.

Entering the gym for the second practice, Dori quickly did the math. Satisfied that the sum of her fears – no other girls – was realized, she ran down to the far end of the court and plopped down on her belly, there to stay for the entirety of the one-hour session. She announced in the car that she was done with basketball.

There were three months left in the season and I was still the coach. I attended every practice and game, taught the boys how to dribble, shoot, play defense, and tie their shoes. Was I happy? Not really. Did I smile? The entire time. I'd get home to find Dori playing Barbies with Jillian and she'd say, "Isn't it funny that my daddy is coaching my basketball team, and I'm not even on it!" The story has a happy ending. The following year, the league rounded up enough girls and I got to coach Dori and all of her little friends on the Barrington Fever.

If the Martyr remains focused on the mission, his players will have a good experience. My boys had fun each week, even if I had to stifle my inner groan every Tuesday and Saturday afternoon. None of them had an inkling that I'd been a martyr to the cause of coaching. They deserved all of my energy, focus and attention no matter what, and they got it. My advice, if you're going to be a Martyr, take it all the way – be a martyr *and* a professional, too.

* * *

And you thought you were just signing your kid up for sports. Who knew that the categories of coaches could rival the number of flavors served at Baskin-Robbins. For all their quirks, those mentioned above share one important quality: they have a heart. Even Mr. Know-It-All and the Critic care about the well-being of their players. In the next chapter we'll encounter some characters within whom a heart might be harder to find.

CHAPTER EIGHT

The Ninth Circle of Hell: Toxic Coaches and How to Avoid Them

Years ago, a fresh wind blew through AYSO's front door. Coach Wayne was a homegrown talent – Loyola, UCLA, and now he wanted to volunteer his soccer expertise to benefit the mini-minions of Region 69. He was open to working with all age groups, to conducting clinics for the players and coaches, and even lining the fields. He was welcomed with open arms.

His value was quickly recognized, his reputation spread, and, unsurprisingly, he was named the head coach of the varsity girls' soccer team at a neighboring high school. Everyone seemed to be happy for the first year or so. Then, whispers of inappropriate behavior grew louder. Overnight, Coach Wayne was gone. No notice, no forwarding address. The soccer community was stunned, but when the story broke, the chatter that preceded his disappearance exploded into a chorus of incredulity. It seems that through social media Coach Wayne had become cozy with some of the girls on the team. Apparently, a few of the more precocious ones had initiated the contact, thinking it cool to be friendly with the coach, but rather than discourage and sever it, Coach Wayne responded. His off-field rapport became evident during games, where the girls he favored, who weren't necessarily the better athletes, received a disproportionate amount of playing time.

The crisis crystallized when a parent found a gift from Coach Wayne in her daughter's bedroom. It wasn't a book of set-plays, or, well, almost anything else that could have been arguably appropriate. Instead the stomach-churning offering was . . . lingerie. The unnerved mom raced to the phone, the families compared disquieting notes, and it became clear that Coach Wayne's affection had been widespread. As the details spilled out, no one could claim that the conduct stretched beyond the unsavory-enough giving of gifts. But had they not discovered this?

These days, similar cases pop up on our newsfeeds with alarming frequency. Not just in sports but in every outpost of society. Yet, no matter how often we read about them, our capacity for shock and disgust is limitless. Coach Wayne's victims were lucky. They got off with a scare, maybe some therapy, and hopefully a life lesson. Had this happened today, Coach Wayne would have been perp-walked to jail, his mugshot lighting up millions of Twitter feeds.

The Coach Wayne story reminds us that danger lurks even in bright sunshine. While most of the coaches you encounter will be honest, caring individuals, there are predators of all persuasions on the prowl. Coaches, teachers, doctors, anyone who comes in close contact with athletes can be suspect. Those seeking to ply their perversions on minors are especially hideous, and they deserve to be exposed, apprehended and dealt with by law enforcement. For the ones who insidiously trade in stolen hopes and dashed dreams, there's a special circle of karmic hell waiting.

Only a smidgen of a fraction of a handful of kids are going to grow up to play sports at the highest levels. The numbers don't lie. Yet that doesn't prevent far too many coaches from employing Con Man 101 tactics:

"Sophie has so much potential, she's way too good for those girls she's playing with now. If she comes with me, I know I can develop her into a truly special player. It's what I do. I can definitely see her playing in college. Starting for (choose a Division 1 powerhouse) *wouldn't be bad would it?"*

What kid wouldn't be jumping out of her cleats, tugging on your arm, with that "please, please, can I" face? For that matter, what parent wouldn't want a coach sizing up her kid that way? If the dream wasn't there before, it certainly is now. Following the courtship comes the honeymoon. The clever predator will champion your child, compliment her effort, and praise her performance. Sometimes there will be whispered confidences or privileged asides disparaging other players to bundle your child even closer. She's on the inside, reveling in the confidence of the coach.

The honeymoon can last a few months, a season, maybe even longer, but eventually the promise of eternal happiness begins to dim. Once it's over, it can get ugly. The sniping and criticism targeted at other girls may shift to yours. It can be sudden and unexpected, perhaps sparked by the arrival of a new player or hiccups your kid is experiencing adapting to a new system.

But when that curtain falls, there's little that can be done to raise it again. The coach is inaccessible or claims that nothing has changed, or worse, will try to drive a wedge between the player and the parent, stating that the parent should back away and let the player take responsibility for herself. Reasonable for a player of sixteen or seventeen. For a twelve- or thirteen-year-old, it's another story.

Coach Juliet was a master of luring players with promises of turning them into stars. A renowned Big 10 point guard back in Ohio, Juliet elbowed her way into the local recreational league, initially as a trainer for its travel teams, and then as a self-professed diagnostician who could assess a player's weaknesses and fix them in a flash.

In short order, she began cherry-picking players to form a satellite of a larger club in the area. With gym time at a premium, she convinced the influential parents of her players to lobby the local school board for control of a space that had for years been used by the program she pillaged and abandoned.

This disregard for the community that offered her a platform was reflected in her coaching style. An icy authoritarian, Juliet would drill her players, yelling at them if they underperformed. Practices were long on running and discipline, short on variety and humor. She claimed that her way was the only way, blaming prior coaches for instilling poor skills and bad habits. She had her players run a pre-season mile around the high school track, hectoring them if they faltered. Parents watched from the stands, either horrified but too cowed to speak up, or seduced by Juliet's propaganda about the brilliance of her methods. The kids were nine years old.

Kim was deeply into her hoops. A Warriors fan from birth, she was overjoyed that her budding proficiency coincided with the golden era of Golden State. While her friends were consumed with Barbie and Ken, she was outside driving to the basket against her older brother and his friends. She played in rec leagues through elementary school, and joined a local travel team in junior high. Now on the cusp of high school, she was spotted by Juliet, whose own club had grown to half a dozen teams.

Juliet invited Kim to join her squad, and Kim leaped at the offer. She brought her "A" game to practice three nights a week, and bought into Juliet's pronouncements about commitment, time management, and even the screwy dictate that homework and tests would never be an excuse for missing training. Kim stayed on top of her assignments, so missing a Juliet practice wasn't an issue. Heading into the summer break, Juliet announced a mandatory training camp in early August, and warned the girls that missing any practices or games would be cause for benching. Kim was concerned as she had long-standing plans to accompany her older sister to her college move-in, but Juliet assured her that she would be OK.

At the August camp, more than a few of Kim's teammates were absent. They were out of town with their parents, or still on vacation, but somehow the compulsory attendance rule wasn't observed by everybody.

Kim didn't really care. She was happy to have a spot on the team, and though Juliet was more of a taskmaster than her previous coach, Kim rose to the challenge. She reminded Juliet of the three days she would be with her sister and once again Juliet gave her the thumbs-up, the reminder not causing much of a stir.

Until it did. After the late August absence, Juliet's tone toward Kim changed. Her comments grew sharper and more critical, mystifying Kim, who watched other girls consistently miss practices without any discernible consequences.

A few days into the fall term, Kim learned that she would be receiving an award for her excellence in Spanish and that the assembly would coincide with an upcoming practice. Rather than be excited by the recognition, all Kim could think about was informing Juliet. Her mom, Brigit, offered to make the call, but Kim insisted that she needed to be the one to break the news. She fought back a battalion of butterflies as she approached her coach who greeted the news with a pained frown and the odd request, "Can they move it to another night?"

When Kim assured her they could not, Juliet frostily nodded and turned her attention to the other girls on the court. Kim retreated to the locker room.

The night of the assembly, all hell broke loose. After receiving her award and the appreciative crowd applauding her back to her seat, Kim glanced at her phone. A flurry of texts from her teammates implored her to leave the program and hurry to the gym. Juliet was running them as punishment for Kim's absence. One girl sneered that receiving an award was no excuse for skipping practice.

The texts continued all night and into the next day. Kim could barely focus in school and when she finally returned to practice the next evening, Juliet confined her to the bench. The session consisted of regular suicides,[1] back-pedal suicides and lateral suicides, with Juliet planting the blame on Kim's sagging shoulders. Kim pleaded with Juliet to take pity on the other girls and let her run. Juliet stood firm, pushing the girls past the brink of exhaustion, all the while channeling their anger Kim's way.

Kim returned home in tears. When Brigit heard what happened, she immediately phoned, emailed and texted Juliet. The coach's

---

1 The suicide is a sprint to multiple, progressively distant lines, dashing back to the start between each leg. Highlighting speed, endurance, and agility, it is exhausting at the best of times. When employed punitively, it is especially draining.

response – that she would only deal with Kim – pushed Brigit over the edge. "My daughter is a minor. You should be dealing with me."

The players continued to bully Kim online. Brigit appealed to Juliet to quash the misconduct but the coach deflected what she considered a challenge to her authority.

As if the situation couldn't get worse, Brigit discovered that Juliet was a member of the group text. She hadn't contributed to the bullying texts herself but she was privy to every damaging comment sent Kim's way. Shocked, Brigit contacted the parent club, which promised to take action, which consisted of waiting for the outcry to die down, and then supporting the coach. Dispirited, Kim left the team.

Prospective parents gravitated to Juliet based on her playing resume and her pitch. Once in the program, dissatisfaction seeped in. Yet many parents felt paralyzed, afraid that if they spoke up, their child would suffer, or that if they left they wouldn't find another team.

In wanting the best for our children we naturally assume that their coaches do, too. We tend to trust first and ask questions later. Hope can blind us to the warning signs. When a coach says all the right things, we want to believe that our kids are in good hands. But words aren't enough.

Actually, sometimes they're too much. Take Miller. Properly, that's Coach Miller, but the middle school girls on the softball team dropped the "coach" and just referred to him by his last name. Miller also taught eighth-grade American Studies, priding himself on presenting the curriculum with an even-handedness that challenged his students to divine his own political leanings (50 percent thought him a Democrat, 50 percent a Republican; I guess he succeeded). Somehow, though, this fairness didn't travel beyond his classroom.

"Miller has no idea what the lives of young girls are like – how they struggle with their insecurities, and self-image. He acts like we are in 1956, he's Paul 'Bear' Bryant and these girls are playing at the University of Alabama." – Team Parent

What Miller failed to grasp was that most of the girls on his team played softball for the love of the game, to relieve the stress of school, and to deepen the bonds of friendship. An articulate booster of that off the field, once Miller stepped onto the diamond, all tenderness and understanding evaporated. He became a drill sergeant, the girls his fumbling recruits. His howl would echo across the field, "What are you swinging at?" or "The play was to first!" The girls would tighten up, terrified of making a mistake. He kept them on edge, lest they incur his wrath and be yanked out of the game.

No one was safe. When an error was committed, Miller would yowl as if someone had stepped on his tail, and throw up his arms in exasperation, then turn to the girls in the dugout and rage at them. Rarely was a word of praise uttered; it couldn't squeeze itself into a sentence saturated with censure.

Unlike coaches that build up their players, Miller was an emotional wrecking ball. He would target the most sensitive, vulnerable girls, and ride them to tears. As in these prior tales, parents sat stewing in their impotence, fearful of the retribution their complaints to the school administration might bring on their daughters.

All of us dream about standing up to bullies. And then we wake up and do our best to get along. Parents need to step in and confront the coach. Diplomatically if possible, but boldly if necessary. Bad behavior should be reported to the organization and if the situation isn't instantly resolved, the kids must be pulled. There are programs aplenty and none of them are worth the abuse.

Coach Wayne crossed the line between acceptable and dangerous adult-child interaction. Juliet ran a program rife with cruelty, bullying both her players and their parents. Miller attacked his players, crushing their confidence and creating an untenable playing environment. Toxic coaches can come in all shapes and sizes but there's a uniformity of warning signs parents must be able to identify.

How does the coach interact with others? Is he attentive and engaged? Do the kids look comfortable or do they tiptoe around in fear of upsetting him? How does the coach justify his approach? The sales pitch of a dangerous coach often sounds reasonable, even inspired. As with Juliet, they claim to know the kids better than anyone. You, too, may be convinced.

When the coach's self-involvement overshadows his concern for his players, the program's equilibrium is upset. Training can become lazy and predictable, with the same drills run every session, endless laps and punitive wind sprints becoming the norm, and the players standing around listening to the coach pontificate. Juliet's timed miles had nine-year-olds being chastised as they were collapsing on the track. All the while, the parents sat on their hands in the stands.

Some parents believe in the value of an authoritarian figure, so their alarm bells don't sound when they see an adult mistreating their children. They buy into the idea that it's necessary discipline. Keeping the kids around for an hour after a game, recapping every play, drilling them in either defeat or victory. Or imposing stringent and uncompromising rules of behavior or attendance. Some threaten "consequences," the politically correct version of punishment. Others will pit players against one another, either physically or psychologically, where the outcome may be divisiveness, rather than personal improvement or team unity.

Social media has evolved considerably since Coach Wayne occupied a chat room with his female players. With Facebook, Instagram, Snapchat and others that materialize daily, the motivated coach can monitor his players' personal lives 24/7. Parents will later say things like, "We knew something didn't feel quite right."

One of the clearest signs that you could be dealing with a toxic coach is unexpected changes in your child's behavior. He shuts down. He shies away from conversation. She stops eating or ravenously consumes everything in sight. He can't sleep or he sleeps too much. Children will take action in their own immature or unfocused way to avoid an unsafe environment. They may throw a tantrum or feign illness when it's time to leave for practice. They may lash out at you or their siblings at the dinner table, or provoke trouble in class. These behaviors could be a cry for help.

Certainly, it could be attributable to a rough patch – childhood offers up a new obstacle daily. Young kids tire easily. They tend to cycle through serial passions with nanosecond half-lives. They may be bored because they've progressed too far too fast. So behavioral changes may not be related to the coach at all. Or, they may portend something more insidious, like trauma, stress or abuse.

If you suspect that your child's coach is a bully, or worse, make your presence known. Start with a conversation; put the coach on notice. Perhaps his behavior has been inadvertent, and once alerted, he'll improve. A truly bad actor, though, won't be able to maintain a facade for long, and improper conduct will reappear. It might improve for your child but leapfrog onto another. At that point you have to be willing to pull your child from the team. Many parents are loath to take this step. They rationalize and second-guess themselves. *Maybe I'm misreading the situation,* they wonder. *Am I making a mistake? Where will my kid go? Will he forgive me?*

It comes down to instinct and evidence. Parents need to trust the former – *if it feels bad, it is bad* – and collect the latter. You're the parent; you get to decide when your child is in an unhealthy situation. Keep copious and detailed notes of interactions and infractions as proof to confirm any allegations later. Don't be afraid to alert the authorities – the club, organization or league management, or family services and the police, should the situation get truly dire.

Considering the number of coaches working with our kids, it's a shame that more of them aren't great. Most are just OK. They won't teach their players much or inspire them to work hard and develop. Luckily, they won't inflict lasting harm, either. The season will end and the kid will transition to another team or another sport. But protecting our children from the bullies and the predators takes vigilance. Our kids are worth it.

CHAPTER NINE

Profiles from the Pantheon

"I just want you to know. I'm a real asshole. The kids will hate me."

Bryan and I looked at each other. We had no choice. Our team's last coach, Jonathan, had nearly died. We should have known something wasn't right when we met him for dinner before hiring him, and while we ate, he nursed a cup of coffee. He was a skinny guy, but during the next four months, we saw him shrink to skeletal proportions. A month into the season, Jonathan landed in the hospital and a few weeks later he was home in England recuperating. A patchwork quilt of coaches got us through the end of the season but here we were, over another meal, with Julio, also drinking coffee (uh oh), whose coaching resume included four national championships and years coaching some of the best youth teams in Southern California. Why would he want to coach Griffie's band of fifteen-year-old underachievers?

Griffie and a bunch of his Palaxy All-Star teammates jumped to club as twelve-year-olds. Tim, who had coached Evan in his club stint, was already coaching a team in their age group, so they slid onto his roster. They bulldozed the competition in their first tournament, winning the championship with a combined goal differential of 67-3. As they collected their medals, they contemplated an ongoing haul of hardware that would drip from their bedposts. Three weeks later, they crashed back to Earth, surrendering three goals in the opening minutes of their first league game. The road remained rocky over the next two years. Tim yielded to Jonathan, who lasted just over a month, and now Bryan, my AYSO and club collaborator, and I were once again searching for a coach.

Julio sat before us, tan, groomed and tiny, but he spoke a big game. Talent wasn't the issue, he explained. What our boys lacked was commitment and discipline.

"I'm going to be an asshole," he repeated. "Can you handle that?"

What choice did we have? We'd tried the nice guy approach with Tim and a more cerebral method with Jonathan. We'd auditioned another coach, Niles, who was ambitious but distant, always looking across the VA field toward UCLA, where he served as a scouting assistant. Our families were becoming impatient; rumblings of defections ratcheted up the pressure. Julio had street cred in spades, but could the boys handle a self-described asshole as coach?

"I, for one, think the boys are ready for the challenge," Bryan jumped in. "Steve?"

Maybe it wasn't the boys I was worried about. To this point, my entire being was dedicated to making sports meaningful through fun and community. Learning accompanied laughter. I glanced across the table at Julio, who flashed a kid-like smile, "Hey, what's the worst that can happen?"

Traffic at rush hour to the VA field was always a bitch. On this night, it was a bitch with attitude. The ordinarily fifteen-minute trip took over an hour. I arrived at the field near the end of practice to see the boys doing push-ups in the mud. Just where you want your kids to be on a cold, damp, January night. Griffie looked up, saw me and gave a little head shake. I was definitely going to hear about it on the ride home.

"All right, everybody up. On the line." A few of the boys bounced to attention. Most of the others struggled to their feet, wiping their hands on their shorts, and moved slowly. "Let's go. NOW!" They bolted to Julio's side. "Who's ready to run?"

"Dad, he literally told us he was an asshole and we were going to hate him." Griffie banged his cleats together, clumps of mud dropping to the ground. He climbed into the car and swung the door shut. "Who says that to kids?"

Julio was true to his word. He barked and he scowled and he got the boys' attention. But he was never mean. He didn't snipe at individuals. He matter-of-factly let the boys know that they should be much further along in their progress, and that laziness and bad habits had contributed to a stall he wasn't going to tolerate. At the first couple of games he perched on the end of the bench, arms folded against his chest and shouted, "Stick your toe in there" or "Get a foot on it!" "COMPETE!" Halftime would see the boys run for their water bottles, then hurry into the huddle.

The losing and inconsistency didn't disappear overnight, but the boys began to respond. Julio's tone softened. There was laughter on the bench. Everyone loosened up. The team won some games, lost others. But the boys realized that Julio's "asshole" posturing had been a ploy to shake them out of their complacency. Once he "had" them, he relaxed, began to joke around, and be the huge, well, diminutive teddy bear who cared deeply about every member of the team.

Four years later, the boys finished their club careers with Julio by their side. Griffie, Jordan, Ben and Gabe (whose stories will follow), and several others had remained in club soccer solely because of their affection for Julio. He taught them to work hard, give an honest effort and be satisfied with the result, whatever it may be, lessons all parents want their kids to carry with them through life. Julio's effect on Griffie and his teammates is something they will always treasure. What could be more fulfilling to a coach, a parent or a player?

We've spoken about John Wooden being the gold standard of coaching. He wrote the book, many books, in fact, and in true saintly fashion he sought to ennoble his players by focusing on their lives ahead of their layups. For all his brilliance, though, at UCLA he didn't have to deal with talent imbalances, growth spurts, erratic attendance – or parents. Players arrived at Pauley Pavilion as elite athletes, whose will to excel elevated them above their peers.

Youth coaches work with less exalted raw materials. Corinne was barely twenty-one when I stole her away from Beverly Hills AYSO to come work for me. OK, so it wasn't as heist-movie-dramatic as that. I'd heard about this young woman with skill and charisma who was training players in our neighboring region. My business was growing in volume of classes and kids, and someone with ability and vision, who just happened to have a little-girl fan base, seemed to be the perfect add. Corinne was all that and more. A decorated youth soccer player with AYSO, club, USC and international professional experience, Corinne took Coast Sports by storm. She had her philosophical head screwed on straight, believing in development over winning, fun over competition, and recreation over professionalization. It was a match made in youth sports heaven.

As predicted, the girls went wild. Not that the boys in classes had any objection to Corinne's games or jokes, but they were a much less discriminating constituency. A two-headed alien could run a class of boys and they'd carry on, unflustered. In a coed class dominated by boys, though, the manic energy of the pre-testosterone set often scattered the few girls to the safety of mommy's blanket. Not when Corinne was around. She was soft-spoken, quick to laugh, and could barely get up and down the field for all the girls hanging on her back, arms and legs. Yet she also projected confidence and a don't-screw-with-me strength that commanded respect.

Which is why Corinne was the first person I thought of when it came time to coach a first-year U12 girls All-Star team. I had gotten myself into a pinch. The previous two years I had coached Dori's All-Star team, the Pali-Cats. Coming into this year, I knew that most of these girls were going to head off to club after the All-Star season, which would leave a big hole in the U12 program going forward. So, in my guilt and with my predilection toward martyrdom (see Chapter Seven), I agreed to create and head coach a second team that would become the A team the next season. Everybody thought I was insane – how could I manage two teams, which would mean four nights of practice each week, and between six and eight games on the weekend – but the logic made perfect sense to me, as long as I had help. I quickly logged a call to Corinne. My stomach stopped churning when she said, "Sure."

Corinne and I "co-coached" the first few practices, though I immediately deferred to her expertise. She had the ability to walk onto any field and instantly evaluate the needs of every player, quickly tailoring a remedial program for each one. For these girls it started with touch and ball control so Corinne instituted the Juggling Cookie

Challenge. The girls were directed to practice ball juggling – repeated bouncing of the soccer ball off of one's foot, or thigh or head, which increased a player's command and confidence – and build up the number of consecutive juggles week to week. At the end of a given period, Corinne would reward the winner with a tray of homemade cookies (which, of course, she'd share with her teammates). Who didn't want cookies? Within a few weeks, the least athletic of the young ladies was recording ten to fifteen juggles, with the winner tallying close to a hundred. The cookies were still a lure, but the across-the-board improvement was the true reward.

Practices were the highpoint on a team marked by game time futility. Inexperience and inconsistency resulted in 8-0, 10-0, and 12-1 losses. It wasn't one thing they were doing wrong; there wasn't one thing they were doing right. Corinne would sit in her chair on the midfield sideline, parceling out nuggets of encouragement or, more often, commiseration, while managing to keep the mood upbeat. I watched, increasingly from the background, as she deftly maintained morale by dialing down the pressure and hyping the fun.

"Oh le le hey oh la la hey faccela vede hey faccela tocca hey" chanted the girls in call and response, with Corinne standing inside their circle before the kickoff. Corinne had learned the chant from a friend who had played in Italy and never revealed the exact translation, which may have been more appropriate for an Italian bachelor party. But it was unique, bonded the team, and pumped up the girls . . . before the inevitable letdown.

As a game got out of hand, Corinne would redefine the stakes. "Don't worry about the score," she'd tell her troops. "Ice cream for anyone doing a step-over." The challenge was on, with Corinne offering the treat to anyone attempting the popular feint, executed by swinging a leg around the front of the ball and planting in that direction, then heading off in the other. Like the crossover dribble in basketball, also designed to unbalance a defender, it is a move taught by every coach and encouraged in training games all the time. But, in contests with consequences, players tense up, fearful of committing mistakes. By lifting the weight from her players' overmatched shoulders, Corinne could persuade them to experiment. Every girl would do that step-over – attackers, defenders, even the goalkeeper. At the end of the season, the team had a massive cookie and ice cream party to celebrate their journey and the dynamically effective leadership of Corinne.

While Corinne rarely raised her voice, Hadi was excitable, loud and profane.

"Get wide!"

"Don't let them throw it over your head!"

"MAKE THEM COUGH IT UP!!!!"

Yet despite the volume there was an undercurrent of playfulness to his beseeching. Evan and his teammates were months shy of ten, and back in 2001, ten-year-olds hadn't had years of private lessons padding their curricula vitae. All-Stars was their first sniff of serious competition. Regarded as the top players on their league teams, none of them had ever participated in a platoon of their peers.

It showed. The boys got in each other's way and lost possession, over-dribbled and lost possession, made poor decisions and lost possession, then blamed each other when the other team capitalized on their self-inflicted woes. Thrown together to create this home for fifteen forgotten boys, neither Hadi nor I entertained the delusion that we could carve this block of stone into a flawless David. But we believed that time, effort and a bottomless reservoir of patience would be a chip in the right direction.

Hadi introduced the "illegal left turn." The term itself, with its promise of mischief, appealed to the boys' imagination. Hadi explained how a dribbler being matched step for step by a defender on his inside would dip his left shoulder and swerve in front of the opponent, gaining an advantage stoppable only by a foul. (With the defender on the other side, the "illegal right turn" became the desired move.) All the best players in the world were accomplished practitioners so its villainy was arguable, yet amateur psychologist Hadi masterfully exploited the appeal of the prohibited as a teaching tool.

Above everything, Hadi knew that for most of the boys, *playing* soccer would inform but a small fraction of their lives, while the memory could last a lifetime. So every chance he got he planned excursions, dinners, and even a trip to Candy Land.

Hadi owned one of the country's premier trail mix and candy distribution companies, with its headquarters located near the airport. Coming home from a tournament in Phoenix, he detoured the team to the company warehouse. At the door, he handed each boy an empty box and then looked at his watch.

"You have ten minutes, starting . . . NOW!" The kids flew down the aisles, grabbing bags of Cherry Sours, Sour Worms, Peach Rings, Gummy Bears, Honey Roasted Cashews and anything else within reach. The stomachaches lasted through the night, but the story of the escapade is savored to this day. The next morning, Hadi was wakened by a call from company security saying the warehouse had been robbed and vandalized. It took a moment for the adrenaline blast to clear before he remembered the kids' joyful pillaging. He hit the snooze bar with a smile on his face.

A coach's connection to a player can be the difference between a ho-hum experience and a life-changing one . . .

Dani was terrified. As a senior co-captain of her high school team, she had worked tirelessly all season, despite little positive feedback from her coach. In fact, on the day she received her acceptance to Penn, he ordered her to run additional laps *for smiling too much*. And now, on the eve of the playoffs, the coach was piling the pressure onto her trembling shoulders.

She reached out to Christian, her club coach and strongest advocate, who had guided her development since her graduation from the Pali-Cats at twelve. He always pushed her to do her best, while reminding her of why, even in her lowest moments, she continued to lace up her cleats. Dani loved soccer. In those early days, when the team would dominate the run of play, but lose on a long ball lofted over the top and a shot that would fizz through the fingers of the 'Cats' well-meaning goalie, Christian would gather his disheartened troops.

"Girls, when you learn how to play, you'll learn how to win."

This wasn't the first time Christian had made this pronouncement. It was his prescription for every team he'd ever coached. He wasn't being disparaging. This wasn't pep-talk material. He was stating a fact of sports, and coincidentally, of life. To get to the next level, you have to master this one.

"When you learn how to play . . ."

Athleticism can open the door, but individual and team development necessarily precede success. Growing up, Christian studied the game, learned the moves of the greats, and incorporated them into his own development. As a coach, Christian constantly sought cutting-edge techniques and drills from books, websites, apps, and the sessions he spied through the fence when Chelsea, Real Madrid, and Manchester City came to the U.S. and trained at UCLA. He would compare what the professionals did to what he would trot out for his younger and less skilled players, and in many cases there wasn't much difference.

" . . . you'll learn how to win."

Christian was a fundamentalist. He encouraged strong individual skills integrated into an elegant team game. If his players did the little things correctly – take a touch, play the simple ball, make runs, keep possession – the big things would take care of themselves. Unlike many coaches who ran generic practices – a warm-up, a few random drills and a scrimmage – Christian planned his sessions to stimulate and challenge his players. He kept them flowing and fun. He had a plan for the season, focusing on building his team's technical and tactical competence one week at a time. He would offer – he didn't push, but it was there for the taking – additional sessions, lessons and beach training for those who had the desire.

"When you learn how to play . . ."

Christian preached perspective. Standing on the sideline, his gaze steady as a lighthouse beacon, he ignored the undercurrent behind him and acted as a protective barrier between his players and their parents. He felt deeply that parents should dial down the pressure – on their kids and on themselves – and allow the learning process to be organic and fun. He understood that if kids enjoyed what they were doing, they would work hard, improve, and keep playing. That would be reward enough. If other benefits accrued, such as making the high school team, or playing in college, the fireworks could be scheduled later. With the future thousands of touches away, the more prudent path was to concentrate on the present.

" . . . you'll learn how to win."

So what happened to all those teams who had to hear this refrain over and over? The ones that took a collective breath and applied themselves to the task, won. They progressed to the highest divisions, claiming cups and trophies and sending the more motivated kids into collegiate programs. The ones that fought it, felt they were too good, or were told as much by their parents, lost. These teams stumbled on, eventually under different leadership, or ceased to exist altogether. Christian wasn't some prescient seer whose vision afforded him a privileged take on the future; he just understood sports and kids and what made them both tick. His commitment to each individual bred a trust that bonded the player to the team, as well as to Christian. Long after their day-to-day player-coach connection was over, he was there as a mentor and a friend. Which is what Dani called upon when she confessed her pre-playoff panic to him. Christian's advice, which summed up his outlook and his approach, was simple:

"Enjoy the day. Have fun."

Dani had a great game.

While too many coaches take themselves too seriously, Coach B understood that working with kids was fun. He enjoyed their spasmodic bursts of energy, their off-kilter view of the world, and their uncomplicated quest for approval. While trying to maintain at least the appearance of control, B secretly reveled in the mayhem.

School sports programs can be inconsistent, and the reason is usually money. Many public school districts across the country have been devastated by budget cuts, and grants, parent organizations, and volunteers have been called upon to cover the shortfall. Private schools with sturdier resources erect facilities that rival those of the top colleges, and they point to their programs and their coaches with pride. Whether public school, or private, however, athletics stands as one of the pillars bolstering the educational model. At Curtis School, elementary home to Evan, Dori and Griffie, the students are privileged to have physical education as part of their everyday curriculum. A coterie of coaches interacts with the kids through their early years, and then in fourth grade, interschool sports begin. The students are placed on teams by skill level and each team competes against counterparts from neighboring schools.

Coach B was the beneficiary of the full Morris experience. He had Evan and his squirrelly squirming for flag football and soccer, Dori and her smothering defense and social priorities for basketball, and Griffie and his torrent of questions for all three sports, for all three years. With B, Griffie hit the jackpot. With Griffie, B needed twelve hours of sleep a night.

It's been posited that Griffie, who hit his growth spurt early and was one of the bigger and more athletic kids in sixth grade, missed making the A team because the only coach who could handle his relentless banter was B, who mostly helmed the B teams. That year, Griffie was a beast. Fastest on the field, he could rip a flag off the belt of a runner with a twenty-yard head start, and he could juke and jive his way through the other team into the end zone.

B could have won every game, piling up ridiculous margins, by handing the ball to Griffie on every play. Instead, he spread the wealth, making sure others had equal and ample opportunities to shine. At the end of the season, the team had tied for the league championship with Curtis's other B team. Fans and families filled the upper field in anticipation of the Curtis vs. Curtis barn burner. I sat perched in the rickety scorer's booth with play-by-play commentators and Griffie classmates Declan and Jake, who predicted a big day for Griffie and a runaway win for B's "B's."

It took only a few plays to realize that Coach Nott – who greeted Griffie after his summer of growth with the question, "Did you park your car in the teachers' lot?" – had other plans for the afternoon. His boys swarmed Griffie every time he touched the ball, snagging his flag before he could dash past the line. On offense, they were able to put the ball in the end zone with ease and regularity. Declan and Jake mirrored the shock in the Coach B camp; Vegas verged on a massive payout.

B never lost his cool; he subbed here, tweaked there, keeping up an energy and a patter that diverted his players from their distress. The boys, cheered and challenged, fought back valiantly, but in vain, and the B's went down to defeat. As disappointing in the moment as the outcome was, B refused to let his boys wallow. Griffie shrugged philosophically. "At least Curtis won."

A lasting image I have of Coach B hails from the Dori era. Curtis was playing bitter rival John Thomas Dye, each meeting bordering on blood sport. During this fifth-grade basketball game, my attention was on JTD's coach, Diana, a portrait of intensity, pacing the edge of the court, chirping at her players. I panned over to see B leaning back on the bench, arms folded, legs outstretched, laughing at some goofiness from subs Dori and her pal Ashley.

This was B. Fun. But also patient, supportive, committed, a leader, a role model, and most of all, a practitioner of what he preached – which, sadly, is too often missing in the coaching world.

If working with younger kids is more art than science, Cooper was Picasso in Adidas training pants. A big, Colts-loving Hoosier with an aversion to shaving, he was a combination Peter Pan and Pied Piper. Not only did he refuse to grow up but his legion of peewee followers would have pushed him off the cliff if he dared to try. His ability to replicate the innocence and exhilaration of his own childhood for a crop of up-and-comers delighted parents as much as it did his wee warriors.

In Cooper's classes and on his rec center flag football, basketball and T-ball teams, no one laughed harder than he did. This unrestrained joy functioned as a protective shield, allowing his players to develop on their own terms. A Cooper-run class was a free-for-all of kids flying into foam tackling dummies, running the base paths backwards, and playing PacMan while dribbling along the lines of a basketball court. He calibrated the level of challenge to the age and skill of his players, knowing when to surge ahead or pull back, basing his choices on the energy and the volume of his kids. No one felt held back and no one was left behind.

Unlike other coaches, Cooper didn't recoil from the parents; rather he threw open the door and invited them into the family – as long as they toed the party line of fun first, development second, and all the rest way further down the scale. Most, seeing the joy in their kids' faces, signed on without hesitation. The few who thought they knew better migrated to other coaches, a hurt that Cooper grievously felt. Not for himself – there were always kids lined up to fill his rosters – but for the kids who would be moving on to coaches who Cooper knew cared less about the calling than he did.

Within a few years of embarking upon my weekly adventure with Evan and his friends, the number of Monday-through-Friday classes mushroomed to twenty. A revolving door of coaches, most answering ads in the *LA Times*, assisted with the teaching. Some, like JT, Katia and Melissa, possessed the perfect blend of silliness, creativity, and patience, but ultimately opted to explore life's other avenues.

The core revolved around Christian, Cooper and Pete, a Brit with scars and a shuffle from four ACL reconstructions and a penchant for telling long, rambling tales about butter-fingered Russian goalkeepers and rampaging gorillas.

"I got a call from a mom who wants to start a class of younger kids," Pete announced as we were hanging out in the shipping container that functioned as our office and storage site at Barrington Park. "Anyone interested in helping me?"

"Younger than the three-and-a-halfs we have now?" asked Christian.

Pete plowed ahead, "It'll be fun. The families seem really nice."

Cooper jumped in. "Yeah, but how old are the kids?"

"They want to do it in the Palisades. We could start a second location."

All three of us, in unison, "Pete, how old are the kids?"

"Two," he responded sheepishly, quickly adding, "But supposedly they're advanced."

I can still hear our laughter today.

Five-year-olds were our sweet spot. Mostly engaged, usually responsive, and always funny, their infectious energy kept us at our best. Our four-year-olds were harder to reach, iffy in their motivation, and spent as much time retreating to mommy's blanket as they did on the field. Our three-and-a-halfs threw tantrums if they didn't get the exact ball they wanted, even though all of the balls were identical in brand, size and color.

Pete's suggestion of entertaining two-year-olds, whose idea of a good time is running away when mommy or daddy says "Come here," left us shaking our heads. Pete went off undeterred. He harbored no illusions that he was going to transform two-year-olds into soccer players. His mission was to make the session so much fun that the kids wouldn't squirm out of their car seats when their parents told them it was time to come back. He listened to their gibberish as if it resonated with earth-shattering import, cheered on their strikes and whiffs alike, and dusted them off after every trip or collision. Keeping it fast paced and loose enough to appeal to ball-sitters and ball-kickers alike, he knew he could win over a crowd of any age.

And he's had them all. From the twos up to his club U19s. His players and parents love him. Why? He's accessible, he listens, and his sole agenda is to serve the needs of his players. Not easy to do in a culture that celebrates winning, scorns losing, and measures a player's worth by how he contributes to both.

He ran his class of two-year-olds into their threes and fours and fives. It went on for years, up through elementary school. After graduating from Pete, they moved on to soccer, basketball and water polo in high school. Pete has moved on to other teams and challenges as well, albeit gingerly after his fifth knee surgery.

Each of these coaches ranks in my pantheon for their dedication to the game, their commitment to their players, and for their belief that sports, approached with passion and perspective, can be one of life's greatest joys.

And then there is Beto.

Beto does this trick. He takes three fingers of his left hand and lays them across his massive right bicep. He presses those fingers into the muscle for a few seconds, then pulls his hand away to reveal three grooves, he calls them waves, rippling across the muscle. Kids never tire of seeing him perform his magic. It catches the attention of grown-ups, too.

Between the lines is where Beto's real magic flourishes. He is a Brazilian Santa Claus, minus the reindeer, gifting all with good cheer and his undeniable love of the game. A professional in his native Sao Paolo, as well as in the U.S. indoor leagues for years after that, Beto enjoys a deep and abiding fan following. His two nephews forged careers in Europe and have been mainstays on the Mexican national team. Yet, considering such a royal pedigree, there's not a grandiose bone in his body. In him, kids sense a kindred spirit. He not only understands them, he is one of them. Just a larger, chiseled version. Beto is without pretension, amused by everything, his booming laugh often making his difficult-to-decipher accent even less comprehensible. With Beto, though, you don't have to hear his words. His warm, crinkly eyes tell the tale: It's a beautiful game so let's have a good time playing it.

Always upbeat and constructive – *which is different from indiscriminately complimentary* – Beto lets his players know they are understood and supported. That what they're doing is meaningful and the more enthusiasm they bring to it, the more meaningful it will be. Soccer has taken Beto places that a poor boy from Sao Paolo could never have imagined and every player that stands before him reaps the benefit of his gratitude.

When a coach loves his game and his role in teaching it, and he has the unique ability to convey that passion to his players, he creates a spell that may never be broken. If you are lucky enough to cross paths with a coach like Beto – or Julio, Corinne, Hadi, Christian, B, Cooper or Pete – your kid's life will be changed, for the better, forever.

CHAPTER TEN

Shoot, Bobby, Shoot!

In the Bible, Abraham came to fatherhood very late in life –
eighty-six when he had Ishmael, and ninety-nine when his beloved
Isaac entered the world. However much he longed for parenthood,
banishing his first-born and nearly sacrificing the younger one framed
for future generations the father-son relationship in all its existential
complexity. A few thousand years later, the Emperor Charlemagne
inhabited the opposite pole of parenting. When hunchback son
Pepin's assassination plot against him was exposed, his deep love for
sonny spared him from the executioner's blade, instead relegating
him to a lifetime timeout in a monastery.

Somewhere between these parenting paradigms lie the rest of us
. . . and Howard.

As a well-respected family therapist, Howard counted many of
our region's parents and players as his patients. He had this way of
looking at you – leaning a little forward, with just the slightest tilt of

his head – that invited you to divulge your deepest secrets, confident that you would be helped and not judged. He was a brilliant listener with insight and empathy suffusing his every word and glance. Strangely this wellspring of patience and perspective seemed to run dry when it came to daughter Amber's athletic pursuits.

A competent, if unspectacular athlete in his youth, Howard recognized Amber's aptitude early and joyfully encouraged his daughter's forays into karate, tennis, softball, basketball, volleyball, swimming and soccer. At nine, Amber made her first All-Star soccer team, and artfully jigsawed the December-through-June demands into a schedule that allowed for winter basketball and spring softball.

Amber's athletic prowess met its match in Howard's pride in her abilities, a pride that was *always* on display. "How great was Amber today?" "Heckuva game Amber played, don't you think?" Lined up watching our kids during a match, Howard would regale us with a description of Amber's game-winning home run the night before, or last week's twenty-point performance that clinched the basketball game. We were all well acquainted with Amber's expertise. But her participation came at a price.

Amber's station as a standout required concessions. Before each of the three seasons I coached her, Howard "negotiated" the terms of her participation. He'd couch the conversation in global considerations. "How could we improve the team?" "What roster changes would make us stronger?" "Should we implement a new formation?" We danced from topic to topic until exhausted, finally arriving at the true root of his concern: "Where do you see Amber playing?"

It was a loaded question. Howard wanted to hear me say, "Forward, of course." But after suffering through Amber's penchant for trying to dribble through five or six players at a time, her allergy to passing, and recognizing her true effectiveness protecting our rear flank, the voice in my head wanted to shout out, "I love her on defense." The correct answer, though, was "Amber will play everywhere."

One of AYSO's governing philosophies held that everybody needed to play every position. Not all in one game, but throughout the course of a weekend, and definitely over the length of the season, a player would rotate around the field. The theory was that playing only one position throughout a youth career could tee up that person for disappointment down the line. What would happen, perhaps, if she got to high school and discovered that there was somebody superior ensconced in her comfort zone? If the coach said, "Sam is a better right forward; we really need you at left back," to an athlete schooled only in offense, the player could find herself languishing on the bench or squeezed out of the sport altogether. Cycling the kids through different positions provides a more holistic understanding of the game while increasing their utility as teammates.

Amber, while strongly preferring forward, was a tenacious defender. Her stifling work in the back contributed to many team victories. Even when anchored at the center of the defense, though, she'd meander up the field until she was hovering around the other team's goal. Howard's chirping encouragement, whether helpful to the team or even to Amber, contributed to a mounting frustration. It occasionally boiled over.

On a gray and chilly January Saturday in Corona, we were soundly stomped by an older team. I called the girls together for a brief benediction. Everybody gathered around – except Amber, who I'd seen sprinting with Howard to the parking lot the moment the game ended.

Howard explained the next day that he bundled Amber back to the hotel to study for a test. Later it leaked out that he had promised

Amber he'd take her to the late-afternoon showing of *Meet the Fockers*. The deeper truth was that their abrupt exit betrayed their displeasure with the performance of the team. And everyone on the team knew it.

Let's pause for a moment for a confession. Perhaps a more "direct" approach with Howard, on everything from his demands to attitude and attendance, would have avoided a situation like this. Amber and Howard could have stayed or left, but the team's tenor would have remained uncompromised. Maybe. Even likely. Our goal as an organization, though, has always been to focus on the kids, not the parents. So we never penalized Amber for Howard's behavior. Maybe there was a smidge of the messianic in our mission. Through team and community, even the most intractable issues could be resolved. I always hoped for the best.

In this case, the worst came first.

Amber and Howard were no-shows for one of the biggest games of the season. My patience frayed, I fired off the following email: "The fact that I had no idea that Amber wasn't coming to this tournament was the absolute clincher in a season of not knowing what Amber's plans were. We all filled out the availability form early in the season, but I sent a follow-up every week primarily because I had no idea if you guys were in or out.

"More often than not I wouldn't hear back from you. I'd make two lineups: one with Amber and one without Amber. I shouldn't have to do that. You were disdainful of the team and it sucks."

That got Howard's attention.

"Steve!" he wrote back. "Oh my gosh! I'm so sorry if we failed to advise about the last tournament. I don't have any boiling-over feelings translating into disdain for the team and neither does

Amber. Perfect, I am not. But rude and inconsiderate I certainly never intended to be."

There was neither intention nor malice in Howard's actions. I believe he took the experience for granted and treated Amber's commitment cavalierly. His response made me wonder how parents can be oblivious to the ramifications of their own behavior – especially super shrink Howard – and how it can enable their children to act similarly.

It also drove home how ineffective and unfair my laissez-faire attitude had been. Had Howard and I had a "come to Moses" conversation at the outset, we could have short-circuited the turmoil. We live, we learn. The situation dissipated over the summer, but over time, Amber's participation diminished as well. She was still a member of the team, but with adolescence and growth spurts, other stars shined brighter. Finally, as the girls prepared to enter high school, and other opportunities opened for them, Amber dropped off the team.

Ten years later, I ran into Howard at the pharmacy. I was genuinely happy to see him again. As we broke the hug, he clung to my arms and said,

"Steve, I owe you an apology."

"Howard, that was so long . . ."

"No, no," he broke in, "back when Amber, Dori, and the rest of the girls were playing, I didn't realize that that moment . . . was the greatest time of our lives."

He paused, seeming to drift off. I was about to fill the silence and affirm his feelings, but Howard wasn't finished.

"The kids. The families. You and the coaches. You created a community, jeez, I miss it. If I could do it all over again, I wouldn't have been such a pain in the ass. I'd have sat there quietly just happy to be watching my kid play ball. Those were the best years."

Howard's words nearly brought me to tears. Years after I'd filed away thoughts of this team, it was still simmering in Howard's mind. What he said, though, echoed everything I've been preaching – and struggling to live by – since my earliest days in youth sports. Community holds the key to a positive, healthy, and memorable experience for our kids. Support their development, downplay the competition, and provide them with camaraderie and fun, and they'll remain focused and happy. A simple formula that we adults too often lose sight of.

Howard's blind devotion to Amber drove a wedge between his daughter and the rest of the team. He saw Amber's athletic ability as exceptional and expected everyone to treat her with respect and deference, which contributed to a distortion of the team dynamic, and encouraged bad behavior all around.

It's a pattern that can run through the entire timeline of youth sports. Early on, if a child displays any aptitude above and beyond the norm, we catapult her onto the fast track of specialized teams and private coaches. The sessions can be expensive and, frankly, a waste of time and money for kids under a certain age.

A group session might cost $15 to $30 per class and run for eight to ten weeks. An hour of private training can range from $100 on the low end to $175 . . . or more. Do young kids really need this? Does it improve their skills? What is the cost-benefit ratio of private lessons vs. group classes? The group fosters socialization; kids need to be with other kids, bouncing off each other, learning when to step forward and when to back off, and through these interactions, they figure out how to meet their needs.

Private lessons, on the other hand, remove kids from a more kinetic environment without necessarily heightening the learning process. Forgoing the team dynamic speaks to a certain parental mindset, one which says, "There's only one person who's important here and that's my kid." No question that we want every parent to unequivocally support his child, but there is healthy and there is myopic. I've received many requests for private soccer lessons for three-year-olds and have had to strain to keep a straight face as I gently explain to the parents the benefits of having the child interact with others in a group situation.

I did succumb once. Val, a tech mogul who survived the '90s dot-com crash, wanted her small-for-his-age son to engage on the field. All of his friends readily dove in, but Nicholas stayed glued to mommy's side. Val surmised, not unreasonably, that if Nicholas felt more comfortable with his abilities he'd be more inclined to join in. So we agreed that a few private lessons could be helpful.

In her Brentwood backyard I laid out my cones, set up some small goals and placed a ball at Nicholas's feet. He looked at it, considered the grid in front of him, then turned and kicked the ball down the driveway. Not an auspicious beginning. I set down another ball and watched it roll after the first one.

"All right, Nicholas, how about if I go first? You just watch."

So that's what I did. I dribbled around the orange cones, then the blue ones, and I stopped in front of a yellow one at the far end of the grid. I turned back to Nicholas.

"See, that wasn't so . . ."

But Nicholas wasn't there. He wasn't in the play structure or in the pool house, and thank god he wasn't floating in the pool. I didn't see him on the driveway, either, and I peeked in the back door.

"Nicholas?"

Val's voice answered. "He's in here." I came around the corner and saw Nicholas slumped at the table, looking like he'd just gone a full ninety minutes against Barcelona. Val was handing him an ice pop. "He says he's tired."

After we discussed Nicholas's non-activity-related fatigue, we decided that maybe we'd try again the following week. I got five minutes of focus from him in the next outing before he collapsed from exhaustion. When Val suggested a return engagement, I politely demurred, thanking her for her generosity, and explained that at least for now, both Nicholas's time, and mine, could be put to better use – his recovering in front of the television, and mine doing anything but private lessons.

I did learn a few lessons "coaching" Nicholas. As young as he was, he may not have been ready for the sport, but situating the lesson at his house tilted the playing field toward disaster. What little kid surrounded by his toys, a comfortable couch in front of a big-screen TV, and a solicitous mom with a plate of chocolate chip cookies would opt to do drills in his backyard, no matter how imaginative and fun, on a hot day in LA? For my part, it was exponentially harder to keep up my enthusiasm and patience with one kid than it would have been with Nicholas and six or seven chums. Energy, like laughter, is contagious. And coaches, like the kids they're working with, thrive on the controlled chaos of a full-on coaching session.

Older kids, eleven and up, are more likely to benefit from private lessons. Temperamentally and developmentally, they may be ready to function in a one-on-one situation. But for younger kids, solo sessions are almost certainly a waste of their time and your money. Still, parents persist, seeking that "leg up" for their kids. And sadly, there's no shortage of coaches lining up to collect the cash.

Suitability aside, for some parents, these lessons comfortably align with their lifestyle. The financial pressure on others may be more acute. Regardless of resources, though, all parents need to be on their guard against the Harold Hills,[1] who, these days, are selling sports excellence instead of boys' bands. They arrive in every town and prey upon our natural desire to help our kids. If they're hawking private lessons for kids younger than ten or eleven, just say no.

Private lessons convey a message of privilege from the parents and the meaning is not lost on their kids. "I'm working with my own coach because I'm special, better or more deserving than my teammates." This sense of entitlement can have an adverse effect on the player and an inverse effect on his development. "I'm so good, I don't have to work harder to get better. The lessons themselves will make it happen." If only . . .

Private lessons aren't the only vehicle for encouraging entitlement. Overzealous family members can inflict their own damage.

William exemplified the loving, supportive grandparent. A genial presence, always welcome at his grandchildren's games, he'd get so carried away when his granddaughter got the ball that he'd shout, "Don't pass, Jessica! Don't pass! Do it yourself!" There was nothing malicious in his enthusiasm. But his stage-grandparenting thrust his kin into a spotlight more appropriately shared by the entire team.

William was an innocent. He loved his granddaughter and rooted, maybe a little too aggressively, for her to succeed. Mel, a dad on Evan's

---

1 Harold Hill is the lead character in Meredith Wilson's *The Music Man*, a con man targeting small-town Midwesterners by selling band instruments and uniforms while promising to organize a band in their community. Falling in love with River City's librarian Marian sparks a change of heart one could only wish on the coaches and programs that prey on our children.

high school lacrosse team, overtly promoted his own agenda. Anytime his son Bobby got the ball, Mel would stand up and shout, "Shoot, Bobby, shoot!" Bobby might have been out of range, mobbed by the defense or neglecting an open teammate. It didn't matter. "*Shoot, Bobby, shoot*" boomed out of the stands. If a teammate took a less than perfect shot or missed a pass to a cutting Bobby, Mel would audibly groan and stomp his displeasure. It became a running joke among the other parents. Almost a mantra. We'd pass each other on the street or in the supermarket and conspiratorially lean in, "*Shoot, Bobby, shoot!*"

I've often wondered if parents ever wake up to the long-term effects that this type of behavior has on their children. So much of their pride is bound up in their kid's performance that when the youngster scores a goal, it's as if they were the ones striking the ball.

Coaches cultivate bad behavior by insistently directing the ball to the best player on the team. "*Pass it to Joey so he can take the last shot!*" "*Get the ball to Susie so she can get us a goal!*" The overall experience is siphoned through the star player's performance. The team may win in the moment, but long term this lopsided treatment will prove detrimental to the development of the squad.

However anointed, there is nothing attractive about the entitled athlete. Raised on a diet of effusive praise and ego inflation, it's small wonder that he is dismissive of teammates and disrespectful of coaches. A classic Victim (as described in Chapter Six), any call that goes against him is greeted with self-righteous alarm: *Are you kidding me? Are you crazy?* He may drop to his knees and raise his eyes to heaven as if beseeching the Lord for deliverance. He didn't invent this display of noxious privilege; it's on television every night and permeates every corner of the culture. Arm gestures and melodramatic genuflection are egregious enough, but bad behavior crosses the line when it devolves into bullying other players and verbally deriding referees.

When Evan was sixteen and nearing the end of his years in soccer, I received a call from Lima, the coach running the club's preseason training camp.

"Steve, I just want to let you know that Evan just quit soccer and left camp."

"What?"

"Yeah, he seemed distracted all morning, but that's Evan. Dogged it during the sprints, but that's Evan, too. And then he came up to me and he said, 'I'm over it. I quit.' He grabbed his bag and took off. He's probably heading over to your camp."

Sure enough, a few minutes later Evan stomped in. He tossed his bag and shrugged, "I'm done. I quit."

This wasn't breaking news. Evan had always been an emotional player, aggressive and mercurial, but overall, someone so electric you couldn't take him off the field. Of late, though, his demeanor had changed. The thrill was gone. He had never been hardworking or disciplined in practice, but when the whistle blew, he came alive. Trying to bring down a ball, with his limbs seemingly headed in different directions at the same time, he could stun the other team with a critical goal or a decisive stop. But the qualities that made him such a compelling competitor contributed to his being a frustrating one as well. If a kid got the better of him at one end of the field, Evan would pursue him all the way back up the sideline and shoulder-check him into the bench. Competition stoked his fire; unfortunately he had trouble calibrating the height of his flame.

Evan's U17 year found the boys pursuing victory in every game, but coming up short in most. In late November, his Galaxy Alliance

Pythons squared off against their crosstown rivals from Pacific Coast Soccer. For years, the "snakes" owned the better record, but as bodies matured and rosters evolved, the differences between the sides had narrowed. In this, the last game of the season, each team could end on a high note and claw its way up the table.

On a blustery day, the wind favored neither side but wreaked havoc on both. A 1-1 draw was about five minutes from the finish when Evan took a pass and blew past a defender. As he bore down on the goalie and pushed the ball to his right foot to shoot, three sharp whistles abruptly ended the match. Both sides froze. Both coaches checked their watches. There was still a considerable chunk of time yet to be played. But the referees were marching off the field, game over.

Suddenly, a blistering barrage of expletives broke the silence. With everyone disoriented by the unexpected stoppage of play, it took a moment to react and locate the uproar's source. I was paying the pizza delivery guy for our post-game celebration when the eruption began. Out of the corner of my eye, I caught Evan at the far end of the field, charging to the sideline, directing his colorful tirade toward the retreating referees. I thought my head was going to explode as I flew onto the field trying to out-scream my son, "Evan, shut up now! Don't say another word!"

I ordered him to the parking lot and into the car, then awkwardly returned to retrieve the player ID cards from the referees, noting the scarlet "R" next to Evan's name. Of course they'd given him a red card. At the team bench, the boys sheepishly scarfed down their pizza, stuffing their gear into their bags between bites. No post-game lolling about today. Goodbyes – and apologies – exchanged, I headed to the car. Before I could say anything, Evan huffed, "I can't believe you didn't support me!"

I was speechless. This was entitlement at its worst. And coming from my own son, no less! We drove home in a most painful and pregnant silence, though I managed to reclaim my voice to rage at him for the next couple of hours. I ranted through a greatest hits of sports themes – good sportsmanship, comportment toward referees, respect for his teammates and coach – then veered into human behavior – anger management, abuse of privilege, entitlement (I couldn't hit that word hard enough).

Evan knew all this, contrition finally bubbling up to the surface. His outburst had betrayed all the teachings that he and his teammates had learned through the years of AYSO and club. But at that point in his young life, he was an uncontrollable bundle of impulses and emotions.

Tantrums erupt at all ages. My cousin's two-year-old was delivering a five-alarm meltdown on a crowded street when a police officer approached.

"Miss, is this your child?" he asked.

To which my harried cousin fired back, "Do you think I'd be standing here if it wasn't?!?"

Outbursts from teenagers, whose newfound size is supposed to dovetail with a budding maturity, can turn heads. A pattern of such behavior portends deeper issues and the earlier they can be identified, the better for everyone. What we don't remedy early will not magically transform later, so we parents need to set limits and boundaries and stick to them. We need to empower our kids, not enable them.

Be wary and ask lots of questions. *What kind of athlete do I want to raise? What kind of adult do I want him to become? Do I care more about his behavior or his achievement?* If this last one gives you a moment's pause, your child is already on a perilous path toward entitlement.

Sad to say, players don't hold a monopoly on bad behavior. But when adults add their toxicity to the mix, the scene can get particularly ugly.

In eighth grade Evan added lacrosse to his athletic repertoire. He was drawn by its similarity to soccer and the primal allure of wielding a big stick. Legally. He improved rapidly and by tenth grade he was playing with one of the elite clubs in Southern California. But this isn't a story about Evan, though it does start with him . . .

. . . because on this beautiful spring morning, I was at Aviation Park in Redondo Beach, planting my lawn chair on the far side of the field with the other parents and fans, to watch him play. He won the faceoff, a hunched-over battle of strength, leverage and quickness, and tore off up the field where he rifled a pass to an attacker lurking behind the net. The team flicked the ball around, getting into a rhythm, maintaining possession, while the long poles of the defense parried runs toward the goal and tried to poke the ball loose.

Suddenly the hypnotic flow was upended as one of Evan's teammates, Clint, taking exception to the tightness with which he was being marked, took his stick and switched from lacrosse to baseball. He swung for the fences but connected with a defender's ribs and felled the player as if he were an oak surrendering to Paul Bunyan's axe. A whistle blew and the referee raced over to where the woodsman was hovering menacingly, daring the tree to get up. A knot of players circled the incident, jostling and shoving each other, testosterone overflowing.

The ref guided Clint out of the cluster and signaled him off the field. He stormed toward the sideline, flinging his helmet at the bench. He passed an adult, who was standing with his arms crossed against his chest, and Clint's head whipped around. He froze, glaring at the man. Then he continued toward the bench where he retrieved his helmet and stuffed it into his equipment bag. Barely an instant later, the adult with the crossed arms charged toward Clint. He clamped the player in a headlock and began pummeling his face with his fist. Immediately a swarm of players and adults descended and yanked the two apart. Each could be seen swearing at the other as they writhed against the arms that were restraining them. Clint finally wrestled himself free, threw his bag over his shoulder and stalked off toward the parking lot.

All of us on the far sideline were transfixed, even if the drone from busy Sepulveda Boulevard behind us drowned out any of the verbal drama. What the hell just happened? Who was this man punching a kid? Something was obviously said to incite the attacker, but what? I sensed there was more to come and about thirty seconds later, we all watched the man sprint up the sideline, chased by a dozen others. Everyone disappeared into the parking lot, which was blocked by the restroom building from our line of sight. When the onlookers filtered back onto the sideline, neither Clint nor his pummeler were there. Shortly after, an armada of police cars, lights flashing and sirens blaring, roared up the boulevard and screeched into the parking lot.

I couldn't wait for the game to end so I could pump Evan for details. He told me that when Clint went off the field, the adult, who was a club official, cracked, "I hope you're satisfied. You just let down your team." Clint's response – "Why don't you suck my b**ls!" – triggered the carnage. Clint's attacking the guy's car prompted the dash to the parking lot. Sure enough, as Evan and I approached my car parked nearby, there was a circle of cops standing behind a black SUV marveling at its shattered rear window. Another officer was taking the statement of the agitated adult. Clint was nowhere in sight.

Indulging bad behavior, by players and, yes, adults as well, should never be an option. Sportsmanship and teamwork are qualities that our young athletes (and their role models) must practice as diligently as dribbling, shooting and defense. As parents we should seek a balance between supporting their sporting dreams, self-esteem and empowerment, and providing a reality check when they career into the realm of the unhealthy. We can be early-times Howard, blinded to everything but the brilliance of his daughter, or late-times Howard, who realized years later how much of the fun he missed.

CHAPTER ELEVEN

Breathe More, Bitch Less

The parents on Griffie's club team were an accomplished lot. The Westside's best and brightest. Every one of them was an exemplar of positive values, and their children gleamed as the reflection of their high standards. Trooping up from the parking lot to whatever field was on the schedule that day, an onlooker could be forgiven for mistaking the hugs and laughter as a family reunion. But once the game began . . .

It had rained the night before and the field at Birmingham High School was pocked with puddles, a patch of mud fermenting in front of the south goal. Our opponent, powerhouse Valley United, peered down from the top of the table (as soccer standings are known), while we were struggling to find our footing several rungs below. So when we managed to squeak in a goal and carry a 1-0 lead into the half, the sideline bristled with cautious confidence.

We knew Valley United would come out of the break breathing fire in search of an equalizer. What we didn't realize was the referees'

155

investment in assisting them.

We haven't yet referenced that lightning rod population – the officials. They will be dealt with, rather, discussed in the next chapter. For present purposes, it should be understood that the referee owns the field. No one – players, coaches, definitely not spectators – can enter or leave it without the referee's permission. He tolerates no dissent. And his word is final. Continuing . . .

Every call, not some, not an equal number – not even a statistically but predictably random number – EVERY CALL favored Valley United. I believe that over the course of a match, referees will make calls that benefit and penalize each side equally. This crew, however, seemed hell-bent on destroying my faith.

After a few whistles against our guys for pushing – and none against the more imposing Valley United, Coach Tim, who even in the tamest of matches manifested a "lively" sideline presence, threw up his arms and appealed, "Mr. Ref-e-reeeeeee." A moment later, one of our guys was bulldozed off his feet right in front of our bench. A reflexive roar went up from the parents. The referee wagged a reproachful finger at our sideline and chased off after the action. The gauntlet had been cast!

The rest of the game, our parents were on fire. Razzing every call, and harassing the man in the center and his ally, the Assistant Referee, our supporters devolved into a chorus of catcalls and taunts. At one point the referee halted the game, and summoned Coach Tim onto the field. After a few moments of animated gesturing and shoulder shrugging, Tim slunk back to the bench. "Hey, everybody, we just have to calm down. No more yelling at the ref."

The truce lasted maybe ten seconds, or until a phantom foul assessed against our guys reignited the outrage. A few of us with leveler heads tried to rein in the others. "Gang, if we don't shut up, this referee is going to find a way to screw us."

"Screw him," shot back one of the dads. This sideline was out for blood. All that was missing were the pitchforks and torches.

Time ticked away and took the boys' confidence with it. The game deteriorated into a jumble of stray passes, ref whistles, missed tackles, ref whistles, frantic defending, ref whistles, protesting parents, whining players, and still more ref whistles. Tim urged the kids to keep their heads, but seeing their parents out of control licensed their own misbehavior.

Full time came . . . and went . . . but the game lurched on. A long pass landed on the foot of their forward deep in our half. Griffie channeled the man toward the end line, where he planted his foot and drove inside toward goal. Suddenly he caught air and planted on his face. From where we stood, it looked like he slipped on the wet turf; Griffie hadn't touched him. The referee, though, adamantly pointed to the penalty spot.

Valley United's star player set the ball down and fizzed the penalty kick past Jordan, our keeper. Immediately, the referee bleated three times, ending the game, 1-1. Our boys were devastated. They'd played their hearts out only to have the referee rip the game from their hands. He then jogged over to face our apoplectic parents, who were bouncing around like agitated apes hurling themselves against the fence at the zoo. The referee grinned. And then gave our sideline the finger!

That referee was awful but our parents were worse. Besides carrying on like tantrum-tossing toddlers, their behavior encouraged the boys to act just as poorly. Two lessons here. Lay off the referees;

they always win. And model the conduct you want to see from your kids. Bad behavior from adults guarantees bad behavior from children.

Nightmare parents pop up in the news with discouraging regularity. Like a head-on collision, it's nothing we want to see, yet we can't look away. We're perversely fascinated by the depths to which our peers will sink, taking false comfort that we could never be as hideous. Except we can. Take the Griffie game during which teammate Victor got elbowed in the mouth and both benches – including parents from both teams! – joined the brawl. Or the Palaxy game where the opposing parents reacted to losing by massing in a menacing gauntlet at the gate. Or the afternoon the parent called me an asshole and threatened to take me to court because his kid wasn't awarded a trophy for a spring program in which trophies weren't given. Or the tiff over sideline seating that flared into a parent pulling a knife on a fourteen-year-old player. There are dozens more war stories, all of them true. To quote Enrique, one of Griffie's teammates, who stalked off the field while adults were throwing punches, "These parents are crazy."

* * *

I grew up in a different world. My parents never saw me play Little League. They never made it to any of my high school soccer games. When my friends and I played touch football in the street, my mom and dad weren't cheering from the curb.

Dads worked, Moms ran the home, and kids went to school, rode their bikes and watched TV. Family time in my house consisted of the fifteen minutes between my father returning from work and my brother and I scarfing down dinner and racing out of the room, leaving my parents to talk about grown-up stuff. I promise that youth sports never entered the conversation. While dedicated to the welfare and happiness of my brother and me, our parents never gave a thought to our sporting lives. If we happened to mention that we'd hit a home run out of Kaufman's lot while batting lefty, or juked John Pugliese out of his Keds en route to the winning touchdown during recess, my dad's lamb chop chewing would not have missed a beat.

Nowadays, dinner table conversation about private lessons, playing time and who's going to do the drive to San Bernardino for this weekend's tournament fill the room. Parents are even more likely than their kids to talk about the day's sports.

Mom: Reed had a good game today.

Dad: Are you kidding? His touch was loose, he couldn't complete a pass and he missed two open goals.

Mom: But he got back on "D," and his clearing header on that corner saved the game.

Those words would never have been spoken in my house. Today, parents are involved in every facet of their kids' lives, sports just being one arena. Forget about "helicopter parents;" we've become a generation of "microscope parents." Everything our kids do is inspected, dissected, and injected with significance. Are they safe, happy, motivated, productive, creative, keeping up, getting ahead, getting along? All valid and arguably noble concerns. Human nature pushes us deeper: How do they stack up against their peers? And the even more insidious: How does this moment fit into a master plan of where they should be years down the road?

Parents have a place in youth sports. How expansive – or intrusive – a place has been debated by anyone who can form an opinion. From our kids' first shaky upright moments, we are their coaches and cheerleaders. We then usher them into Mommy & Me and Daddy & Me classes (both of which often end up as Nanny & Me classes), where we're still integrally involved. We sit back when they enter preschool sports classes and either cower like the Coach Ray parents or man the blankies and water bottles as in the classes I've offered.

Once they become old enough to join organized teams and leagues, the doors of opportunity open wide for us. We can be bit players or flaming divas depending upon how much responsibility we want to assume. If we enter this realm, where the meaning of life can be distilled down to the bouncing of a ball, there are standards and practices we need follow.

Bronze Level Sports Parents

We all lead busy lives. Adding sports may be more a case of shoehorning than slipping them into our schedule. But the benefits far outweigh the burdens. The commitment we make is not only to our kids, it's to their teams and coaches as well. If they're in a recreational program, practices will likely be once a week; a club or travel program will train two, maybe three (four is not unheard of) times weekly. Our responsibility is dropping off and picking up on time. It's the same on game days, though "on time" could mean an hour before the whistle. You may ask, "What's the big deal if we're a few minutes late?"

Practice slots are meticulously scheduled back to back through the afternoon and evening. If a player comes late, it bites into a coach's time with the team. On game day, punctuality is even more critical. The devoted coach has spent hours devising his lineup, and last-minute tweaks due to tardiness or uncommunicated absence can throw off the entire scheme.

Collecting your child demands a similar discipline. Your coach has his own family to get home to, and asking him to babysit your child stretches his job description. Obviously, emergencies and unforeseen instances will impact this arrangement, but as a rule, timeliness is a nonnegotiable condition of participation.

In the wild and woolly days before live scans and lawsuits, a kid at the field by himself fifteen or twenty minutes after practice would have been tossed into the coach's car and deposited at home. Since the late 1990s, however, AYSO's Safe Haven Child & Volunteer Protection program has discouraged a coach from being alone with a child other than his own,[1] one of the reasons we insist that parents claim their kids on time.

One year I had Jackson, a low-key kid in a screaming neon Barcelona jersey, whose parents seemed impervious to punctuality. After the second week of Jackson and me shuffling our feet under a setting sun with Evan firing off angry looks from the front seat of our car, I urged Jackson's parents to consider his feelings and my own kids waiting for dinner.

"Coach Steve, we're so sorry. It will never happen again."

Apparently "never" doesn't have the half-life it used to. The next week, they were late again. The Division Commissioner weighed in with mom and dad, dangling the threat of diminished playing time if the trend continued. The fourth tardy drew the ire of the Regional

---

1 *AYSO'S Safe Haven: Making it Safe For All Players and Volunteers* (2017), p.16. Designed to safeguard both the players and those who work with them, the Safe Haven Child & Volunteer Protection program details everything from coaching comportment and recognizing the different forms of abuse to field inspections and environmental hazards. Under the list of Supervision Protocols it states that "No adult should ever be alone with a child other than their own child."

Commissioner, who stated that she was authorizing me to drop off Jackson at Fire Station 19 if mom or dad weren't there on time to collect him.[2]

The end of practice resembles the Fall of Saigon, minus the helicopters being toppled into the sea. A cascade of kids streams toward the parking lot as parents in idling cars, some double parked and impeding traffic, hurry to get them home. The quagmire, dense and impenetrable, miraculously clears in about ten minutes.

When I looked up after packing my gear, Jackson was gone. I sighed in silent victory.

"So we don't have to wait around?" Evan grabbed the ball bag and started for the car. Funny how helpful he could be when he was hungry.

I teased, "Not unless you want to work on your . . ." Just then, across the now empty field, I saw a flash of bright yellow moving in the foliage near the far fence.

I had a sinking feeling as I neared the bushes.

"Jackson? Jackson, is that you?"

Big brown eyes blinked back at me.

"Why are you in there?"

He shimmied his way out, then approached me, head down, like a puppy caught chewing on a pair of slippers.

"Jackson...?"

I could see his gears spinning through a litany of excuses before dropping his shoulders and blurting out the truth.

---

2 Punishing players for their parents' transgressions is antithetical to AYSO's mission of uplifting children. It has to be something persistent or extreme for the most draconian measures to be exacted. In most cases parents respond before the axe falls. Sometimes changing teams, practice fields or schedules, or getting assistance with finding carpools will ameliorate a stressful situation.

"My mom told me that if she wasn't here when it was time to go I should hide in the bushes so I wouldn't get in trouble."

Did you ever hear anything more heartbreaking – and infuriating – at the same time?

Jackson didn't get in trouble, but his parents were put on notice that if one of them wasn't present for the entire practice each week, he would be dropped from the league. Happy to say this ended the pickup problem, Jackson finished the season and Evan made it home on time for dinner.

Bringing the proper gear is also compulsory. In soccer, that means *both* shin guards, *both* cleats, proper socks and an *inflated* ball. This should be easy enough, until a shin guard disappears under the bed, a cleat gets wedged behind a car seat, and one sock vanishes in the dryer. Proper planning dictates that all of these items should be located and packed the night before, but nobody's perfect. If possible, a second set should be handy and stored ready to use. It might get a little pricey, but I'll never forget the words of wisdom offered by my pal Ken when I complained that Evan was lobbying for a second pair of cleats.

"Get him the shoes. Be grateful he's not into horses." Ken's reference to the unconscionable sums required to pursue the equestrian arts hit home. I bought the cleats.

Other Bronze Level parental duties include replying to emails, attending meetings, bringing snacks when assigned and . . . supporting your kids by watching them play.

Coming to games can be one of our greatest joys. Sitting in the stands or populating the sideline, basking in the energy of our mini-me's rollicking around the field (if they're younger) or executing with

163

creative precision (if they're older), validates our original sin of having them. Some parents show up with signs, banners or mounted Fathead photos. Others settle in with a latte and the *New York Times.* The default minimum is a love for your child and an hour of patience.

Cheering is highly encouraged. Shouting expletives, criticizing officials and denigrating opponents is not. The mom who strode onto the U10 field, mid-game, to call the referee an asshole crossed an obvious line despite her disingenuous defense that she didn't realize she couldn't do that. Somehow all the little boys looking on with gaping jaws did.

A full-throated, positive endorsement can rouse a team to greater effort. In the roar of the crowd, though, singular voices often get lost, not reaching one's precious child's ears. Most of the time, that is . . .

On the field, Ben's focus was unwavering. Team captain and center mid, he was as smooth and efficient as a blackjack dealer, effortlessly pinging passes, while mindful of everything swirling around him. Crowd noise, no matter how boisterous, rarely disturbed his concentration. Yet one voice without fail could worm its way through his defenses and echo through his core: his mom's.

Getting to games wasn't easy for Hadar, an attorney who worked downtown. But the opportunity to see her son play was something she eagerly sought. Being in the stands with her friends, trading notes and sharing stories, made the outing even better. When Ben whipped in a cross or prevailed in a tackle, Hadar would punctuate the moment with a rousing, "Yay, Ben!" On the other hand, any infraction called against her precious baby provoked a stream of semi-coherent invective loud enough to shock both benches. Early on, Ben warned his mom that she wasn't allowed to talk at games. If he heard her voice – his seriousness evident from the tightening of the sinews in his neck – her attendance privileges could be revoked.

Over the years, Hadar missed many games. Luckily, husband Jeff, a more sanguine supporter, brought home detailed reports.

The loudest sidelines in recreational leagues like AYSO can be found in the least consequential divisions – 5U, 6U and 8U. Parents and coaches go bonkers watching their juniors frolic around the field. There are no stakes beyond which kids are the cutest or having the best time, yet you'd think you were watching a World Cup final. By the time you're a parent in 14U, you're just happy that your child still wants to play. You cheer at appropriate moments and the rest of the time you're scrolling through your emails. And that's how it should be.

It's a magnitude of intensity madder in the travel leagues, where "the future" looms over the present, and even the most reverent spectator is screaming on the inside. Additionally, there's the belief that the more vociferous the support, the better the player will perform. Doesn't work that way. Kids metabolize volume as pressure.

With certain hard-core parents, there's little correlation between their fervor and the age of their child. Perhaps a holdover from the days when they were their toddlers' first "coaches," they can't seem to let go despite the harm their interference may cause. Yet non-coaching parents need to leave their advice at home. Contradictory comments confuse players – they want to heed their coach, but feel allegiance to their parent – while undermining the authority of the coach.

Aidan's dad, Charlie, used to station himself opposite Aidan's position in the defense and pepper his encouragement with instructions. Gavin's dad, Yuri, would shout his tips in Russian. The most flagrant violator was local news anchor Dean, who would stalk the sideline following son Austin's flight up and down the field, criticizing everything poor Austin did – or didn't do.

In these situations, most coaches opt for gentle persuasion over confrontation. I can attest to numerous emails and sideline sidles, admonishing parents to please curb their "enthusiasm" during games. Once apprised, some cease and desist. Others temporarily refrain, then mosey away from midfield to make their mischief farther down the line. Recalcitrant cases court danger when they sneak around to enemy territory to vent or cheer. Opposing parents don't take kindly to interlopers.

Parents need neither force nor volume to inflict injury. When they view the experience solely through the prism of their own child's performance, it blinds them to the feelings of others.

As on Evan's first All-Star team, the position of goalkeeper on Dori's Pali-Cats was a communal one. No one begged to stand in the line of fire, but for the good of the team, a few opted to share the misery. Mackenzie's shoulders would hunch into her neck, and her eyes would well up before donning the pinnie and going out to the field. And then she'd fearlessly throw her seventy-pound body into the fray, diving, swooping and flying to turn away every shot.

Cami was a more willing volunteer. Her three older sisters were keepers, so shot-stopping was in her blood. It just wasn't in her hands. During one fourth quarter she fell victim to a barrage of rapid-fire goals. At the end of the game, she fled the field, embarrassed and weeping, into the arms of her mom, Nancy.

Everyone gathered around to console Cami. Dori and Jillian, defenders during those ten minutes of infamy, tried to comfort their teammate. Nancy patted her daughter's back.

"It's OK, Cami. It wasn't your fault. Your defenders let you down." Stung by the blame, Dori and Jillian crept away.

Cami's mom was right . . . and wrong. For the ball to even get close to Cami, her teammates had to have been derelict in their duties. But not just the defenders, all of the players. The over-dribbling forward who coughed up the ball, the midfielder who dove in and missed the tackle, and yes, the defender who stepped too soon and was out of position to thwart the attack. Team error led to the shots that devastated Cami. But to pin the blame on two specific girls was unthinking and cruel.

Nothing was going to make Cami feel better on that chilly after-noon. A warm hug and a hot chocolate might have helped. Seeking solace for her daughter, there were a million other things Nancy could have said, all of which would have been a more constructive, positive way of handling the hurt. All could have started with "Cami . . ."

". . . it was unlucky. Nobody could have blocked those shots."

". . . that's soccer. Sometimes the ball bounces your way, some-times it doesn't."

". . . you played your heart out. I was so proud of you."

". . . it was nobody's fault. It's the team that wins and the team that loses."

". . . you'll get 'em next time. Let's go home and eat badly."

Well, maybe not advocating poor food choices, though many a time that's been the go-to response for anyone who's lost a tough match.

As parents we have to consider the long-term effects of what we say to our kids. Sugarcoating difficult truths isn't the answer, but rescuing them from their feelings doesn't work either. Handling hardship is a teachable skill.

Cami had a rough outing. It wasn't Dori and Jillian's finest hour either. But Dani, Emma, Jordan, Mikaela, Raleigh, and both Mackenzies played their own parts in the shellacking. If deflecting responsibility by assigning blame is our default reaction, isn't that what our kids will do, not just now, but as they grow up? Shouldn't we encourage them to be resilient, maintain perspective, and accept responsibility? Isn't it our responsibility, our purpose even, to teach them? If so, it's a lot easier to start when they're young; adolescence provides a whole different set of challenges.

Divorce and Youth Sports

One of youth sports' finest features is its ability to foster family bonding. Yet when the family is already fractured, as in cases of divorce, the field can be another battleground on which warring parents can inflict further suffering on each other and their already victimized children. Sometimes the parents are oblivious to the toll they exact. Other times it's a calculated strategy. When such conflicts play out in team sports, the carnage is widespread.

When kids don't show up on days a vindictive parent has custody, the team pays the price. When scrapping spouses miss carpools, send players without proper equipment or forget their snack responsibilities, the team feels the pain. But the ones who suffer the most are the kids caught in the middle.

Chase's parents were trapped in a bitter breakup replete with recriminations and court orders. Due to the delicacy of the situation, Mom asked me to be an advocate for Chase. She apprised me that due to pending legal action, Dad was to receive no emails, no favors, and no acknowledgment whenever he was around. My job just got tougher. Trying to stay out of the family drama, I tailored my actions to what was best for Chase in the moment. But there were times conflict could not be avoided.

The morning game was over and Evan's Pali Xtreme piled into several cars to head off to lunch. I was last to leave the field, and found Chase and Dad looking lost in the parking lot, not knowing what to do or where to go. Conscience wouldn't let me leave them out so I asked, "You guys want a ride?" They hopped in and we drove to lunch. That night, I received an email from Mom castigating me for betraying her trust by buddying up to Dad. Further, she stated, Chase no longer wanted to come to games because he didn't feel safe or protected.

I reiterated my concern for Chase, and expressed regret that he was a pawn in a larger battle. Subsequently, we only saw Chase on Mom-custody weekends. The situation was upsetting to Chase, and uncomfortable for everyone else associated with the team.

In this case, Mom was sincerely concerned about her son's welfare and safety. In another situation I was close to, one parent's actions were shamefully sinister.

It killed Gordon that Brenda, his twin sister, his YOUNGER twin sister, looked down on him. Literally. At ten, Brenda was three inches taller than her minutes-older sibling. Likely to be resolved in adolescence, the size issue paled in comparison to a more intractable one.

Their parents' marriage dissolved when the kids were four months old and the rancor between them still blazed white hot. Mom devoted every waking moment to making sure Gordon and Brenda were active and happy. She grew up playing sports and instilled that love in her kids, who grew to be fiercely dedicated athletes. But anything that Mom supported, Dad protested. He weaponized the kids and wielded them as a cudgel against Mom, ostensibly the only discernible use they had for him.

He balked at Mom enrolling them in sports, moaning when the scheduling conflicted with his own priorities. They would be AWOL from soccer practices to watch his golf lessons. They missed their teams' playoffs when Dad loaded them into a car for a weekend in Phoenix. That is, they sat with a nanny for the six-hour drive. Dad flew.

He lobbied to place them in an inferior basketball program because it was a few blocks closer to his house than the league they were thriving in. He threatened Mom with court, complaining that Gordon and Brenda cold-shouldered him when he came to their games – which he actually never came to. And while trying to undermine their participation in sports, he complained about their weight, capriciously kept them from food, and forced them to do miles on a treadmill. The kids were seven. Tragically, his efforts to harass his ex-wife exacted a toll on his children, while creating problems for the coaches and others who were trying to help.

While there are more malefactors like this floating around than we choose to believe, most parents are unambiguous advocates for their children. They love coming to games and many indicate a desire, within the limits of their available time, to involve themselves more robustly in the experience.

Our paramount concern, as coaches and team parents, should be the well-being of these kids, who are reluctant participants in a situation not of their own creation. Without distorting the dynamic of the team, we should be sensitive, supportive and patient. Realize that these brief hours with us each week may be their only respite from the tension at home, and our efforts actually make a difference.

Silver Level Sports Parents

There is a middle ground between spectating and running the show. You're itching to do more than the former but there are compelling reasons why the latter is not an option. Work and family commitments, travel schedule, confidence, and expertise can be disqualifying factors. Fear not, you can still make your impact felt in smaller but nevertheless significant ways, either at the field or behind the scenes.

If you're searching for a position with a lofty title, one that confers deference and respect, but in most cases involves a light workload, look no further than Assistant Coach. In some sports in some leagues and with some coaches, the assistant is expected to be ready, willing and able to step in for the head honcho. But if Shakespeare's King Henry IV was bemoaning the weight of his responsibilities when he said, "Uneasy lies the head that wears a crown," the heads of most assistant coaches aren't lying that uneasy.

There aren't long, deliberative nights, they aren't bothered by unhappy parents, and if they wind up having to coach and the team gets toasted, little blame will affix to them. Yet gifts and gratitude will come their way at the end-of-season party.

Still, there's considerable value in implementing strategy, assisting with roster moves, warming up goalkeepers, shagging balls, and even tying players' shoes. In a coach's absence, the assistant assumes the helm and hopefully he or she has been trained, certified and paying attention. I've seen assistants who know little more than that their kid is on the team try to manage a game. It usually isn't pretty.

Short of enlisting as an Assistant Coach, other valuable contributions are taking photos or shooting video, designing social media platforms, setting up goals, and lining the field, though the last task should be executed with caution. Haphazardly discarding paint cans may result in a surprise when arriving in the morning; offensive language and anatomical doodles sprayed across the blacktop can put a damper on the day.

Every team needs a Manager, someone to organize communications, devise snack schedules, supervise directions to the field, and arrange meals, parties and get-togethers. Even though the Manager functions primarily behind the scenes, teams with a superior administrator are readily differentiated from those with a looser grip at the helm. Everything from timeliness to appearance to general comportment reflects the work of the Manager's hand. They are the unsung heroes who, in just a few hours a week utilizing a strong set of skills, shape order from chaos. Think of it as power without the glory. If you want or can handle both, though, we need to move on to the next order of sports parenting.

The Ten-Year Window

Foreshadowing

Stirrings

The inspiration

*Barrington
first class*

First steps

The Team

The Team

King Kong Dori
Photo: Jeff Amram

Basic
training

175

Daddy, we're going to be late

Early classes

Early classes

*Taking AYSO
by storm*

*Chicago Bulls
v Blue Rockets
(names chosen by kids)*

*Just won? Lost? Had a
great snack? Could be any
of the three…*

Photo: Art Streiber

*Wicked
Strawberries
(name chosen
by coach)*

Happiness is halftime with mommy

Griffie and Will, first U6 practice, fetal position

Yellowjackets

Be nice to Kyle
Photos: Nick Kokotakis

Pali Xtreme

*Goalie Evan
dribbling
downfield*

3 monkeys

*Griffie crashing
the Python
championship*

The agony....and the ecstasy

Pali-Cats

High-five line humiliation

Best time at tournaments

Gatorators

U10 size mismatch

184

Palaxy

Palaxy referees

Galaxy high-five line

What it's all about

Classic "Victim" pose

Pali-Cats and mascot Estaban

Ref Dori

Pal Real

Fearsome

Devil-Cats mayhem
Photo: Chuck Ryant

Galaxy Alliance Pythons

Galaxy Alliance Devil-Cats

Real Moms Wear Cleats

Blink and you'll miss it…

FCLA B98s last dance in Vegas

CHAPTER TWELVE

Raise Your Hand and Change Your Life Forever

"So how do you think the team is doing?" Ken, my original All-Star interrogator, speared his scrambled eggs. In the next chair, coiled behind his mustache and ready to pounce, Lou studied me. They had cornered me at the end of practice the night before and asked me to breakfast at Mort's, the neighborhood deli, which was low on ambiance but high in local flavor. I'd sped down the hill after carpool, which in the mornings was more like driving a busload of sullen prisoners from the courthouse back to the jail. The invitation had been unexpected, but I instantly saw the direction it was headed. My spoon froze in my bowl of granola.

"We're getting better."

This was our third year together. Evan and the original bunch of Pali Xtreme misfits had morphed into a powerhouse for their second U10 season, collecting medals and championships nearly every weekend. We were now the younger team in our first year of U12, and once again, victories cropped up as often as water parks in the Sahara.

I smiled at Ken and Lou. Did they want unvarnished honesty or a tuchus-full of smoke? At the next table, a three-year-old Isaac Newton was testing gravity with a fistful of Cheerios. His slightly older brother was knocking over every water glass and cackling with delight. The toddler in the high chair began to cry because why not. Mom was outgunned.

"We're not winning many games." Ken's tone belied the nonchalant way he was pushing around his food. Lou had yet to speak. But his stare was making me uncomfortable.

"Well, the teams we're playing are bigger and older than we are, but the boys are figuring it out. Once they get used to the speed of play and the physicality, results will come."

"And when will that be?" Lou had found his opening. "It's February. We've been at this three months already. We've won what, two games so far? Steve, I know you and Hadi are doing all you can do, but I don't want Johnny to lose interest."

There it was! Using his son as a human shield. Johnny, like the rest of the boys, wasn't fond of losing, but he didn't seem overly frustrated or even embarrassed. Lou was pinning his own dissatisfaction to Johnny's no. 14 jersey.

The mom at the next table was losing the battle. Barely nine o'clock in the morning and her face was already raising the white flag of surrender. Yet I wished I was sharing the table with her and her monsters. I would have happily been splattered by oatmeal if it got me out of this.

"Guys, I understand your frustration. Losing is no fun. But we've talked about this. When you're the young team in a two-year division, you're going to get slotted against the older kids, and we'll lose more games than we're used to. Next year we'll be the older team and we'll kick ass again." It seemed logical to me.

"… if Johnny still wants to play." Lou's mustache was angry and beginning to snarl on its own. Perhaps worried that it would jump off Lou's face, Ken put a hand on his friend's shoulder.

"Stevie, it's just that Henry really wants to play in college."

"Johnny's got his heart set on Cornell."

I couldn't stand it any longer. "The boys are eleven! Winning games now isn't going to get them any closer to college. They should be focused on learning how to play defense, and passing, and not shooting right at the goalie. If they're already worried about college, let them get a head start on their SAT prep."

Hardened faces, unmoved by reason, glared back at me. Finally, Lou dropped his eyes to his plate.

"Steve, maybe you're not the man to lead this team. You're a nice guy and all. But maybe we need to find another coach."

"Wait, you're firing me? Is that what this breakfast is?" I was up on my feet now. Even the unruly kids from the other table were turned in my direction. "You can't fire me. I'M A VOLUNTEER!"

Gold Level Sports Parents

Being a chauffeur, a spectator, a ball wrangler, an assistant coach or a manager may fall short of your dreams of participation in your child's athletic journey. And if writing a check to ensure access while conveying the illusion of true involvement, preferred by many these days, leaves you unfulfilled, perhaps you're primed to take the plunge into an immersive volunteer adventure.

How about signing up for Division Commissioner? As the title describes, you would be in charge of an entire age grouping, say 8U girls or 14U boys. The responsibility comes with an almost god-like power, in that your prime directive is building the teams. (Some organizations employ a draft, where coaches select their own players, but the Division Commissioner still mediates what's fair and foul.) Altruism doesn't flow through everyone's arteries and some use their post to stack their kids' teams. Most volunteers, however, are diligent practitioners, seeking team balance to provide each player with the same shot at a fun and productive season.

The job isn't all unchecked authority. The commissioner spends about three weeks during the summer creating the teams. She then spends the next three months justifying them, broadly speaking, in the form of roster changes (Tiffany has timpani lessons on Tuesdays, Nigel's cooking class moved to Monday, both need to be on new teams), parent complaints (my kid's coach only plays his own kid at forward) and other issues (we have USC season tickets so our games need to be first thing in the morning). The position is both unifying and polarizing.

Exhibit A: Two texts received by our U12 Girls' Commissioner on the same day – within minutes of each other, in fact.

1) Betsy, thank you so much for the most wonderful season. My daughter's team didn't win a game and only scored two goals. But the girls, under the miraculous direction of Coach Brian, had a fabulous time.

2) Shame on you, Betsy. You should wear darker clothes so no one sees you. Then again, no one really cares about you, do they? I'm sure if they did, you wouldn't be so vindictive.

To elicit such conflicting reactions, the commissioner holds hands, slaps wrists, works magic, and stays up to all hours returning phone calls, emails and texts. With over two hundred kids in some divisions, there can be some pretty late nights.

Going to sleep only slightly earlier are the coaches, who come to their position from a number of avenues. Many were players, former recreation, club, and college athletes, whose own careers are receding further into life's rearview mirror. Others never played the game at all. Almost all join the ranks at the request of their kids, some of whom can't wait to play while others condition their participation on the presence of mom or dad at the helm.

With my wild man raring to go, my entry point was the White Tigers, a gaggle of five-year-old goofballs, led by Evan and his pal Jacob. Along for the ride were Alex, whose timidity won him the ironic moniker Secret Weapon (which wondrously sparked him into action), Sammy, an athlete in a hurry, his one gear being overdrive, and Bryn, who beamed with pride as she outhustled and outmuscled every boy on the field. There was also Ian, dubbed Mr. Defense for closing his eyes and reaching out a leg to accidentally stop a break-away, Jacob W., whose parents carted him to the field still asleep for our eight o'clock games, and Ryan, who spent most of his time in training beefing with his older brother Jeffrey. At game time, Ryan stood around confused that his quarry couldn't rumble with him out on the field. (None of these wee warriors grew up to become professional athletes. In high school, three played soccer, one played basketball, and Sammy tackled football. He became the only college athlete, pursuing his dream at Delaware. At twenty-seven, only Jacob still has ties to sports, working in the front office of the Golden State Warriors. Most of the others have moved into the arts – music, film, painting and design, with a couple in politics and business – proving that there is life after youth sports.)

My most enduring takeaway from the White Tigers, though, was a love for coaching that remained undiminished for two decades. I loved everything about it.

The kids and their rainbow of personalities, their desire to be fun and have fun, I remember it all. I loved the August coaches' meeting, the excitement of gazing at my roster for the first time and making the introductory phone calls to my new parents. "Hi, my name is Coach Steve and I'm thrilled to welcome you to..."

I loved creating practice plans and designing drills, inflating the balls, loading up the car, driving to the field. I loved being early, first out to the field, and luxuriating in the solitude as I set up the grids. I loved watching the first car roll up, with an excited kid tumbling out of the back seat and racing out to greet me.

I loved spending time on my lineups. Three days before the game, I'd take ten minutes to pencil in a rough substitution pattern. Who would be goalie in the fourth quarter, who would start the game, when would certain players sub out? The next night, I'd cogitate a little harder, move kids around to different positions, strengthen the defense. And the night before the game, I would lock it all in. I'd stare at the page, tally the number of quarters each player sat, and check for fairness in rotating positions. And then I'd put it to bed.

I loved waking up on game days; it didn't matter how ungodly the hour. I'd bound out of bed, toss one of my kids in the car, and finally wake up about a half-hour into the drive.

I loved training the coaches. I loved working with the greatest unsung filmmaker, Colin, to make videos of each team. I loved crafting my write-ups of our weekly tournaments. And I loved being part of the soccer community.

One of my duties as regional head coach was to greet the new families coming out to register. With my own experience of jumping onto the end of a line reanimating memories of nervous excitement, I would approach the newbies and deliver my welcome spiel, which also contained a coach recruitment pitch. It went something like this:

"Good afternoon, everybody. On behalf of AYSO Region 69, I'd like to welcome you to your new family. AYSO is the largest youth sports organization in the country with 650,000 players playing on 50,000 teams, staffed by 250,000 volunteers. By virtue of your being here to endure my speech today, you are now a volunteer. You've probably seen in the registration materials some of the categories you can sign up for – assistant coach, team manager, field set-up, picture day manager, a few others. I'd like to speak to you today about becoming a coach.

"Why a coach?

"Well, we hardly know our neighbors and all the kids on the block go to different schools. Is there anything that can bring us together? How about working toward a common cause? And dedicating ourselves to making a difference? Providing our families and neighbors with a sense of community, which simultaneously expands and shrinks our universe. The deeper our involvement, the more people we know, and the more connected and vital we feel.

"We spend our days chained to our desks and tethered to our phones. Time passes and we stand still. Escaping the confines of our business and social lives for even a few hours a week can be liberating. When you're coaching, you are in the moment instead of planning for it, worrying about it, or missing it altogether. There's nothing but you, the kids, and a ball.

"From the stands, watching your kid play, you may be lucky to vicariously relive your own childhood. If you're coaching, there is no barrier between you and the experience. You can be a kid again . . . without the math tests or the French homework.

"As a coach, you'll be a leader in the community and a hero to your kids – how often do you get to be that? – modeling behavior and the values we want all kids to embrace.

"The season races by in a three month burst, but the memories last forever. Years from now, you'll be rolling down the aisle in the supermarket when you feel a tap on your shoulder. You'll turn to see this giant hovering over you whose face awakens glimmers of a tiny kid you vaguely remember. "Hi Coach," he'll say in a deep baritone as he reaches out a meat hook to swallow your hand. "Remember me? I just wanted to thank you for everything you did for me that year on the Red Dragons. It was the most fun I ever had playing sports." You'll float out of the store, maybe even forgetting what you went there to buy.

"The knowledge that you're enriching your community, enhancing the lives of its kids, and bonding ever tighter with your own will keep you warm for years to come."

By the end, the words would be tumbling over each other as they fought their way out of my mouth, and breathless, I'd look back at the crowd, expecting a chorus of "huzzahs" and a mad rush to grab the coach applications I brandished in my hand. Instead, I'd see polite smiles, some nods, and a few moms grabbing the shirts of their squirrelly kids trying to get away. It didn't matter. If I weren't already coaching, I would have signed up right then.

Anyone willing to assume the role of coach deserves our respect and support. I say this with the caveat that any adult that interacts with our children merits vetting and scrutiny. But once our questions are answered and our apprehensions assuaged, it's time to let the coach . . . coach. This applies to when the kids are on the field, when they're in the car, and when they're at home.

It's easy to defer to the coach at the field. He's the maestro orchestrating his minions in a symphony of synchronicity. In his dreams. More likely he's trying to explain a drill to a knot of knuckleheads, whose attention span after a long day of school rivals that of a gnat. If he's lucky he'll find the sweet spot somewhere between chaos and order. We parents back off and give him his space, grateful that *he's* the one taking charge of Tommy, and wishing he could help with homework and dinner, too.

While the risk of physical injury is inherent in sports, the car ride and the dinner table present more existential dangers. The parent steaming about the game's outcome and criticizing the coach during the ride home is, unfortunately, universal. But blaming the coach is a more pernicious attack than the one mounted by the other team. It undermines his leadership and sows doubts which can affect the child's motivation and effort. We parents need to leave the game on the field, respect the decisions of the coach, and strive not to subvert his authority.

What happens when the coach's vision for our kids doesn't align with ours? Dad sees Ashley as a striker, but the coach plays her only on defense. Xander misses practice to study for his midterm, then starts the next game on the bench. Charlotte pooches a goal punt, and the other team capitalizes on her mistake to bang it home for a score. The coach goes ballistic, and sits Charlotte in the second half.

Each of these scenarios is certain to spike a parent's blood pressure. Ashley is eight, the games mean nothing, why can't she play forward? School should be a priority and Xander's preparation for his test should be commended, not punished. Charlotte volunteered to play in goal when no one else would step forward. Why should she be humiliated for a mistake?

Confronting a coach in the moment, or after the whistle, or in the parking lot, is a recipe for failure. Game time emotions run hot, and if a coach feels threatened by a hostile parent, his fight or (more likely) flight response will trigger. The smart money advises us to be patient and see how the situation plays out over time. Holding our tongue is generally a better strategy than speaking our mind. We should count to ten, and neither text nor tweet in anger.

The 24-Hour Rule

Six days a week, parents are free, even encouraged, to contact the coach with concerns, issues or questions. Game day should be like the Sabbath, a day free of confrontation. You're stressed, your kid is stressed, and yes, the coach is stressed, too. The game unfolds quickly, with emotions soaring and crashing like a ball flying from one end of the field to the other. Errors abound and everyone – players, referees, and coaches – make them. Whether or not they affect the outcome, often an ache will lodge deep in your chest. Unless excised, it may metastasize, spreading a gloom that can affect your dinner, your evening, and your very outlook on life.

The natural impulse is to lay your troubles at the feet of the coach. He's the root cause, right? So we plop down at the computer to compose a blistering email designed to bring him to his knees. As we write, we get even more churned up as we replay over and over his affront to our child. We finish with a wrathful flourish and hit "send" – and immediately a sickening sensation lodges in our stomach. Are we second-guessing ourselves for overreacting? Or realizing that emailed rage rarely begets a mollifying response? Blood will have blood...

A better prescription for PGSD – Post-Game Stress Disorder – is to take a "timeout." Smolder, stew, even write that email if the demon inside insists. But don't send it. Pace and curse and swear to the heavens. But don't reach for the phone. Mold a voodoo doll out of Play-Doh and acupuncture the hell out of it. But, whatever you do, *do not* drive to the coach's house.

If, after a feverish night endlessly replaying the outrage in our heads, we waken to the same fire and fury, then go ahead and send the email or make the call. Chances are, though, the therapeutic properties of time and sleep have calmed us. Maybe even opened our eyes to consider the other side, to realize that the transgression was inadvertent, or minor, or our own mood refracting the events on the field. Ultimately, the parent who exercises restraint will get the better result.

Coaching Your Own Kid, Or: Tell Me Again Why I Signed Up to Do This?

Coach Chuck had it easy. His son Jared, at eleven, was already a full-blown mensch. Not the biggest kid, definitely not the fastest, but the way he was able to see the field and visualize the game, distribute the ball to all the right places at all the right times, and above all command respect by the way he carried himself and treated others, made him the best player on the team. He was the embodiment of the compliment "coachable." Chuck was already a committed, sought after coach. Jared made him a winning one as well.

Even under the most propitious circumstances, coaching is not for the faint of heart. Molding a roster of unevenly skilled players into a team demands preparation, organization, patience, perspective, a sense of humor, and a whole lotta luck. It ramps up several degrees of complicated when your own kid is in the crowd staring back at you.

But that's why most of us are coaches, right? Beyond our own desire to wield the clipboard, the choice to coach usually comes in two flavors: our kids desperately want us to, or they won't play unless we do.

Evan had to shed his preference for Coach Ray to accept Coach Dad as legit. Once that hurdle was cleared, joining AYSO with me as his coach was the next step. He made me work for every dollar I wasn't being paid.

At his mercurial best Evan never met a drill he couldn't destroy. Two-man passing through a lane of cones? Evan would aim for the cones, much more fun knocking them down. A simple touch drill with a partner tossing the ball to be volleyed back? Evan preferred knocking the ball over his partner's head, giggling as his teammate had to run to retrieve it. In the larger picture, all harmless. In the moment, distracting, frustrating, and practice halting. It was a godsend the U8 year that a movie-star mom generously made room on her blanket for timeout mode Evan.

These early years presented an equally exasperating game-time Evan. He was energy incarnate, dysfunctionally applied all over the field. Still, he exhibited flashes of brilliance and I succumbed to the "potential-expectation trap" I spoke about in Chapter Four. I bristled at what I perceived to be the squandering of his talent. Why didn't he want to go outside and knock the ball around? Why wouldn't he practice his juggling in the driveway? Why was he always goofing around at practice while his teammates were taking it more seriously?

Let's concede that he was young – six, seven, eight, nine – with all the inconsistencies of focus and interest that were appropriate for his age. Digging deeper revealed causes that were specific to Evan as well as routinely rooted in the "coach's kid" experience.

For Evan, soccer was a thing. It wasn't *the* thing. And it wasn't the *only* thing. Fish tanks, video games, drawing, and sleepovers with friends beckoned strongly when he wasn't in cleats. So my pressing for him to be more devoted was a waste of breath.

The more primal impetus for his behavior took me a while to grasp. Here I was, his dad, attending to eleven other kids that weren't his siblings (who he had no choice but to share me with). Sure, I was paying attention to him as well. But it was 91 percent less attention than he felt he should be receiving. Obviously he was going to figure out a way to set himself apart from the masses, and if deriving negative attention was that way, at least it was attention.

This is a common reaction for kids whose parents are their coaches. In the abstract, it's a great idea. "Dad's my coach. I'll feel so special!" Then confronted with all these hangers-on in the huddle, it's a disorienting and deflating, "What the heck!"

Some, like Evan, act out obliquely. Dori rarely gave in to histrionics. Her way of grabbing back the spotlight was to sing out, "Daddy, watch me. Watch me!" She could be executing a trick or falling over the ball, as long as my eyes were on her, she was happy.

Griffie didn't want the attention, period. If I congratulated him for something he'd done well, he'd grunt and shrug. If I pointed out something that could be done better, watch out. Griffie had a rigid and specific understanding of how he should play the game. Calling out to him with adjustments broke his concentration and added to the pressure he put on himself. He would bark that he was doing what was asked or that his was a smarter way to go. Racing up and down the field carrying on a running dialogue with me on the sideline, his protest could erupt into a full-blown tantrum. That sweet little face scrunched up in tear-streaked frustration, arguing as if his life depended on it, then quickly refocusing to clear the ball, before launching right back into the fight.

So how do we manage this psycho-familial minefield and keep the season on a positive trajectory? A wise man counseled me to say this to my kids:

"At home, I am your father and you get me all to yourself. Here, I am the coach of the team and it's my job to make sure that everybody – including you – has a good time. But whether at home or on the field, I love you."

It worked . . . for a few minutes . . . the first time or two I tried it. Below, however, might be a longer-lasting prescription for successfully coaching your own kid:

1. Know that your kid wants you to coach. She thinks it's cool that everybody looks up to you. Don't let her down.

2. Fairness and consistency are key. Whatever rules, codes or systems you institute, apply them to every player equally.

3. Don't favor. Either your kid or any of the others. When a coach sets his own child above the others (through advantageous playing time or preferential positioning), hurt feelings and resentment spread among the other players and parents. It's OK to make them feel important. Just don't fashion the entire team culture around them.

4. Likewise don't punish. Sometimes coach's kids complain that dad is solicitous to others while critical of them. Be self-aware to prevent this injustice.

5. "You have to set a good example." Ugh. This is the least productive thing you can say to your child. Understand the

inherent pressure of being the "coach's kid." Don't compound it by expecting him to be better, more cooperative or a harder worker than everyone else. He may be your kid, but he's still a kid.

6. Rather than impose expectations, model the positive qualities you want from your child and her teammates. Be honest, respectful, patient, and forgiving.

7. Communicate with your child. Make her a partner. Share what you're planning for practices and games. This is an area where it's OK for the familial bond to shine. No one will care if your child blurts out that World Cup is on the agenda. But your child will feel closer to you for this tidbit of insider information.

8. In the moment, emotions run high. Dial yours down to a simmer.

9. If conflict with your child flares, postpone the battle until you're home. Revisit quietly, later in the evening. His defenses will be down, as will yours.

And the most important . . .

10. Regularly revisit the question of who you're doing this for. You're allowed to be part of the answer, but your child should always be at the top of the list.

With the coaches squared away, it's time to send in the refs. They're the whistle-wielding, knee-sock wearing, last line of defense between the rule of law and anarchy on the field. Like the sporting version of blind justice, they play no favorites and have no rooting interest in any contest. They serve one master: the game itself.

Committed to ensuring a safe, fair and fun environment, most prefer to fulfill that mandate in as invisible a fashion as possible.

Attention drawn their way indicates a universe out of balance. And yet, in the heat of combat, with bodies flying and passions flaring, odds are good that any given call will trigger a chorus of outrage from 50 percent of the attendees. Multiply that by a hundred routine-to-consequential calls during a game, and we're talking about ground fertile for conflict.

To thrive in this war zone, a referee needs fast-twitch mental reflexes, a bulletproof ego, and severe hearing loss, this last to ignore the shrieks and cries pelting him from all sides. Eagle Eyesight is optional as most of the participants and spectators will think the official is vision-impaired.

The referee is Wyatt Earp with a red card replacing his six-shooter, Chief Justice of the Supreme Court with only two sidekicks instead of an unwieldy eight, and King Solomon whose baby is the fate of the match. That's a lot of power consolidated in one individual. Most referees exercise it with the restraint and wisdom of an Atticus Finch. Folks like Schneidy and Hinshaw, Chuck, Brad, Kremer and Lee, guys whose kids aged out of the program years ago but who continue to race up and down the field for the love of the game and their commitment to the players. Then there's Rex Sebastian.

A veteran with thirty years of experience, all smiles and collegiality before the game, once the ball was played, he devolved into a whistle-happy grim reaper. No one was safe. Players would be whistled for the tiniest bump and threatened, "Next time, it's a yellow card." If they looked to the sideline for explanation and Rex heard the coach's soothing, "It's OK, just play your game," Rex would blast that whistle again and call out, "Coach!" With all eyes boring into him, the coach would slink out into the field and Rex would admonish him with, "Positive coaching, coach. Next time I'll have to send you off." If the coach protested that he was merely trying to support his player, Rex would cut him off: "Back to the sideline, coach."

The Rex Sebastian Show bumped along like a car caught in stop-and-go traffic. Any momentum mounted by either team would be blunted by yet another whistle. It was unpleasant to watch and no fun to play. Even his assistant referees patrolling the lines would shrug or mutter under their breaths.

Once, a mom on my team, fed up with Rex intimidating another player, lost her cool, "Why don't you pick on someone your own size?"

Rex wheeled around and scanned the sideline for the source of the complaint.

"Who said that?"

No one responded, not a Spartacus among us, so Rex singled out an unsuspecting victim and tore into her, reducing her to tears.

I found myself one Saturday the recipient of a Rex Sebastian spotlight dance. It was an early morning game, and Evan's team, the Riptide, was playing as if still in bed. I shouted across the field, partially in jest, definitely in frustration, "Hey boys, you should have let us know you weren't going to show up today." A few of the parents chuckled, as did some of the boys, acknowledging my gentle jab. Rex's bleat nearly pierced my eardrum.

"COACH!" I followed his wagging finger to the center of the field. "Coach, positive coaching only!"

"And what about positive reffing? You blow the whistle every ten seconds, then yell at the kids for trying to play the game. This game is for them, but you hijack it and make it all about you. Stuff the whistle in your pocket and LET THE KIDS PLAY!!!"

I left him in the center of the field with his jaw bobbing, sputtering gibberish, and strode triumphantly back to a round of high fives at the bench. The game resumed and a chastened Rex didn't utter another word or signal another stoppage of play. Both teams left the field happy.

Actually, I didn't say any of that. But I thought it *really* hard. I slunk back to the coach's box and suffered with everyone else through the end of the fits-and-starts match.

Why does the league allow Rex to keep reffing, you ask? Well, sadly, fewer and fewer souls show up each year willing to do the job. Rex's antics may ruin the game for everyone but having no one to take his place will cancel the game altogether. Which is worse?

This probably hasn't been the most seductive pitch for raising your hand to ref, but let me offer up another side. The Palaxy team carried a roster of sixteen players, a hefty number for 7-vs.-7 U10 games. To find playing time for that many boys we entered nineteen tournaments and ensured that players got to as many weekends as possible. The system worked well, with the least involved player still attending 50 percent of our games. In order to run an operation this size, we needed a referee pool hefty enough to cover three or four games a weekend. Every family had to provide a trained and certified referee to the cause. The dads and moms got into it and we became a stylish crew, opting to purchase almost all of the available referee colors – traditional yellow, royal blue, Kelly green, black, and the rare ruby red.

We had the hard-core volunteers like Rick, Cyrus, Dan, Steve and Jan, many of whom were also coaches, and all of whom relished their time as center refs. Sergio, Scott, and the three Davids took a more relaxed approach, conveniently forgetting to pack the high socks or the referee-standard black shorts. JT was the most casual. On numerous occasions he was busted for yammering on his cellphone while he was supposed to be hustling down the sideline keeping apace of the last defender.

Marcy was new to the game, but realizing its growing significance for our family, and wanting to be part of the 24/7 soccer conversation, she readily grabbed the socks and flags and hurried out to the line.

Her style could best be described as holistic. She reffed the players and kept the sideline in check as well. The moment she sensed any contradictory chatter from the parents behind her, she would turn and thrust out her flag.

"If you think you can do better, here ya go . . ." She never had any takers.

Some of the most confident referees are the contingent of twelve- to eighteen-year-olds who have grown up in the game and love it so much they want to give back in any way possible. They grab the reins of authority and officiate for kids not much younger than they are. If their command is at times shaky, their knowledge is freshly acquired and accessible. Sideline boors, however, make no concession for age and aim their sniping at these young heroes. In our region, a zero tolerance policy for criticizing youth referees earns these blowhards an escort off the field. Preserving and protecting the community outreach of these young ones overrides our patience for unthinking adults.

Referees are a tight-knit clan, forged in the fire of game time, and brimming with almost identical stories of obnoxious parents and energetic players. It's their love of the game, and their dedication to seeing it played safely and fairly, though, that keeps them donning the socks, grabbing the whistle, and taking care of our kids.

Platinum Level Sports Parents

If you harbor grand ambitions, a passion for civic service, or have an inordinate amount of free time, perhaps league administration is worth a shot. I didn't realize I had any of those qualifications when Jeff, Renaissance man and six-year Region 69 Coach Administrator, brought me onto the board. Slyly seeking his successor, he asked if I'd like to attend a meeting on a national proposal to dispense with weekday practices and move to smaller-sided games for the youngest kids. I was flattered, and with my own program catering to this age group, I readily agreed.

From that meeting, Jeff invited me to sit in on the larger board gatherings, and a year later he popped the question: Would I become his deputy? Before I knew it, he was waving goodbye and I was sitting in his vaunted seat at the far end of our rowdy, why-should-the-kids-have-all-the-fun? conference table. Over the next fifteen years, as I trained and certified the coaches, enlisted professionals to work with the kids, operated as a velvet hammer writing tons of alternately inspiring and admonishing emails, and coached twenty league and All-Star teams, I also had a front-row view of my own kids as they grew up. While my commitment was total, I interacted with folks who made my tenure seem part time.

Debbie and Dick were lifers. Like most volunteers in the organization, they began as a young family with little kids eager to kick a ball. Dick coached and refereed. Debbie pitched in where needed, her energy and problem-solving acumen drawing her more deeply into the organization. She ultimately rose to the rank of Regional Commissioner, the head honcho, the grand pooh-bah, the boss of bosses. She was the embodiment of the axiom, "You want to get something done, find the busiest person in town to do it."

Debbie buzzed with the energy of the Tasmanian devil and attacked problems with the never-let-go tenacity of a Jack Russell terrier, while drawing upon her encyclopedic knowledge of everyone in the community to serve and protect the interests of Region 69. She didn't manage it all single-handedly, but it seemed like she did, navigating every field closure, parent complaint and coach overreach with assurance and an unshakable integrity. There was no one who could match her dedication, drive, and frantic functionality.

Husband Dick, while happy to cede the spotlight to his effervescent spouse, performed his own nimble feats of political legerdemain. He spearheaded the acquisition of field lights for the high school, employing his presidency of the Boosters Club to improve conditions at both the school and within AYSO, while helming teams and officiating matches long after his two sons and a daughter aged out of the program.

Debbie and Dick gave everything, including their front porch, to Region 69. Spilling over with bags of balls, cones, uniforms, paperwork, checks, plaques and anything else league-related, the porch was the flood plain of their commitment to the community. Almost forty years in, their vitality undiminished, they now shepherd their grandchildren through the program.

And then there were George and Richard and Janet and Bob, for whom service was a sacred trust. Over his tenure, George held every position in the region. Coach, All-Star coach, referee, Division Commissioner, Regional Referee Commissioner, and Regional Commissioner, while also serving a stint on the National Board of Directors. Richard procured every soccer ball and distributed every uniform for a generation. Janet volunteered her way through the ranks to step into Debbie's capacious shoes as head of the region. Every blade of playable grass has been lovingly tended by Bob. These and scores more were the behind-the-scenes prime movers that yearly propelled the league onward.

Girls Just Wanna Have Fun

So, when do the referees get to join in on the party? Or the coaches or the team managers? What about the division commissioners, the set-up folks or even the long-suffering parent chauffeurs, all of whom have obligingly made sure that their kids got to play ball? For a long time in our region, there was a weekly Saturday afternoon "coaches" game, though in actuality, anybody who appeared was thrown onto the field. Other than that there wasn't much.

Too long ago, in evaluating this landscape, I saw a paucity of opportunities for adult women – mostly moms – to experience the game. The ones I knew all had kids in the league, and had been enthusiastic volunteers. Many were athletes in their own right – Pam played competitive tennis, Maren had run track, Jody had been voted her high school's best athlete, Jill was a confirmed gym rat, Mary Beth and Melissa could do it all – but none had ever laced up a pair of cleats for themselves. So I created a Moms' Soccer program to offer women:

- a new group of friends unrelated to their kids' classes or schools
- the opportunity to get out of the gym and into a fresh mode of exercise
- a chance to play a team sport, some for the first time
- the opportunity to play a sport their children were playing
- a way to let them see how hard their kids were working and increase their empathy for their kids' efforts

Twice a week we'd meet at Barrington Park, on the same field trod by Evan and his merry men, and spend about forty-five minutes learning skills, then finish the session with a scrimmage. In the beginning, we offered Tuesday and Thursday sessions, based on who could attend on which day. Through the grapevine, the Tuesdays would hear about the Thursdays, and vice versa, and a friendly rivalry developed. Each would ask me which day was "better?" Discretion dictated my answer, which was a self-protective, "Both are great." After a while, the vagaries of scheduling forced some moms to switch days. Others, bitten by the bug, wanted to play twice a week. The cross-pollination of the classes served to dispel the jealousy and tighten the bonds. As hoped, new friendships formed as a deep affection for the game developed.

Sometime during the second year, several of the more ambitious moms asked about playing competitively. Were there other women in the area who had already been playing? Was there a league they could join? Could they participate in a tournament like their kids? Sure enough, we found another local group, most of whom had been playing for years, and welcomed them into our cozy bunch.

Shifting time commitments and a few injuries thinned the ranks, but six or seven of our OGs are still playing today, recreationally, on league teams, and in tournaments. Our little experiment succeeded on every level. The women added "adult athlete" to their already impressive CVs. They learned to appreciate their children's experience while playing a sport that they weren't exposed to as kids. From volunteering for their kids to competing themselves, these women journeyed along a road that allowed them to richly realize the fulsome promise of sports.

* * *

During my tenure in youth sports, I've watched volunteerism get a bad rap. From a bountiful pool of prospective coaches in my early days, it's now a struggle to scrape up enough bodies to lead a division's requisite number of teams. How do we account for this decline in magnanimity?

Stirrings were evident in the early 2000s, when we prosecuted two wars with no military draft and 1 percent of the populace shouldering the entire burden. The message that there would always be someone else to pick up the slack embedded itself in the national psyche. A more visible manifestation was the rise of the app and its ability to grant our every earthly desire with the tap of a finger. In this instant-gratification society, fortified by DoorDash and TaskRabbit, our personal preoccupations supplant any responsibility we feel toward our community.

Tell this to the people who populate these pages. They'd shrug, *"Sure, giving to others takes time, commitment and effort."* And they'd concede that the generosity and nobility of volunteering may not be for everyone. But then they'd draw close and whisper the not-so-secret truth of volunteering: It's fun. Rewarding and fun. And they wouldn't trade those hours for anything.

So put down your phone, stick your checkbook back in the drawer, and look around. I bet somewhere in your community there's a line waiting for you to jump on the end of.

CHAPTER THIRTEEN

On the Road to Find Out

Childhood is a mad dash from birth to college, crammed with moments and memories frantically stitched together by family and community. For parents, it can seem like Human Whack-a-Mole. You get one kid back from an ear infection, then the other one drops his science project in a puddle. No sooner is the mud scraped off than a feud erupts in the friend group. Throw in carpool, afterschool activities, enrichment classes, religious school, and dance, music, and art lessons, and you've got neither enough arms nor hours to make it all work.

Youth sports provides no respite from the craziness. It's rife with moles of its own. *Is Ella good enough to make the team? Is the team good enough for Ella? Does Ella even want to play this sport?* Yet, bursting with all the elements of high drama – spectacle, passion, elation and devastation – the full measure of life can be experienced in a season, or a game, or even a shot. Kids thrive on these peak moments, the built-in camaraderie, and the opportunities to test – and push – their limitations, with the unbridled joy all of this can bring.

The more of these moments that parents can share with their children, the tighter the family bonds will be. (The key word is "share," not to be confused with "dominate" or "overwhelm.") While children are the primary beneficiaries of the virtues enumerated above, there has to be some quid pro quo for parents, too. Altruism stretches only so far. There has to be some salve for the parent whose work-crammed weekdays slide seamlessly into errand-filled weekends. "If I'm sitting on a sideline somewhere," a parent may validly feel, "something important isn't getting done at home."

I received this email from one of our team parents: *Jeremy loved his first tournament. He asked, "Do you think I can be with all my same teammates next year? Do you think I can make the A team?" I asked him what was the best part of the weekend and he said, "My header goal, the best pizza in the world and the spitball fight at the pancake place." I think he's hooked.*

Sounds like dad was, too. I can relate. I remember the lightning-strike headers that brought me cheering to my feet, the roof-of-the-mouth-charring pizza in Victorville, and the monumental all-restaurant spitball fight (followed by the meticulous all-restaurant cleanup) that would have gone viral had YouTube yet been created.

The players garnered the accolades but they held no monopoly on the fun. We parents, as the chauffeurs, outfitters, schedulers, travel agents, and bottomless bankers, drove thousands of miles, bundled up in the snow, dove under tents in the heat, endured myriad meals of runny eggs and rubbery fries, sacrificed time with our spouses and other children – and loved every minute. Well, maybe not *every* minute . . .

For many families, "the road" presents a Rorschach test of the entire youth sports experience. Some parents prefer a five-alarm tantrum or an up-all-night baby than an hour in the car. Moms and dads would flip coins, with the loser enduring an excruciating 8 a.m. kickoff, squinting into the glare of the rising sun and the grass so dewy their shoes would stay wet till noon. Some would manufacture scheduling conflicts, and park their kids with others committed to making the drive. That's how badly some folks resisted the ride. Sleepovers before game days were frowned upon as the attendees usually did their sleeping on the field.

But for those able to see more than the white lines speeding by, these drives offered an opportunity. My friend Army tells it this way:

"The best parts of AYSO were driving Augie and Sadie to faraway games, and having a chance to have the greatest talks with them because it was just us driving somewhere to play a game . . . It didn't really matter what game because we were playing a different game – the game of life. The games of fathers and sons, fathers and daughters, mothers and sons and daughters, and sometimes all together – on a road trip, in search of ourselves and each other. And then – there was 'the game' and the highs and lows of competition, the victories and defeats, that prepare us all for the games and competitions ahead. Ahhh, those days that we will never get back again. But we will always carry them forward with us."

My rides with my kids rarely offered such profundity, but just hurtling toward the next patch of grass was exciting. I remember one sunrise, zipping along the 210 to Rancho Cucamonga when, cresting a hill, I found myself heading straight into a bank of backlit, billowing red-orange clouds. It felt otherworldly, even spiritual. I reached over to my dozing daughter, "Dori, you gotta see this."

"Dad, stop." She shrugged me off. (I suspect that if I had handed her my phone with a photo of the phenomenon, she would have at least cracked open one eye.)

219

As the coach, who had to be to the field early anyway, I found exhilarating the challenge of rising at ungodly hours and getting ready with the lights off, knowing Marcy still had several more hours to spend in Snoozeville. Evan was a beast to rouse, snoring through alarms, shaking off my gentle taps, "five more minutes"-ing me till he somehow staggered into the back seat when it was time to go. Dori and Griffie were troopers, Dori setting her own alarm, Griffie relying on his internal version. All three of them would pack into the car with blankies, pillows, and headphones to grab as many more zzzzz's as they could.

Later games offered the possibility of conversation and connection, if not as frequently as Army recounts above. From the put-upon "*Da-aaad*" when they didn't want to engage, to the chirpy downloading about school or friends when they were less guarded, the content was less important than the time together. We shared familiar rhythms and easy shortcuts, touched on pressing fears and long-range dreams. Cocooned in the car, breathing the same experience, it was immediate and timeless.

And almost always accompanied by music. During Evan's U8 days, when he played on the polo field below Will Rogers' ranch, we'd wend our way up the hill to Bruce Springsteen's "Badlands," with me pounding out the lyric on the steering wheel.

"*I believe in the love that you gave me, I believe in the hope that can save me...*"

Two years later we crammed his entire All-Star team into my car and raced through the streets of Huntington Beach, with them hanging out the windows barking "Who Let the Dogs Out" at amused pedestrians. Dori, Jillian and sister Casey swayed in the back seat to "The Hamster Dance." Griffie was dictatorial, commandeering the radio dial when he climbed into the passenger seat. "If I have to sit in the car, I get to choose the music!" Ellie Goulding and EDM propelled us from San Bernardino to Santa Barbara.

Like adherents to the Postal Service creed, we barreled through every caprice of weather. We braved snow coming through the Palmdale pass, and winds that swept my SUV across three lanes en route to Apple Valley.

Then there was the slog through the Noah's Ark-magnitude deluge, wondering how the girls were going to play when I couldn't see past the edge of the hood. The famed Riverside Locomotion tournament prided itself on never canceling its games, weather be damned. Dori was prepared with extra cleats, a bag full of socks, a hair dryer for her uniform, and an exuberance that strained against her seatbelt.

"It'll be fun to play in the rain," she declared.

Sure, for her. But coaching in this inclemency, with my lineup smearing across the whiteboard and the cold penetrating multiple layers to nestle in my bones, was going to be no picnic. The windshield wipers groaned from exhaustion.

"It's gonna be great," I agreed.

* * *

Traditionally in parenting, everything from caregiving to imparting values flows from adult to child. The same directional current generally applies in youth sports. Parents deliver services — driving, feeding, writing the check — and kids reap the benefits.

What about opportunities to learn from our kids? We can't spy on them in school, and they clam up when we intrude on their social interactions. But on the field we're front-row orchestra to their process. Can they win with humility and lose with grace? Will they surprise us with acts of selflessness, like pumping up a player lacking in confidence or deferring to one with less skill? How will they react to adversity, and can they fight through it to emerge stronger on the other side? Sometimes what we learn from our kids is more literal.

Dori's Pali-Cats' victory at the Section 1 Championship catapulted them into the Tri-Section tournament, the apex of the AYSO pyramid. Over 1,200 U10 girls league teams funneled down into 250 All-Star teams, and here we were in the final four. An extraordinary accomplishment. Unfortunately, with top scorer Dani AWOL for a family function, and dependable defender Raleigh nursing a creaky knee, the battle was going to be uphill. When Mackenzie, our speedy right winger, arrived with a sore throat, I was less than enthused. Mom Erin waved away my concern.

"She'll be fine. I gave her two teaspoons of cough medicine."

Nooooooo! The hypochondriac in me, well versed in the effects of over-the-counter medications, knew that a doped-up Mackenzie might meander ineffectively around the field, handicapping our chances further. I asked the nicest human ever to grace one of my teams how she felt.

Mackenzie yawned. "OK, I guess."

Crap.

Castaic was our semifinal opponent. Their prime weapon was a lanky center forward with a penchant for pounding the kickoff into the goal. But as play began on a very wet Field 5, the game appeared to be ours. The forwards were clicking up top. The defenders erected a mighty wall in the back. And Cami in the goal barely touched the ball. We camped out in Castaic's end pushing toward an inevitable goal. But in soccer, the only certainty is uncertainty. And Castaic didn't get here because of their attractive uniforms.

After the half, a giant sinkhole swallowed us whole. A give-and-go, a missed tackle, and two shots on target left the Pali-Cats sputtering. Dori raced over with urgency. "Dad, Mackenzie's half-asleep on 'D.' (Damn that cough medicine!) Move her up front, maybe she'll wake up." Dori was right. Even from across the field, I could see Mackenzie's eyelids drooping. "Mackenzie! Switch with Jillian."

Within seconds, Emma on the wing cut through a knot of defenders and sailed a cross to Mackenzie, who, as if smooched by Prince Charming, magically stirred. She settled the ball and finessed it past the diving keeper. With the girls playing AND coaching – thank you, Dori – we were back in the game . . . even if we didn't stay there long.

Castaic slipped in a third, soul-crushing score and it was off to lunch at the mall. Propitiously, a pet store with pet-able pets adjoined the restaurant. A few hours later, we rallied against rivals Culver City to snag third place. But that morning, it was Dori to the rescue, seeing clearly what I was unable to fathom.

* * *

Even for the diehard parent, the "fun" of waking in the dark and riding in the rain can survive only so long. There has to be a more gripping motivation for sustaining this over a period of weeks, or months, or even years.

Increasingly, we consult technology for our answers. The internet and social media have made the world more immediate and more consumable, yet they have also exacerbated a fracturing which threatens to overwhelm our lives. The fear of losing control of our destiny steers us to sites that confirm our biases while tuning out anything that seeks to challenge them. What separates us is often more compelling than what brings us together.

On a local level, this Balkanization expresses itself in our estrangement from our neighbors, whom we don't know and whose kids all attend different schools. We come home from work and disappear into our screens, either to keep working or to view life from a safe remove. What's lacking is community, those ties that bind us to each other and enhance our lives in good times and bad. Church groups, civic and charitable organizations, even political alliances can fill the void. But few interactions have the power to close the gap in the same transgenerational, transformational, and transcendent way as youth sports.

I've been blessed to be part of three rewarding and enduring soccer communities, one for each of my kids. With Evan it was the Pythons, an assemblage that lasted deep into club; Dori had her Pali-Cats and Devil-Cats, and Griffie belonged to the freewheeling Palaxy, with its next chapter at FC Los Angeles.

My entry into this world was a serendipitous fluke. As described, my decision to helm (with Hadi) a newly-spawned "C" team for Evan and his peers, sealed my fate for the next dozen years. The original core shed some pieces and appended others, resulting in a team, in every sense of the word. They were each other's best friends, as they skateboarded, paint-balled, went to movies, and navigated the rites of adolescence together. Through their teens, as some migrated to other pursuits, and schools and social groups claimed others, their connection remained vital and supportive.

A parallel path was forged with the families. The moms and dads of Evan's teammates became the first set of new best friends I'd made in the decades since college. It was an imposing parent body. A top-of-the-line Hollywood attorney, a renowned anesthesiologist, a Harvard MBA on the board of several charitable organizations, a patron of the LA Philharmonic, the owner of a public relations firm, the CFO of a major snack-food brand . . .

The men were equally as accomplished, with even a CIA agent in the mix. Actually he was a building manager, but his low-key demeanor, his habit of cupping his mouth while speaking on his cell, and the wad of bills he flashed to pay for meals, fueled conspiratorial fantasies. This was the group I greeted every Saturday morning at a middle school or recreation center somewhere along the sprawl of the Southern California freeway system. Communication was key, and a steady stream of emails kept everybody flowing in the same direction. If you didn't stay current in the correspondence, though, you could get lost . . .

One morning just before game time in Moorpark, I noticed that Chris was missing. I hadn't heard from his parents about ill health or a competing obligation, and it was unlike them to ever be late. I called dad Kip, who picked up in one ring.

"Everything all right? Where are you guys?"

"At the field, but I don't see anyone."

"We're way down near the far end, just keep walking."

"No no no. I literally don't see anyone. There's no one here."

Now I was confused. One of those cognitive disconnect moments. There were hundreds of kids and families all around me. Then it dawned on me . . .

"Wait. Where are you?"

"Palmdale."

"Palmdale??? That's next week. We're in Moorpark!"

"Holy shit!" I could hear Chris through the phone. "You screwed up, Dad."

Kip didn't need to hear it from me. In fact I think he had already hung up and was flying down the 14. Sixty-seven miles and forty-five minutes later, he screeched up to the field. Chris, adrenaline pumping, ran himself silly for the last five minutes of the game. It took Kip until Palmdale the next week to catch his breath.

The bottom line was that it didn't matter where we went as long as we went there together. We'd endure the weekdays to arrive at the weekends, when we'd crowd the sidelines, cheer for our kids, shag balls, split lunch tabs, snooze through movies (except for the classic *Paul Blart, Mall Cop*), return to the field, cheer some more, go home, get up and do it all again. Weekend after weekend. We had each other's backs and, more importantly, those of each other's kids.

On a good day, the drive to Diamond Bar is a brisk forty-five minutes away. But on the 10 or the 60, there are few good days, only windows that aren't awful. Each year my All-Star teams made the pilgrimage to play in Diamond Bar's Cottontail Classic. Of the three, Dori and her Pali-Cats managed the highest finish, when they narrowly lost the championship to Culver City (whose coach cunningly worked the referees for a goalie interference call that nullified one of our scores). Of more lasting note was Dori forgetting to pack her cleats all three years she played.

I hounded Evan, who could barely be bothered, to check the contents of his soccer bag before hitting the road. Griffie would forget socks, cleats, shin guards, his shorts . . . until we finally adopted a verbal checklist to certify he had what he needed.

But Dori was the most organized of the three. She took pride in laying out her school clothes the night before. And prior to a soccer tournament she would catalog everything she needed and make sure it landed in her bag. Somehow, some way, on three April Saturdays in three successive years, cleats didn't make the cut.

The first year we made the stomach-clenching discovery moments from the field. She couldn't play in the slippers she was wearing, and there was neither the time nor the inclination to hurry home and back. If the girls had been older, we could have banked on someone having an extra pair, but they weren't that acquisitive or jaded yet.

Here's where the community paid dividends. Dani's mom, Laurie, had let me know she'd be getting to the field right at game time. Perhaps she hadn't left home yet. A quick call confirmed my hope and Laurie detoured for the shoes.

In year two, Dori's tears moved Marcy to scrap her work plans, bundle a reluctant Griffie into the car and deliver the shoes. And to complete the trifecta, Jillian's mom, Pam, driving carpool that day, scoured the neighborhood and discovered a children's shoe store that was open early. Luckily they carried cheap but functional soccer shoes, a size too small but – beggars and choosers, right? Without the bonds of community, Dori would have sat moping on the sideline.

As AYSO gave way to club, the twin necessities of being more competitive and filling up the roster resulted in the teams becoming more diverse. They took on a Latin flavor, with players coming from greater distances and socioeconomic circumstances to join in. It became a richer, more profound experience for all of us.

The reality of life's inequity only became a factor on trips down to San Diego when some of the Hispanic players' parents wouldn't come along. The party line chalked it up to the dads having to work, but the parents confided that it was dangerous for them to be so close to the border. It was a wake-up call that resisted easy answers, or any answers at all. This intrusion of politics into youth sports had a sobering effect, highlighting our differences and showing us the limits of compassion and hope. The politics of the moment offer little insight into how this situation will resolve for the better. But, somehow, for the sake of all our children, it must. One thing is clear, community – the community of caring and purpose – is going to have to contribute to the solution.

* * *

What happened to Dori's hopes of playing in a deluge?

The tournament that billed itself as weather-resistant buckled after a few flashes of lightning. We had just limped into the parking lot to find cars filled with disappointed kids . . . and relieved parents. Dori's groan and my cheer cancelled each other out.

Driving home was out of the question. No one on the team had the stomach for another crawl and our hotel reservations were beyond the refund deadline. A flurry of calls determined that our best option was . . . lunch.

No one really cared about the quality of the mac and cheese at the Mission Inn, Riverside's signature architectural wonder, at that moment overrun with pent-up soccer kids and their cranky parents, but as the girls colored and poured every condiment on the table into their glasses of milk, we parents devised a soccer-less game plan.

Mom Erin, dispenser of cough syrup, found a roller rink in the Yellow Pages. (Remember them?) Off we went. You could choose skates or blades or a seat on the side but the hours rolled by and when we departed around four, the skies were blue, the sun was out and the games were still cancelled.

Kids love swimming pools. The temperature outside could be soaring into the hundreds or sinking into the teens. Doesn't matter. A pool, some friends, and the promise of milkshakes will keep any young girl or boy happy. The adults took over a bank of lounges, grabbed a stack of towels, and kept the food and libations flowing. The conversation centered on – what else? – soccer. Our gratitude that our girls loved it – and were good at it – our contentment in the company of each other, and how we couldn't imagine spending our weekends any other way. Looking back from the other end of the run, that glow has become an ache.

CHAPTER FOURTEEN

Winning the 1-1 Tie:
The Dynamics of Competition

"Sometimes you win and sometimes you learn…"
– John Wooden and John Maxwell

Evan's second year of U8, his team, the Golden Zapdos (it was the height of the original Pokemon craze), was winless through the first nine games. His team the year before, the Red Dragons, had gone 0-for-10. Heading into the final match of the season, Evan's two-year U8 experience was a cellar-dwelling bust. As luck would have it, we were paired against the league's other winless squad, coached by the division's other Coach Steve. As the teams took the field, there was a buzz that belied the quality of the competition. Somebody's losing streak was ending today.

Fueled by hope and promise, the match was a pendular affair, with momentum swinging from one team to the other. It was Athens

231

vs. Sparta in a low-stakes battle for redemption and dignity. Despite our boys playing an asphyxiating defense, the other team squibbed in a goal. For an instant, Evan and his mates lapsed into their all too familiar "here we go again" malaise. But, encouraged by the sideline's wall of support, the boys rallied to bang home an equalizing goal. The dust cleared on a 1-1 tie.

The referee summoned Coach Steve the Other and me to the center of the field.

"Gentlemen, how would you like to play an overtime to determine a winner?"

Coach Steve and I looked at each other, both of us at a loss. AYSO rules expressly forbid additional time, mostly because of the compressed schedule of games running back to back from early morning to late afternoon. The whistle blows, that's a wrap. A tie was a tie. But this ref, perhaps cognizant of the struggle both teams had faced this season, was offering the chance to throw off the mantle of losing. It was an attractive proposition. I looked into Coach Steve's eyes. He was definitely considering . . .

And then both of us snapped to our senses.

"No, thanks . . ."

" . . . we're good."

We shook hands and headed back to our benches, both of us proud of the 1-1 tie we'd each just won. It felt as satisfying as if we'd just won the league title. Our long-suffering parents were rapturous, twirling their sons, tossing them into the air. It was a fantastic way to close out the season.

It wasn't just the thrill of victory the boys were vying for. Whether at seven they could articulate that they were also striving for dignity, redemption, and respect, the intangibles were definitely on the line that day. Few would argue that by any traditional definition a tie could be considered a win. Yet no one who witnessed the unrestrained celebration of both teams would dare dispute that everyone there was a winner, arguably more so than if one team had sent the other home in defeat. This is why when we talk about victory and defeat, we need to redefine our terms.

Competition, in itself, is healthy. We push ourselves to do our best, striving against resistance and obstacles, while comparing our efforts to those of others. Some form of "winning" is usually the goal. But for kids, who need to learn how to play before they can actually compete, the pressure to win can turn a healthy impulse into a burden. Prematurely keying on results rather than on development negatively impacts the entire sporting experience.

Prevailing forces in society want us to believe that success is a zero-sum game. If we're not winning, we're losing. We're either up or down, happy or sad, rich or poor. Reality resists such a narrow casting of life's possibilities. Suppose, though, that we live in a binary world, where constant winning is the desired state of being. We thrill to the accolades, amass a mountain of cash, and insulate ourselves from the dangers beyond our door. But we risk becoming stale, our biases calcified, our growth stunted.

Winning reinforces what we're doing and why we're doing it that way. If we're always right, why change? Why do anything differently? Why experiment? Adversity forces us to dig deeper or reframe the question. The genius of youth sports lies in its ability to wring meaning from every trying, frustrating, and unsuccessful moment that makes up the majority of every game. Whether a contest ends in victory or defeat just fulfills our human need for closure. Therefore, when dealing with kids, it behooves us to emphasize effort over outcome. Encourage them to seek solutions when faced with setbacks. Find joy in the journey.

Mike Singletary, the Chicago Bears' Hall of Fame linebacker, once said, "You know what my favorite part of the game is? The opportunity to play."

And as Olympic champion Jackie Joyner-Kersee said: "For me, the joy of athletics has never resided in winning. I derive my happiness as much from the process as the result. I don't mind losing as long as I see improvement or I feel I've done as well as I possibly could. If I lose I just go back to the track and work some more." (The fact that she rarely lost shouldn't undercut the sentiment.)

Obvious in these inspirational quotes is the primacy of fun derived through hard work and determination. With patience, results will come. And winning isn't everything.

When kids pound their fists into the turf or kick basketballs into the rafters or fling their bat after a strikeout, we're seeing the balance tipped the other way. Occasional flare-ups of frustration are understandable as part of the natural march toward emotional maturity. Some of this behavior may even be coded in our DNA, an offshoot of the "fight or flight" response. In most cases, cooling tempers lead to high fives and continuation of play. Then there are the pugnacious players who interpret any slight or hard tackle as a personal affront, the previously detailed Vigilante. They'll bounce back to their feet, fists poised and nostrils flaring. Unfortunately, every televised football, basketball, hockey or you-name-it game highlights these dustups times ten. Social media posts fan the flames even higher. All of which reinforces in young minds that outbursts and inappropriate aggressiveness are the norm. The crazier, the better. More eyes, more likes, more wins.

Children also learn about the negative aspects of competition from their parents, who are frequently more invested in the outcome of a game than they are. A child's memory refreshes within moments of leaving the field. Definitely by the time the chicken nuggets and French fries land on the table. (Parents may be consumed by the contest for hours after. Coaches bear the burden the longest, often carrying it through the week and into the next game.)

We should encourage kids to let go and move on, as a balanced relationship to winning and losing augurs a more successful approach to life. For kids there will always be another game, another opportunity to strive and compete, and in competing, to succeed.

The first tournament in the six-month-long All-Star season is the Beverly Hills Sportsmanship Cup, held before the holidays in December. Sportsmanship is heavily promoted, with the awarding of trophies to the teams displaying the highest level of regard for their opponents and the game. (Hardware can also be won through the conventional scoring-more-goals metric.) This was going to be the first outing for Dori's U10 Pali-Cats, and in my own perverse display of organizational sportsmanship, I left Dori off this inaugural roster. No nepotism in this outfit.

Our team was young, small, and inexperienced, a trifecta of shortcomings that proved insurmountable as we lost all four of our matches. Our first game, tackling a towering team from Diamond Bar (Dori's future allergy), was eye opening. Watching these graceful giraffes glide up and down the field, toying with us before scoring at will, foreshadowed the months ahead.

End of game rituals revolved around some version of the high-five line. Many of the girls' teams opted for the tunnel, a gauntlet formed by the victors standing in two lines with hands joined overhead. They would chant an upbeat if innocuous cheer while the losing team filed through. (Occasionally the losing squad would emerge from the tunnel and form one of their own as a final salute to the winners.)

On this day, the Diamond Bar ladies unveiled an iteration I'd never seen, getting down on their knees to create a tunnel with a much lower ceiling. Our girls were forced to crawl through on their tummies while the winners chanted, "We are proud of you, we are proud of you, hey hey hey" over and over again.

"Oh no, this is not happening!" Exploding past me onto the field was Victoria, Lacey's mom, who began bowling over the Diamond Bar-ettes and yanking our Pali kittens to their feet. Their attempt to humiliate our girls thwarted, the victors skipped back to their bench. Our girls, unsure of what had just happened, retreated behind Victoria. At the sideline, still seething, she turned to admonish the troops.

"Girls, you don't crawl for anyone!"

Ten shocked little faces nodded back. It wasn't sportsmanship's finest hour. And Diamond Bar didn't take home that trophy.

Did Lacey's mom overreact? Maybe a bit. Was it fair for the Diamond Bar girls to rub our kids' faces in their defeat? Definitely not. But this is what can happen when players – often abetted by their coaches – feel entitled to flaunt their victories. Goodwill evaporates and tempers flare.

Over the years I've witnessed a litany of high-five line abuses. Kids shuffling through with closed fists punching the open hands of their adversaries. Or spitting on their hands just before slapping their opponent's palm. There was the scandalous affair of one team trading the customary "good game" for "bad game, you suck!" These five-year-old malefactors didn't even know the meaning of bad sportsmanship, but they triggered a torrent of inflamed emails and some tearful apologies before the next game.

Good sportsmanship is often described as winning with grace and losing with dignity. It's embodied in fair play, having respect for the rules and honoring the traditions of the game. Good sportsmanship stresses integrity, and consideration of teammates, opponents, officials and spectators. Mark Twain colorfully characterized it another way: "It's good sportsmanship to not pick up lost golf balls while they are still rolling." This more or less sums it up.

We want our kids to exhibit good sportsmanship on and off the field. We want them to be as generous to their opponents as they are to their teammates. We want them to walk away from a game with their heads held high, neither arrogant in victory nor petulant in defeat.

The Brentwood School boys' varsity soccer team used to play the squad from Christa McAuliffe, formerly the Kilpatrick Camp, the juvenile detention facility made famous in the film *Gridiron Gang*, starring Dwayne "The Rock" Johnson. The game matched two diametrical programs, both in terms of resources and rosters. Brentwood, an academically rigorous private school with state-of-the-art athletic facilities, is nestled within an affluent Southern California neighborhood. While the school prides itself on its commitment to diversity, the vast majority of its students – and soccer players – come from more privileged circumstances than the residents of the locked-down dormitories at McAuliffe. Brentwood's roster was always set in October. The McAuliffe eleven frequently changed from game to game as its composition depended on students currently in custody. Looking into the faces of the McAuliffe boys as they filed onto the expansive campus, with its students moving about freely, always triggered a twinge of sadness. Without knowing why these boys were where they were, nor trying to blot drops spilled from a bleeding heart, it was a difficult juxtaposition to fully grasp. On the other side, they were getting to play in aspirational surroundings, and perhaps the experience could inspire a positive life change.

The game itself was usually a mismatch. The McAuliffe kids gave it their best shot but despite featuring individuals with skill, the inconsistent roster doomed them to an underwhelming effort. Brentwood goals lit up the scoreboard, but after the first few, no one cared to celebrate. Both sides were aware of the disparity in station, yet they treated each other with respect born of honest and hard-fought competition.

At the end of this contest during Griffie's senior year, as the Brentwood parents were laying out the post-game sandwiches and pizza, they looked across the field to the McAuliffe boys, who were quietly packing up their gear. Instantly it was decided to welcome the McAuliffe boys into the feast. For the first time all afternoon, their smiles could be seen. They gratefully joined in, and for a few moments, at least, the values of generosity and sportsmanship had real-world, real-time consequences.

Red Gatorade and the Yu-Gi-Oh Stratagem

The Mercy Rule was created in most youth sports to counter unchecked competition, which can lead to lopsided scores and bruised feelings. Welcome to the Blowout, a phenomenon whose dimensions are familiar to anyone who's ever laced up a pair of sneakers and engaged in any form of athletic contest. One team is strong, the other meek, and the powerhouse takes no prisoners in an efficient immolation of its opponent. Here, Goliath kicks the crap out of David.

Every MLB season there are a few scores in the 20-3 range. Early fall college football games between top-ranked contenders and patsies looking for promotion and gate money can yield 56-0 shutouts. The Palisades Charter High School water polo team posted a playoff score of 34-0. Tell me, where is the love?

Skewed scores occur frequently in the youth ranks, where teams may be "stacked," or draft and random selection formats create imbalances that exploit inconsistencies in players' skills and development. These disparities can be magnified by – and let's be generous – an unwitting coach, aggressive parents, and untamed kids, all who equate domination with fun. Games quickly get out of hand with one team running up the score and the other team running for the exit. There are no winners when this happens. It's recreational sports at its least uplifting. When my stronger teams found themselves across the ball from a hapless squad, and the glint of goal greediness would sparkle in their eyes, I used to ask, "How much better can you feel by making your friends on the other team feel worse?" The wise guys would blurt out, "a lot," but most got the message.

In an effort to level the playing field and make it fairer for all, our AYSO region adopted a version of the Mercy Rule. Less a rule than a mindset, it stipulated that once a score ballooned beyond competitive recognizability, the advantaged team should amend its tactics to focus on aspects other than scoring, while offering the struggling squad a chance to get back into the game.

Many people subscribe to a more Darwinian view of sports: you win some, you lose some – and some you lose badly. Quite a few of our AYSO folks took exception to our Mercy Rule guidelines. *Why is AYSO so worried about coddling the losers?* they wanted to know. *Losing is a fact of life. Why penalize the winners?*

Our response began with a reminder that we are a recreational organization, where development and community come first, and fun is our paramount goal. If you're a kid or a coach or a parent whose team is being pounded, there is little fun to be had. We used to say that if you went up 3-0 or 4-0, you should call off the dogs. But that was vague and it didn't account for specific game conditions.

So we discussed with our coaches how to analyze a blowout, what to do if you find yourself on either side of the divide. Preparation is the key, knowing it's unrealistic to expect kids to suddenly switch gears from attack mode to a more measured approach in the middle of a game. Appropriate adjustments have to be learned and practiced ahead of time and the signs of a shellacking need to be identified:

- If you line up against a team that has no substitutes on its sideline or one that will be playing short;
- If your team towers over the kids on the opposite side;
- If your team takes the ball and easily scores two goals within the first few minutes of the game . . . and the other team's response is to lose the ball back to you on the ensuing kickoffs;
- If you go up 3-0 in the first or second quarter and the other team appears to have no answer for your dominance . . . by 4-0 in the first half, you should have a pretty good idea that things will not get dramatically better.

Best not to scream out "No more scoring." The intended effect, to slow down the onslaught and give the other team the appearance, if not the reality, of a chance will be completely sabotaged by such a blatant announcement.

In practice and before the game the coach must counsel his players. He should devise a code word – a name, a number, a saying – so that the kids can recognize when to launch into anti-slaughter mode. At the same time, review the tactics the team will employ to make the game productive and challenging for themselves. The trick is to foster an opportunity for learning, not impose a punishment on the players.

Simple fixes like switching attackers to defense and defenders to the attack, or moving the right side to the left side, can be the first things to try. Placing players in positions they are less familiar with can result in stemming the slaughter as well as stretching the players' capabilities. Try allowing shots only from crossed balls or taken with the weaker foot. Play keep-away with a set number of consecutive passes before a shot. Change the focus of the game while keeping it interesting for the stronger players without demoralizing the weaker ones.

The Gatorators, Griffie's U10 league team, was a squad drowning in talent. There was Matthew, previously spoken of, who was unheralded before the season but quickly identified as the league MVP; Miles, who was so fast that everyone else appeared to be frozen in blocks of cement; Cooper and Scotty, precocious athletes whose game IQ set them above the competition; Jordan, big and raw and just learning how to make the most of both; Ryan and Cole, who were capable of playing anywhere on the field; and Griffie, the wild card. When he wasn't racing up and down the field arguing with me, he was dropping his shoulder and imposing his will on the opposition.

Early in the season it became apparent that this was a team few others could match. Left alone, they were capable of tallying ten to fifteen goals a game. This put me in a bind. As the league's head coach, I was tasked with maintaining fairness and addressing its violations. Any advantage exhibited by one of my teams directed unwanted attention my way. Most years it was a non-issue. My teams were average to not bad, so no one could charge that I'd grabbed all the best players. Besides, I didn't make the teams, the commissioners did. Although, in deference to the amount of time I devoted to the program, they would quietly throw me a player or two. I got lucky with the Gatorators.

All right, in the interest of going unburdened to the great beyond, and because the statute of limitations on this has long since passed, let me be honest. For this team I lodged a few more requests than usual. Matthew hadn't played the previous year so no one knew how good he was. But what I saw at camp blew me away. Jordan's sister Dani was with Dori on the Pali-Cats and he and Griffie were friends. Cooper, Miles, Scotty, Ryan, Cole – I knew them all from classes and camp. So . . . this team was a tad more handpicked than my others.

There. I confessed. Consign me to soccer hell. I'll go willingly.

At the time, though, this super team presented a super challenge. I had to prevent them from tearing up the league. My plan was two-pronged. I would keep our strongest scorers at the back during the first half and play those less clever at finding the back of the net up top. While our best athletes weren't taking shots, they were adept at keeping the other teams away from our goal, so through the first half, the game was inarguably competitive.

After the break, though, I had to let my horses run free. Boy, were they ready. Teams wouldn't know what hit them. Matt could flip a ball up from his foot to his head, pop it over the defender, then guide it into the corner of the net. Miles would pass the ball down the sideline and outrun the other team to catch up to it and score. Cooper and Scotty could give-and-go their way down the field and the one closest to the goal would knock it home. Griffie was more power, less finesse. He'd straight-arm a defender to the ground, run over him, and slip the ball home with his left foot. At the other end, Jordan and Ryan sacrificed their bodies to seal our goal tight. It was almost symphonic; if Francis Ford Coppola hadn't co-opted "Ride of the Valkyries" for *Apocalypse Now*, it could have been our soundtrack. And it all could have gotten out of hand.

So I instituted Red Gatorade. That was our code to put the kibosh on the scoring. Once we got up two or three goals, I would call across the field, "Red Gatorade," and add a number after it, say "10" – "Red Gatorade 10." That meant that the boys couldn't take another shot until they'd completed ten consecutive passes. If the other team touched or tackled the ball away, the count had to start again. These boys were so good, they probably could have strung together thirty or forty passes, but for the condition of the field. Barrington Park, home to my earliest Evan classes, had deteriorated over the years. The City of LA tended to it only intermittently and the gophers took full advantage. They had a flourishing megalopolis beneath the lumpy and pockmarked field. Occasionally in the heat of the action, a tiny head would poke out of its hole, and all the kids would stop to coo at the adorable intruder.

"Red Gatorade" kept us within the bounds of good sportsmanship, and the boys accepted its constraints willingly. They enjoyed playing a game within the game. And the teams they consigned to defeat were usually buoyed by their strong showing in keeping the game close – even if they had our help. *Ssshhhh…*

The Mercy Rule also has applications for the team on the "ouch" end of the beating. Some coaches send up the white flag and spend the game consoling the players. "You never had a chance." "The deck was stacked." "You did the best you could." Nonsense. There are still ways to win while losing.

Coach Corinne has her players concentrate on achievable goals, both individual (everyone executes a step-over move) and team (everyone touches the ball). She redirects the focus away from the score and emphasizes the opportunity to improve.

More aggressive approaches include defending dangerous opponents with one or even two players, effectively sandwiching them and choking off their access to the ball or making them work harder to get it. Maybe pack the defense and keep more bodies between the ball and the goal – "Parking the bus," as it were. Leave a hopeful forward up top, right on the shoulder of the last defender. Maybe he'll get lucky.

All the good intentions in the world, however, are no match for a mob of motivated five-year-olds. They are as incapable of following directions to string passes together, or to shoot only with their weaker foot, as they are to stand in a line without pushing or shoving. So asking them to take pity on a weaker opponent was an "ask" too far. I scrolled through my checklist of coaching and parenting strategies: encouraging good sportsmanship, leading by example, appealing to their better nature – all of them nonstarters – and skidded all the way down the slippery slope to bribing them. Which brought up the oft-debated ethical question: can something good come out of doing something bad? I certainly hoped so.

Drawing upon my knowledge of Griffie's current obsessions, I offered the boys a deal. If they let the other team score, and weren't too obvious about it, I would get them all Yu-Gi-Oh trading cards. On a team where half the kids didn't care if they were playing or sitting out, suddenly every hand shot up. They all wanted in.

The good news is that in U6, it's common for players to trip over the ball. Suddenly, though, the entire team looked like vaudeville performers slipping on banana peels. The ball pinged off George's shin guard. Down he went. Moments later, the ball rolled toward JoJo just as, amazingly, an 8.5-magnitude shaker seemed to rumble right beneath his feet. He toppled over. Every time the ball landed in the vicinity of one of our players, they belly-flopped in the most dramatic fashion, with grunts and cries and howls.

Watching all of his teammates quake and tumble, Edmund felt left out. Standing alone in the middle of the field, the ball a good thirty yards away, Edmund just collapsed, then popped up, smiling. "Did I do it right, Coach Steve?"

The referee cast me a suspicious eye. I smiled and shrugged. He blew the whistle to end the half. The boys bounced off the field, bubbling with pride.

"How was that?"

"Did you see mine?"

"When do we get the Yu-Gi-Oh cards?"

"Boys, sssshhh, not so loud." I thought I caught the coach across the field looking my way, so I turned and leaned down to the team. "You can't be that obvious. It has to look accidental." Who did I think I was talking to? I could barely teach them how to dribble, but here I expected them to perform like professional stuntmen? There was a bigger issue. "And they didn't score a goal. Try to fall down closer to our end of the field." Off they went.

On the second-half kickoff, the other team, which, to this point, hadn't mounted the whiff of an attack, was off and racing toward our goal. Our entire squad took off in pursuit. Right before the goal, they caught up and were about to win back the ball, when suddenly, as if as one, they remembered why they were there. It wasn't about soccer. It wasn't about sportsmanship. It was all about the Yu-Gi-Oh cards. In that instant, the whole team hit the deck, like strike-struck bowling pins. And miraculously, the ball trickled into the goal.

When the dust cleared and the game ended with the score Yellowjackets: many; Other Team: 1, the opposing coach approached me with a huge grin on his face. He reached into his pocket and slapped a twenty into my palm. "That was our first goal of the season. The cards are on me." He patted me on the back and trotted off to his ecstatic son.

In my years of coaching kids, I've seen a lot. But I'd never seen this. In Griffie's first year of U8 our team was the Soda Jerks. (My assistant, Coach Marty, had suggested the name. The kids had zero idea about its ice cream and soda fountain origins, but it sounded silly, which was enough.) Competitively, the team fell into the "not bad" range; it won a few games, lost almost as many. But in a match toward the end of the season, we found ourselves playing Coach David's no-name wonders. They were a squad of futility; had the Bad News Bears played soccer they would have kicked these guys' butts. The upcoming match with the Soda Jerks promised to be a wipeout.

In my capacity as Region 69's defender of the faith and exemplar of good sportsmanship, I knew I had to take preemptive action. Drawing heavily on the Mercy Rule, I approached Coach David and offered to restrain my strongest players, through substitutions and positional placements, through the first three quarters, after which I'd be obligated to let them off the leash.

David nodded, seeming to indicate it was a deal, and we retreated to our opposite sidelines. The game unfolded as planned. Our attack was intentionally neutered, and Coach David's boys, encouraged that they were in the game, fought valiantly. At the end of the third quarter, the score was knotted at nil apiece. Their shackles removed, my most lethal lineup took the field. I held my breath, hoping that the slaughter wouldn't be too bloody. That's when I saw something I'd never seen on a soccer field.

"Hey, Dad, look what they're doing," Griffie called out. "This is going to be great."

All eight of Coach David's boys were lining up, side by side, on the goal line. As they waited, trembling, Griffie and the Soda Jerks brought the ball down the field and stopped for a moment to regard this most unusual defense. Then it was ready, aim, fire...and the barrage of shots began.

A rocket blast thudded into one boy's stomach. He dropped with a sickening moan. The team closed ranks around him as the ball ricocheted back to one of our boys. The next shot caromed off another player's thigh. He winced in pain, but stood his ground. By this point, the fallen warrior had picked himself up and rejoined the phalanx. Another shot – *BAM!* – and another one bit the dust.

The shots kept coming, the bodies kept dropping, but we weren't scoring and they weren't yielding. One man would go down, another would edge into his space. More shots, pinging off chests, legs, even heads, as both sidelines groaned. But Coach David's boys valiantly and defiantly stood their ground. The firing squad lasted for a full eight minutes before the referee bleated the end of the torture, and the game.

Coach David's kids were ecstatic, if slow, in joining the high-five line. My Soda Jerks were shell-shocked, but graciously congratulated their more-than-worthy opponents on a job well done. Some may regard Coach David's exploitation of the "insider information" I provided as Machiavellian. Others may recoil at the bombardment unleashed upon the unprotected defenders. What I witnessed was an extraordinary demonstration of courage, team unity, and crafty coaching. The entire game had been informed by the Mercy Rule and both teams had come away winners.

I've been fortunate to be part of teams competing to achieve larger goals. Evan and Dori's All-Star teams made it to the state championships (with the Pythons winning and the Pali-Cats capturing third place). Griffie's Palaxy medaled in fifteen tournaments, taking first in ten of them. These teams were exceptional on the field and off. The coaches and parents framed the lessons of life in sharp foreground focus.

Yet, for some, the primary competition lies within. They struggle with illness, insecurity, and other demons real and imagined. Their years in youth sports furnish them a proving ground where they battle self-doubt and emerge as stronger, more integrated individuals.

CHAPTER FIFTEEN

Kids Triumphant

You would have had to search far and wide to find a less athletic little girl than Lizzy. At her preschool Sports Day, when the most taxing event was running in a straight line for thirty feet, Lizzy broke down in tears. Behind an excruciating shyness, occasional glimpses of an already sharp intellect would leak out. But sports weren't part of this package. Parents Ann and Jon had other ideas, so they provided her with three dirt-streaked and scabbed-up younger brothers, whose 24/7 physicality forced Lizzy to compete, or else.

I caught up with her a few years later on the soccer field, where excellent footwork and elbow-throwing tenacity helped her find a home. She became a card-carrying member of the Pali-Cats, plying her pull-back twist and turn into goal-seeking opportunities, and generally thriving through the happy suffering of our early years.

One day I noticed that her already gangly frame was sharper and bonier. Her energy level was low and girls who previously had been unable to push her off the ball were nudging her aside with ease. She seemed antsy and uncomfortable, and would slowly jog around our huddle at halftime, her feet constantly moving, like a kitten with sticky paws. Ann and Jon were on the case, taking Lizzy to doctors, exploring her waning vitality, stomachaches and overall lethargy. She missed practices and tournaments due to the flu or mono or whatever diagnosis the experts were blaming for her pain that week. Finally, they admitted her to the hospital, which was when the diagnosis of Crohn's successfully summed up her symptoms. Her teammates were thrown, ten-year-old girls aren't supposed to be ill. Especially affected, Dani spent hours at Lizzy's bedside, doing her best to inflate the spirits of her teammate and friend.

One of the most crushing concessions to her condition was her parents' removing her from the Pali-Cat roster. Well, putting her on "Injured Reserve." She wouldn't be strong enough to play for months, if ever again. But Lizzy was a fighter; she fully planned on returning to action. Even when recuperating at home, still so frail, she would ask her parents to bring her to our games. After every tournament I would write a recap, "The Kitty Litter," and send it to the parents. Lizzy, not content to just watch her teammates, asked if she could do the reporting.

Game Day, Chapter Two: By Lizzy

...After what felt like forever, it was time to get back onto the field. Game 2 shaped up as THE contest of the day. Hemet, the black and pink-clad champions of Area N, had beaten our end of day opponent, Chino Hills, 2-0, so if we could get through them, we'd have a strong chance of getting to Sunday. The Hemet girls looked us over during warm-ups and with a sneer, dispatched us to the discard pile. They figured they were made in the shade. But Pali-Cats dine out on the role of underdog. Dis and dismiss us. Underrate us. Plan your victory party. And then let us do our stuff.

She wrote that at age ten! Mighty impressive, wouldn't you say? Lizzy slowly recovered and made it back near the end of our third and final campaign. She had to scrape the barnacles off her game, but her feistiness was in full force, as true as it was the day she donned the Pali-Cat gold and black. Lizzy drifted out of soccer, and to a passion that was well suited to those restless feet – running. She relocated her talents to the track, where she excelled in the 800-meter and 1,500-meter distances for her high school. She piggybacked her brilliance onto an already stellar academic career and leapfrogged across the country to Harvard, where her running eventually took a back seat to learning and life.

Throughout her journey, Lizzy's competition was with herself. Striving to make her mark, overcoming the limitations of illness, and landing in a place she was always destined to be. From the little girl who balked at running in a straight line to the one setting records on the track, her courage pushed her beyond anyone's wildest dreams. Except maybe Lizzy's.

Jordan had two expressions. One was serious, thoughtful; you could see her synapses sparking as she considered a question or processed new information. More frequently experienced was her smile. It liberated her being and exposed a spirit at once swashbuckling and innocent. It was this spirit that she brought to her first year on the Pali-Cats.

Jordan wasn't the most dynamic eight-year-old athlete, but on a team that lost the majority of its games, she fit right in. While most of the girls laughed their way through the season, letting go of the weekly beat-downs within moments of leaving the field, Jordan's mood darkened as the season progressed. She seemed to internalize the defeats, and carried the frustration of losing to practices, in both her attitude and her interactions with her teammates. It took a while for the news to emerge that her parents were in the process of divorcing. Jordan would shrug off our concern, downplaying the effect of her domestic woes on her Pali-Cat participation. But it was obvious to everyone else as her malaise insinuated itself into the team's morale. Jordan was no longer Jordan.

Through the following summer and fall, the situation festered. When it came time to construct the second-year All-Star team, Jordan was no longer competitive with her peers. Understandably. But on a team with a finite roster, and a dozen athletically worthy candidates all vying for Jordan's slot, I had the heartbreaking task of not inviting her back for year two. She quietly accepted her relegation to the B team, suppressing the sting every time she saw her former teammates practicing on the other side of the field. The season began bumpily, indifference masking her pain and clouding her performance.

Around mid-season, something changed. Whether consciously or not, she realized that there was little she could do to affect her parents' happiness. So she concentrated on her own. It wasn't easy. She applied herself in training, tirelessly working on her skills, each improvement fueling the next. Battling through setbacks and plateaus, her confidence slowly built back up. And after a while, the smile that could lift everyone around her returned. Her reunion with the Pali-Cats the next year was a slam dunk.

After that successful season, she moved to club, and over the next few years, her trajectory toward excellence progressed uninterrupted. By the end of her last high school season, she had become one of the best, most indispensable players on the field. No one would have blamed Jordan for giving up back in U10. The youth ranks thin considerably as kids get older, with many leaving for reasons far less dramatic than divorce. But Jordan was built of sterner stuff, and discovered the will within to compete for her own athletic survival.

There was no kid more coachable than Ethan. Always willing to work hard to learn and develop, his was the most rapt expression staring up at me in the huddle. He was a student of the game, striving to improve his skills while seeking a deeper understanding of tactics and strategy. Any instructions were unfailingly executed.

"Ethie, go play goal."

"You bet."

"Hey, we need you on defense."

"Anything you say."

"Play up top, go score a goal."

"I'll do my best, Coach Steve."

His best was always pretty damn good. A member of our three AYSO All-Star teams – the Paligators, Palaxy, and Pal Real – and charter member of the Galaxy Alliance B98 club squad, Ethan was totally in the mix having fun with his teammates, but when a steady presence was required, Ethan was the go-to guy.

Nobody's perfect, and Ethan's Achilles heel was a pair of legs seemingly encased in lead. Opponents would fly by and poor Ethan, head down, arms flapping, would flail to catch up. It was painful to witness. Making matters worse, puberty lengthened without strengthening him. Slow is bad; slow and weak is insurmountable.

In selecting the team for its U13 year, Coach Tim delivered the devastating news that Ethan was being sent down to the second team. After absorbing the blow of having to say goodbye to his teammates of four years, Ethan, like Jordan in the story above, recommitted himself to redemption. He worked on anticipating the flow of the game and positioning his body to offset velocity issues, and built himself up to increase his power and presence. Within a few months, his efforts were rewarded; Coach Tim invited him back onto the squad.

But not every inspirational tale comes with a happy ending. In the winter, Coach Tim left the team, and his replacement, Coach Jonathan, opted to clean house and start fresh. Cuts were made, and as the blade got closer to Ethan, I vainly lobbied on his behalf. But Jonathan had neither the context nor the patience to gain a true appreciation of what made Ethan special. Within months of his return, Ethan was once again dropped from the team.

Rejected once, Ethan was able to fight back. Rejected twice, Ethan plunged into a darkness no light could penetrate. The prospect of returning to the B team felt like the ultimate defeat. How could the game he loved so much betray him this way? His parents and I shared his tears, but even as we were worrying about his next steps, Ethan surprised us. He quieted his pain and insecurity long enough to practice with his new/old team. It wasn't the same. Competitively it wasn't close. But it was soccer. And over time, it was in his commitment to his passion that he found his peace. He became a team leader, challenging and inspiring all around him to greater effect. The team started seeing better results and Ethan's self-esteem soared. Once he won the competition within, everything else fell into place.

The Ethan that emerged from this trial was, on the surface, the same Ethan he'd always been. But probing a little deeper revealed a stronger sense of purpose, an understanding of the healing power of hard work, and a reservoir of empathy he's utilized many times since to help others suffering their own plights.

Winning for Lizzy, Jordan, and Ethan had less to do with mastering a skill or besting an on-field opponent and everything to do with fighting through illness, divorce, and rejection, devastating for anyone but potentially crushing for kids. Their efforts to emerge healthier and happier on the other side imbued them with a strength of character certain to ensure their success far beyond the white lines of the playing field.

As Emmett Smith, the legendary Dallas Cowboys running back, said: "I may win and I may lose, but I will never be defeated." I think I know who he was speaking about.

CHAPTER SIXTEEN

Size Matters…But Don't Let It

The groan could be seen if not heard. A sigh of disappointment followed by downcast, shaking heads. Even from across the field it was obvious that Gabriel's imminent entry into the game was not being welcomed with universal approval. It didn't matter if the team was leading or behind, though introducing him into a losing effort added hand-wringing to the critics' reaction. Warming up on the sideline, Gabriel felt the pressure. A starter, scorer, and go-to component of the All-Star Palaxy, in club he now lived on the bench, his game time slashed, his confidence shaken. His skills were sound, his touch sharper than most of his teammates. But Gabriel suffered from the unforgivable in competitive sports: he was small.

It wasn't much better for Ben. Like Gabriel, a magician on the ball, whose crowning U10 moment was his single-handed slicing and dicing of Palaxy to capture the Area P championship for his West LA All-Stars, Ben also suffered from the same vertical malady as Gabriel.

When others, flush with hormones, started sprouting and adding rippling muscles, Ben, by comparison, seemed to shrink. Though he was masterful on the field, puberty-blessed opponents had little trouble swatting him away and capturing the ball. In another milieu, this size mismatch would have been labeled bullying. On the soccer field, it was considered bench-worthy. Gabriel and Ben spent a lot of time together.

Griffie, on the other hand, went to sleep at the end of fifth grade a little kid with a squeaky voice and woke up for sixth grade a head taller and an octave deeper. Remarkable was the reaction of those who hadn't seen him over those three summer months. Where he had been dismissed by his classmates as a quirky chatterbox, he was now seen as a powerful figure whose words resounded with import. In flag football and basketball he shined, but in soccer he flourished. His technique wasn't up to that of Gabriel and Ben, but his speed, dynamism and effect on the game made it difficult to sub him out.

Size matters in youth sports. Bigger is, in most cases, better. Growth is capricious and unforgiving. Puberty can just as easily be a hero or a villain. It's not entirely random; the children of 7-foot parents have a reasonable expectation of being tall. Likewise, the children of 5-foot parents may feel their diminutive future preordained. Everyone hopes that their child will be tall; even beyond the sporting world, our culture tends to give privilege and respect to those who can see above the crowd.

When Evan was two years old, we consulted a doctor about his pigeon-toed gait. The physician took X-rays and reported back that based on how open his growth plates were, Evan would likely be 6-foot-2 or taller. Marcy and I were stunned. Neither of us tops 5-foot-9, and though a search of our respective family trees could produce a few six-footers, we were surprised that Evan would crash through that ceiling. (He didn't, maxing out at the family 5-foot-9. And we came to appreciate that his turned-in foot would translate to superior speed on the soccer field. In hindsight, it wasn't the most productive doctor visit.)

Early growth may be accompanied by a precocious display of coordination and speed, which would naturally convey an advantage to the young athlete. This phenomenon is thoroughly detailed in an article called "Early and Late Bloomers in Youth Sports: Lessons for Parents," by Brooke DeLench.[1] According to DeLench, some of the advantages an early bloomer tends to receive are:

- More positive reinforcement and encouragement from adults;
- Earlier and more extensive socialization into sports;
- Access to better coaching, facilities, and competitive experiences (i.e., places on "select teams") and
- The benefit of a "residual bias" from being viewed as a talented athlete at an early age.

But DeLench goes on to explain: "Although numerous advantages are conferred on an early bloomer, if your child experiences early success in sports, such success also has some downsides." An early bloomer:

- Is often able to exploit his or her physical ability without having to work as hard at developing skills as less precocious players in order to stay competitive. When the others catch up physically, they may end up being better players because they have been forced to develop their skills while they grew into their bodies.

---

1 Brooke DeLench, "Early and Late Bloomers in Youth Sports: Lessons for Parents," www.momsteam.com (2017)

- Often has to try to live up to heightened expectations; this may lead him to practice and play more (e.g., multiple teams during the same season, for instance) than his young body can handle in order to live up to his reputation. Playing under this kind of pressure often leads to burnout and all that extra wear and tear on his body can lead to overuse injuries.
- May define himself by whether he wins or loses; if he or she is unable to maintain the success he had early in his athletic career, if that self-image is shattered, the results can be disastrous and may lead her to quit sports altogether.
- May tempt her parents to push her to specialize too early and/or train too hard. Excessive training too often leads to burnout and/or overuse injuries, some of which don't show up until high school or college, but can be traced to excessive training when the player was nine, ten or eleven. Parents need to avoid being lulled into valuing short-term success more than their child's long-term future. If they don't, they may be placing their child's physical safety and emotional health at risk.

As DeLench notes, bearing the weight of additional expectations can create unwanted pressure, both self-imposed and from well-meaning adults. Some kids can measure up to the hype; others buckle or walk away. I know teenagers who are 6-foot-5, with the physical gifts of a star tight end or a point guard. Yet these kids gravitate toward art and music, not sports. It takes self-awareness and courage for kids to push back against preconceptions of who they should be, based on the superficiality of their physical appearance.

In U10, the Pali-Cats lined up against the squad from Hollywood-Wilshire in pool play of the Area P championships. The centerpiece of the Hollywood team towered over everyone by at least a foot. Even more striking was her bright green hair, dyed to match her uniform. In earlier games, we watched her toy with opponents as she powered in goals at will. The kitties were quaking.

When our turn arrived, the girls employed a strategy of distraction. At least two shadowed Hollywood's behemoth the entire time. If she threatened to break away, we had a third Pali-Cat waiting to step up. The 'Cats were pesky, stalking her at all times. This attention affected her touch, and balls she managed to reach she misplayed or passed out of bounds. Her teammates, unused to seeing their leader neutralized, wilted. The Pali-Cats prevailed.

Flash forward a few years. The girls, now fifteen and playing club on the Devil-Cats, were thrilled when a girl named Jessie came to try out. She impressed everyone with her warmth, her self-deprecating humor, and above all, her ability. Watching her play, there was something about her that felt familiar. And then it hit me. Jessie was Hollywood-Wilshire's giant, no longer green-haired and humungous. She was actually middle of this pack, in terms of height.

At nine, our girls characterized Jessie as mean and aloof. She was "the enemy," whose size intimidated them, so they painted her in terms that bore no relation to reality. Still an imposing athlete, Jessie now was welcomed with open arms.

For some early bloomers, this precocious prowess can be a curse. Take the five-year-old who moves around the basketball court with the ease of a baller three times his age. The whispers ripple through the crowd.

"Did you see Jack make those three-pointers? That kid's going to the pros."

As Jack's "reputation" grows, celebrity follows. He's treated differently. Rules are bent or abolished altogether. His boosted and, soon, bloated ego affects his every interaction. Daily concerns disappear as there's always someone doing, getting, covering, and assuming responsibility for him. His exalted existence becomes less a privilege than a right, enabling bad behavior and imprudence. Insulated from his own life, Jack never develops the emotional fortitude to match his physical gifts. Entitlement, immaturity, and lack of preparation undermine a meaningful future.

Everyone knows at least one Jack. A more common ending to this scenario plays out much earlier, likely in adolescence, when the early bloomer is caught and surpassed by his peers. Whether later or sooner, though, the curse will collect its due.

Late bloomers encounter a different set of issues. Aside from being overlooked for recognition, these athletes can be the last picks in that Darwinian meat grinder, the playground. This inattention can spill over onto league teams, where they may struggle for playing time. With less time comes delayed development. And those who improve on a slower track might not receive the proper consideration from top coaches and programs as they get older.

By all measures, Tyler was one of the most valuable players on the team. He controlled the middle of the field with an agility of body and mind. His resourcefulness was legendary. He once scored a goal with his groin, as he thrust it at a ball screaming across the goal mouth. Sacrificing procreative security, he "crotched" the ball into the net. It was this freewheeling approach that endeared him to his teammates. But puberty, in its mad dash to anoint everyone on the team, took its time with Tyler. While everyone added height and heft, Tyler remained bite-sized. As thirteen turned into fourteen, and fifteen rapidly followed, Tyler went from invaluable starter, to first man off the bench, to frustrated sub, to "sayonara." Height had claimed another victim, ending the marriage of soccer and Tyler.

As in most of these cases, Tyler's hormones finally arrived, and by graduation, a newly-minted six-footer crossed the stage to receive his diploma.

Later development is hardly uncommon, though its ancillary effects in terms of socializing, dating, and generally not standing out can be profound. But when we accept that differences among children are nature's way, we can help those affected mitigate anxiety and stress. Tyler thrived in Ann Arbor, now flourishes in start-up culture, and certainly wasn't stymied in any lasting manner by the timetable of his development. Arguably, the challenges he fought through made him a stronger, more capable adult.

With odds against them, it's no surprise that smaller athletes often out-work, out-hustle and out-fight their taller teammates. All through her AYSO years, Samantha wore jersey no. 2, befitting her status as the most petite on the team (no. 1 traditionally went to the goalkeeper). Lining up before the game, she'd ignore the smirks from opposing players because she knew something they were about to learn. On the whistle, Samantha transformed into a heat-seeking missile aimed straight for their goal. An alchemical combination of speed, pluck, and stubborn undeniability, she'd outrun or out-muscle all who stood in her way, stuffing their condescension into the back of the net. Respect trailed her all the way back to midfield.

Katie was a Dori teammate during U15 and U16. Even the more diminutive girls were giants next to Katie, who barely cracked 5-foot-2 standing in cleats on hard turf. For a small girl, she played a big game. The first one to every ball, whether on the ground or in the air, Katie employed pace, power and an unshakable self-confidence to outplay heartier opponents. Seeing her outleap girls a foot taller always brought the other team down to earth. She paid for her ambition, frequently limping off the field with bumps and knocks. But her spirit was unrelenting. Waving away ice packs and Advil, she would be back in the fray, forcing the action.

Kyle was also a battler. At birth, the tinier of twins – as "older" brother Drew never let him forget – he was also marked with a heart defect that required emergency surgery with a follow-up chest-cutting planned for his teens. Scary stuff to have looming, yet compounding his woes was a cruelly delayed growth spurt. Even as Drew was lengthening, a stiff wind could have swept up Kyle and deposited him across the street.

Kyle built a career exploding everyone else's expectations. In the U11 playoffs, stationed at central defender, Kyle, barely kissing 5 feet, matched up against a 6-foot-2 attacker. The taller boy beamed like it was Christmas morning and Kyle was his present. He couldn't wait for his teammates to pass him the ball. He's still waiting. Every ball that landed within striking distance, Kyle darted to and cleared away. A few years later, still small but just as brave and seeking a greater challenge, Kyle left a team of his friends to join one of complete strangers. He more than succeeded, indeed making himself indispensable. It's ironic that the player with the damaged heart proved to be the one whose heart beat the loudest.

Parents and coaches need to remember that size guarantees nothing. A coach may see monsters warming up on the other sideline, then look down at his munchkins and fret about the slaughter to come. Yet the comparison can be deceiving and the undersized team, with a roster of overachievers, will shock their larger opponents. Here is where an emphasis on skills development pays dividends. In the near term, there may be no answer against a player of size and pace. Over time, however, the player with the sharper skills, mental engagement, and unwavering spirit will prevail.

When the clock strikes adolescence, and hormones begin to exert their mystical power, everything changes. Your gangly twelve-year-old no longer possesses the cuteness of nine, and within this newly noxious mixture of hair, sweat, and attitude, lies a struggle for coordination and mastery. Advanced eight-year-old athletes at thirteen may need to confront aching knees and sore feet before recovering their abilities. Some glide through the transition; others struggle to get comfortable in their new skin. Some may move on to other sports that better fit their physicality, and still others may drop out of athletics altogether.

In the past few years, studies have purported to correlate a person's body type with the sports he would be best suited for. Parents have latched onto these conclusions to home in on the sports in which their children will find success. According to these studies, shorter, stockier kids make good weightlifters; those with a more V-shaped frame, wide shoulders and narrow hips, tend to favor soccer and baseball. Tall works for basketball, sprinting, football (and these days, just about everything). The truth is, if your kid is Shaq-sized, a mite like Messi, or standing anywhere in between, the most important criteria for athletic success is interest and enthusiasm. If your child loves the sport he's playing, and he's determined to develop, that's the right one for him.

Brooke DeLench outlined a few more lessons for parents of kids of all sizes:

1. Take a balanced approach. Do not get too down if your child is not immediately a superstar or too high if he is. The important thing is that he continues to play, to develop and learn new skills.

2. Emphasize the process and the journey, not the results achieved; therefore,

3. Avoid praising the *outcome* and instead praise *effort*;

4. Help your child see herself as a whole person, not just as an athlete;

5. Be realistic about possible reasons for early athletic success. Make sure your child understands that early success is not a guarantee of future success (and vice versa).

6. Select a sports program that understands child development. Pick a program that recognizes that variability in the way children's athletic talent develops by offering all children a chance to play as long as they want to.

Despite their superior ball skills, Gabriel and Ben were labeled a liability by some of the parents. They were small and slow, a decided disadvantage in testosterone-fueled U14. A few of the dads actively lobbied for them to be dropped from the squad. Coach Tim, to his everlasting credit, refused. He, like all rational observers, knew that the boys would grow. Their parents, while well below the NBA threshold, were tall enough. Tim strongly believed that it made no sense to cut talented, hard-working kids with positive attitudes who were temporarily at the mercy of their genetics.

"They're thirteen! If they win or lose a game now, does it really matter? But if I keep them on the team, they'll be a huge help at sixteen."

His thankless task was trying to balance the team's needs with those of Gabriel and Ben. Their minutes fluctuated with the level of the competition and Tim's sense of their ability to contribute. But when it became apparent that they were staying on the team, some of the other boys, seeking a more competitive situation, moved on.

No surprise that by sixteen Gabriel and Ben were peering down at some of their suddenly shorter comrades. With their size now working on their behalf, their already finely-tuned ball skills and game IQ helped them stand out for all the right reasons. That fall, we played a match against the team the "malcontents" and their parents had joined. Ben spent the entire game besting these boys for the ball, and Gabriel scored twice right in front of the formerly raging parents. It was a moment of redemption for Ben and Gabriel, vindication for Tim, and validation that time and patience would solve the problem of size for athletes who give their heart and soul to their sports.

The point is that size can be viewed as either an advantage or a disadvantage, depending on where your child falls on the scale. But for the motivated child – with enlightened parents – it can be a stage of opportunity and learning in a productive and happy lifetime.

CHAPTER SEVENTEEN

Money Talk$

"I'm tired of hearing about money, money, money, money, money.
I just want to play the game, drink Pepsi, wear Reebok."
– Shaquille O'Neal

Once upon a time, in a sepia-toned past, kids went door to door peddling raffle tickets to raise money for their little league team. For a hundred bucks, dry cleaners, diners, and banks could splash their names across the front of the uniform, and hang a team picture on their wall to broadcast their philanthropy. Nowadays, a donation under ten grand barely merits a patch on a jersey sleeve. Money in youth sports is almost as significant as it is in the professional ranks. Though we're not talking about stratospheric salaries or mega-dollar endorsement deals, the expenses involved in maintaining what used to be a free-play environment are staggering.

Youth sports has mushroomed into a world of high-stakes competition where success is increasingly determined by financial viability. You gotta pay to play. With coaching, training, gear, nutrition and all the ancillary costs, youth sports in the United States has morphed into a $17 billion per year industry.[1] This doesn't include the $7 billion per year in travel expenses that we rack up getting our kids to and from games.

"Youth sports tourism wasn't even a category four years ago, and now it's the fastest-growing segment in travel," said Dave Hollander, professor at New York University's Tisch Center for Hospitality, Tourism and Sports.[2] "You've got millions of kids involved, parents spending thousands of dollars, and cities building facilities to host events and chase tourism dollars. It's just huge."

In 2017, more than 36 million kids, ages 5 to 18, played youth sports. Curiously, according to The Aspen Institute's Project Play,[3] most sports have seen major attrition over the past decade. "In 2015, 56.6 percent of children between the ages of 6 and 12 played team sports at least one time during the year… [But] the percentage of children between the ages of 6 and 12 who played basketball, baseball, soccer, football, volleyball and wrestling on a regular basis has dropped since 2008 (SFIA, 2016)." The expense of participating causes parents to delay enrolling their children, or convinces them to remove a child who's already playing.

Parents have to scrounge for the loose change caught beneath their couch cushions to cover the rising cost of sports-related activities.

1 Christina Corbin and Lydia Culp, "The human cost of raising youth sports to a '$17 billion' industry," Fox News, https://www.foxnews.com/sports/youth-sports-17-billion-industry-human-cost (April 30, 2019)

2 Mark Koba, "Spending big on kids' sports? You're not alone," www.cnbc.com (January 13, 2014)

3 "Sport for All Play for Life: A Playbook to Get Every Kid in the Game," Sports & Society Program, The Aspen Institute's Project Play (January 25, 2015)

While recreational programs may cap out at a few hundred dollars a year, club expenses could soar to $3,000 or more, and that's before uniforms, tournaments and travel are factored in. So why do we spend so much of our financial, emotional and physical capital on sports?

Start with it's fun and there's nothing like it. In a top five, you could realistically assign spots one to four. But in the interests of probing deeper, there are a surfeit of reasons, social and cultural, that can explain the phenomenon.

Mashing together the idioms "keeping up with the Joneses" and "the grass is always greener" sheds light on one major rationale. When we look around and see the kids at school or in the neighborhood committed to sports, it moves us to ask questions like, *"How come I'm not doing this for my kid?" "Am I a bad parent if my kid isn't on a travel team?" "Shouldn't my kids have the newest Nikes and the hottest gear like everyone else?"* And the topper: *"What does this say about me as a parent?"* Our psyches have been poisoned, our parental competence challenged.

For some parents, the hopes and expectations of their kids playing at a higher level drive the conversation. They believe that an early start in sports may benefit their kid when it comes to making his high school team. And while they're fantasizing about the future, why not visualize their kid starring in college?

Forbes reported that 67 percent of parents (who participated in their survey) held hopes of their children earning athletic scholarships to college, and 34 percent figured their kids would move on to the Olympics or go pro.[4] Though the level of spending required to facilitate those dreams "didn't leave a lot of financial wiggle room

4 Bob Cook, "What Drives Parents' Youth Sports Spending? Don't Underestimate Peer Pressure," www.Forbes.com (August 1, 2016)

for feeding college or retirement funds," it wasn't a big deal for these parents. Universally, they considered the added expenses an investment in their child's future.

Peter grew up on Long Island loving the Jets and the Mets, then came to LA and added the Clippers and the Angels to his roster of passions. He attended games, collected gear, knew the players – Peter was a fan's fan. When he and Donna married, he looked forward to sharing his love of sports with his kids and eagerly anticipated them fulfilling their own sports destinies. Daughters Stevie and Sammy were going to be ballplayers. Both played AYSO soccer and rec center basketball. Through elementary school, Sammy even spent several years as the only girl on Encino Little League baseball teams. Eventually it was time to move from hardball to softball and Sammy aced the transition, perching herself on the pitcher's mound.

Peter was only too happy to further the cause by chipping in for weekly pitching lessons. At a hundred dollars an hour they weren't cheap but excellence had its price. Only problem was, Sammy's sunny disposition got increasingly cloudy every time she headed out to softball. And when she announced on the eve of ninth grade that she was quitting the game, Peter was gutted. He protested her decision, tried to convince her to reconsider. But Sammy shut him down with the unassailable, *"Dad, I'm afraid of the ball!"*

Parental best efforts are thwarted by the irresistible caprices of youth every day. As well they should be. We can lead those ponies to the mound but we can't make them pitch. What we need to realize is that our kids have a better chance of owning a professional team than ever playing on one. Perhaps these statistics can provide some context:

"There are over 7 million high school athletes. But only enough college roster spots for 2 percent of them. And only 1 percent of them get full rides to D1 colleges." That's according to NCAA Athletic Scholarship Statistics.[5]

To me that's game, set, match. But let's delve a little deeper, while also defining our terms.

Division 1 (DI) consists of schools that compete at the highest level of intercollegiate sports. They are often the bigger schools, with the largest athletic budgets, grandest facilities and the most scholarships to offer. Think of Michigan, Notre Dame, Stanford, USC, Ohio State, Texas, Alabama, and Duke, for example. Ivy League schools also compete in DI, though they do not provide athletic scholarships.

Division 2 (DII) is the next level in the athletic hierarchy. While there is overlap among all three divisions, DII differentiates itself as a being a step down competitively from DI, while still providing scholarships for its athletes. Some DII schools are Adelphi, Azusa Pacific, University of Bridgeport, and San Francisco State.

Division 3 (DIII) schools do not offer athletic scholarships. They are often smaller, more academically-prestigious institutions such as Johns Hopkins, Tufts, Amherst, Emory, and Bowdoin. They consider their academics to be lure enough, and to many that's an accurate assessment.

Here are the numbers for several sports (a link to a complete breakdown of the progression of players from high school to college to the professional leagues can be found in the footnote).[6]

---

5 "Odds of a High School Athlete playing in College," ScholarshipStats.com (2019)

6 "Probability of Competing Beyond High School," NCAA, www.ncaa.org/about/resources/research/probability-competing-beyond-high-school (April 3, 2019)

- 487,097 play baseball in high school. 35,460 of them (7.3%) continue to play in college. 10,716 (2.2%) play in DI programs. 10,753 (2.2%) play in DII programs. And 14,126 (2.9%) play for DIII schools. Still seems like a lot of kids playing.
- How about Women's Basketball? There are 412,407 playing in high school. 16,614 (4.0%) make it onto college teams. Roughly the same number, 4,950 players make it onto DI and DII squads (1.2% for each). And 6,599 (1.6%) have careers in DIII.
- Men's Soccer. 456,362 are on the pitch through high school. It drops to 25,072 (5.5%) in college. 5,933 (1.3%) play in DI. 6,845 (1.5%) make DII teams. And 12,322 (2.7%) get to wear the colors of DIII schools.

Three-quarters of all plant and animal life died in the mass extinction at the end of the Cretaceous era sixty-five million years ago. The drop-off in sports participation from high school to college is even more precipitous. Let's take it to the next step and examine players moving from college to the pros.

Of the 35,460 NCAA baseball players, 775 (2.2%) are drafted. What started as a high school population of almost 490,000 funnels down to fewer than 800 in the minor leagues. Way fewer get that golden ticket to the bigs.

Of the 16,614 women playing college basketball, only 34 of them are drafted into the WNBA. That's two-tenths of 1 percent. And from the 412,407 young ladies we started with in high school . . . Yikes.

Men's soccer. Of the 25,072 flying up and down the fields in college, 75 are drafted to play at the next level. Three-tenths of 1 percent. Again, a whopping 456,362 boys playing in high school whittled down to fewer than 100 making it to the pros!!!

The odds of riding a specialized route into a fully-sponsored future are microscopic. The early specialization of our athletes leads down a path of intense competition that's also financially depleting while offering no guarantee of a "pay off" at the finish. We parents might have to return to dreaming of our kids becoming doctors and lawyers and accountants. Almost anything is more realistic and attainable than a career as a professional athlete.

The truth about scholarship money is equally as sobering. Only six sports award "full rides," where tuition, room and board, books and some living expenses are covered. These "head count" sports are football, men and women's basketball, women's gymnastics, tennis, and volleyball. Athletes in these DI programs are either given full scholarships or no scholarships. Every other sport is considered an "equivalency" sport. Schools are assessed a specific number of scholarships, which the coach can slice into smaller pieces to spread the money around to more athletes.

Parents may shell out tens of thousands of dollars (even hundreds of thousands in extreme cases) in the decade their kids are in the youth sport system and receive, perhaps, $2,000 a year back in scholarship money. The math doesn't add up.

Yet that doesn't stop people from chasing the dream. Maybe this will:

Playing high-level college sports will be a full-time job. According to an NCAA survey, "playing football required 43.3 hours per week; college baseball, 42.1 hours; men's basketball, 39.2 hours; and women's basketball, 37.6 hours. Because of the huge time commitment, as well as time away from campus, Division 1 athletes will often not be able to major in rigorous disciplines, such as the sciences and engineering."[7]

---

7 Lynn O'Shaughnessy, "8 things you should know about sports scholarships," CBS News MoneyWatch (September 20, 2012)

In Division 1, your commitment to your sport takes precedence over everything else – academics, extracurricular activities, social life, and sleep. Your sport is your job, which is one of the prime arguments in favor of NCAA athletes being paid. While universities are making millions of dollars from the efforts of their athletes, many players, even those on scholarship, struggle to make ends meet. Schools see it another way. They're offering their athletes a free education. The argument rages on.

Division 3 schools' focus on academics over athletics presents its students with a more well-rounded experience, giving them the opportunity to partake in more of what the school has to offer. A DIII athlete still spends a considerable amount of his time on the field or in the gym, but it's a significantly lesser level of commitment than that of his DI brethren.

Whereas Division 3 and the Ivy League schools in Division 1 don't offer athletic scholarships, the athletic departments will generally be given an allotment of applicants that they can shepherd into the system. Coaches can lend their influence during the admissions process, which will help some who might not get in based solely on their academic profile. Elite club programs, high-level tournaments, college ID camps, highlight reels and interviews, while upping the monetary outlay, can pique a college coach's attention, and many parents consider this the cost of doing business. They hope their "investment" may one day yield an email that reads, "Welcome to Harvard."

With the speed of a cheetah and the relentlessness of a charging rhino, Alex plowed a swath through any defense unlucky enough to challenge him. Modest and unassuming off the field, his flashy game-time play caught the eye of numerous college coaches. Injuries, a byproduct of his blistering style, prevented him from vying for DI consideration, but DIII Wesleyan University in Connecticut courted him. Alex glowed after getting the call that he was going to be included on the coach's list of recruits. He cruised through senior-year soccer season, earning First Team All-League honors, barely able to contain his enthusiasm about playing at the next level.

And then this call came. "I'm really sorry, I don't quite know what happened," began the Wesleyan coach. Alex's grades, which wobbled after a concussion he suffered junior year, had dropped him below the admissions cut. The coach, thinking Alex would be admitted on his merits, didn't exert the extra "push" by including him on his list. Hanging up, Alex was crushed.

Here's where the story gets strange. The previous summer, before submitting any applications, Alex attended a football ID camp at Brown University. And with his soccer-strong leg, he was able to launch fifty-yard field goals. Naturally, the Brown coach took notice, but Alex's heart belonged to Wesleyan and that was the end of it. Until it wasn't. After the Wesleyan debacle, Alex reached out to the Brown coach, and within weeks, not only had he been admitted to Brown, he was handed a football uniform.

Freshman year he suited up but never entered a game. Still, being part of the team brought with it an instant friend group and lubricated his social transition to college. Something, though, wasn't right. He missed the flow and physicality of soccer. He loved Brown, he liked football, but soccer had always been his passion.

After the season, he met with the soccer coach, convinced him of his commitment, and traded his shoulder pads for shin guards. True to the convolutions of Alex's story, an injury glued him to the bench, ultimately freeing him up to focus on his future in the business world.

One valuable takeaway from Alex's experience is the active role an athlete must take in the recruiting process. Alex initiated the contact with the Wesleyan coach, and his participation in the Brown football camp led to the impression he made on that school's staff. When Alex's Wesleyan dream disintegrated, he quickly mobilized to devise and execute Plan B. Parents, school athletic departments and recruiting services can do only so much. Like everything else in this realm, it boils down to the desire and drive of the athlete.

Even when the recruitment process functions smoothly, how can we parents know, when our kids are five or six or ten, whether Brown or Wesleyan, or Harvard or Stanford, or any of these academically rigorous schools, will be an option years down the road? Or if our seven- and nine-year-olds may be skilled enough to play at powerhouses like Ohio State, Michigan or Texas? Unless they're 6-foot-2 and superhumanly coordinated in sixth grade, for the most part we can't. There is no way to predict the scope of our kids' athletic future.

Over the past decade I have encountered more and more parents reaching for their checkbooks to ensure an edge for their kids. Whether securing top-of-the-line coaches or setting their sights on the most competitive teams, there's a feeling that the access money conveys will translate into a tangible advantage.

Look no further than the college admissions scandal that broke in March 2019. The implicated parents went to extraordinary lengths to secure their kids' spots in the most competitive programs. From rigging their SAT and ACT scores to falsifying their athletic resumes to writing horrifyingly large checks, those involved applied an "ends justify the means" rationale to legitimize their actions. Until they got caught, of course.

I'm not arguing that there's a scaled-down equivalent in the youth sports world, but an unhealthy number of individuals and organizations would consider parents derelict if they didn't spend what they could or otherwise work the system to advantage their kids. In this way, parental insecurity is unapologetically exploited by systemic greed.

Altruism is proclaimed – *we want what's best for your child* – but the machine runs on cash. Give us your money and we'll get your kid into – *choose one* – club, high school, college. (Only the most shameless programs promise a career in the pros; many tout college, then append "and beyond" as code for a stint at a higher level.) Picture the Sarlacc from *Return of the Jedi*, a gaping maw with tentacles and teeth in the desert of Tatooine that greedily gobbles up anything dropped within its reach. Welcome to pay-to-play youth sports.

Still, some families possess the means and the inclination. They may say, *we know there are no guarantees but this is what we want for our kid.* I would suggest that they consider the desires of the child. (Seemingly obvious but you'd be surprised.) And, if this is something the child longs to pursue, they should check in periodically to assess whether his interest remains resolute. Once roaring down the tracks, this train can be difficult to stop.

Many parents are understandably reluctant to mortgage their lives to have their kids run, kick and catch. Others don't possess the financial wherewithal to take the high-priced route. Thankfully, there are other avenues that will get you to the same destination without an endless outlay. Most programs provide scholarships. There are also benefactors in the community willing to help deserving families cover the necessary fees. And then there are the truly generous . . .

Alex's mom, Linda (different Alex), knew he would grow up to play football. But after a session of soccer classes, American football was jettisoned and Alex was on his way to becoming a devotee of the world game. He played on all the top club teams, competed in the highest echelon tournaments and was primed for a college career. But life, in the form of surfing, injuries, and surfing injuries, changed Alex's plans. His younger brother Nicky was an even more avid soccer player, and the team of his teens was one of the best in California.

What Linda encountered, as she chaperoned her boys through the sport, was a demographic dependent upon donations and philanthropy for access to teams and tournaments. More striking was the number of these kids who, for cultural and financial reasons, never made it into the pool for college consideration. It's something U.S. Soccer is finally waking up to as it witnesses an entire population of athletes absent from the top levels of the sport. Determined to do her part to fix the system, Linda created the Soccer Scholars Foundation which:

". . . identifies young soccer talent throughout California and the New York metropolitan area, who have the potential and desire to play college sports yet lack the academic, informational and leadership support to achieve that potential. SSF provides guidance through Mentors and Enrichment Programs – utilizing strategic partnerships, an online forum of shared resources, and unique opportunities for academic and personal development."

In four years, Linda and SSF have already helped more than sixty kids matriculate into colleges they would otherwise not have had the access or the resources to attend.

Activist parents like Linda are striving at the grassroots level to change the complexion of youth sports by generating opportunities for all of our kids. As yet in their infancy, and needing a constant infusion of engagement and resources, these efforts reinforce that giving back to the community makes us all a little bit better.

It's easy to stumble blindly, not knowing where to turn for scholarships or other opportunities to defray some of the financial burden, but families in need should not be afraid to ask. Surely fewer than six degrees separates us from someone with the answer.

With initiative and some leg work, we can always find opportunities for our kids to play, regardless of the economics. Despite what unscrupulous coaches may say to lasso kids at an early age – "if you don't join now, there won't be room later" – there are always slots to be filled. Coaches with open spots will work with parents on a financial accommodation.

As money has flooded the youth sports universe, we parents have to exercise vigilance to ensure fairness, accessibility and opportunity for all kids, without regard to financial resources. And for our own kids, we need to maintain perspective in finding the right fit and resist the lure of an uncertain future in favor of embracing the benefits of the here and now.

CHAPTER EIGHTEEN

Going Pro at Nine

Only a handful of years ago, the youngest teams that club and travel programs offered were for nine-year-olds. Most kids that age were still registered in the recreational leagues, preferring to wait another few years before jumping ship. AYSO and other programs more than adequately, and often exceptionally, served this clientele through U10 and into U12. Then the paradigm shifted. A few clubs, seeking an earlier tap into the pipeline, began to build teams for eight-year-olds, with "pre-academy" squads formed to entice those who were six and seven. In true *Field of Dreams* fashion – "if you build it, they will come" – families started leaving the recreational environments at an earlier age. The drip quickened to a flow, and pretty soon, entry-level teams at clubs were flourishing at the expense of local AYSO regions.

Why? What was the hurry?

Parents who for years were happy that their kids were having fun in a less-pressured environment suddenly began pointing fingers at the inconsistency of volunteer – read: parent – coaching. *My kid isn't developing as quickly as he should be.* My question – what's the rush? – was usually greeted with some uncomfortable harrumphing before a stammered "w-w-well, some of his friends are already in club, and I don't want Joey to be left behind." The dreaded "I want him to fulfill his potential" intruded into every conversation.

We've got a generation of parents living in an always-connected universe where everything is just a touchscreen tap away. Patience and perspective have been sacrificed on the altar of instant gratification. No longer does development occur over a period of years. Nowadays, parents can't understand why Johnny hasn't become a superstar by the end of his first practice. I'm exaggerating only slightly. Technology never sleeps, information refreshes every few minutes, and this steady bombardment of glowing content has affected not just us, but our kids as well. It makes sense that in this climate, superlatives – newest, biggest, best-est – will be eagerly pursued.

To be fair, the premature evacuation from recreational to club can't be pinned solely on aggressive and competitive parents, or their altered brain waves and behavioral patterns. In some cases, recreational leagues have sputtered in satisfying their mandate to mix fun and learning in a family-friendly environment. Many have been slow to recognize the changes in society, and they stubbornly cling to policies and procedures that drive their customers into the welcoming arms of the more competitive programs. One example is AYSO's "all volunteer" ethos and its continuing refusal to allow its referees to be paid.

AYSO has justifiably been proud of its charter as an organization staffed by volunteers. With a population of players hovering around 650,000, the 50,000 teams are staffed by 250,000 volunteers. That's a lot of time and energy committed by parents, grandparents, siblings, students, and other generous souls within the community. Even in difficult times, someone can always be convinced to coach. Drumming up referees is a gnarlier task. Some feel their grasp of the laws is shaky so they shrink from the very public responsibility of having to apply them in the moment. Most cite the catalog of horror stories of sideline abuse by spectators. Almost all would rather pay a few extra dollars in fees to have the league hire professionals. Yet the tradeoff – volunteers who, because of their kids, are invested in the program vs. hired hands, who, in many cases, possess vision and judgment that isn't that much better – isn't unequivocal.

AYSO has slammed the door on this proposal, even as it has relaxed restrictions on remunerating coaches. (Team coaches still cannot receive pay, but regions can set up coaching clinics and instructional opportunities that circumnavigate the rules.)

Club programs want only two things from parents – their kids and their money. They'll supply everything else, including the referees. It's one of the primary reasons cited for the flight from AYSO. "I don't have to volunteer and, specifically, I don't have to ref. Here's my kid."

Yet, are parents expecting too much from both recreational and competitive programs? Are we impatient with the pace of childhood itself? If adulthood is marked by the narrowing of options, with our choices limiting what we can do, why are we so eager to impose this agenda upon our children? Youth is fueled by a frenetic energy optimal for exploration and discovery. It's messy and it's fun. So why are we hell-bent on shutting it down?

When we weigh the relative merits of recreational vs. competitive sports, the conversation has to include a discussion of "specialization."

In the good ol' days of the twentieth century, kids played multiple sports, usually a different one each season. Where I grew up, the fall choices were football or soccer, with winter hosting basketball and wrestling. When the melting snow gave rise to spring, we headed outside for baseball or lacrosse. Everyone took the summer off, either to go to camp or head to the beach. The cycle started again once we went back to school after Labor Day. (None of this present-day school beginning in August nonsense.)

But the whirlwind of specialization has changed everything. More kids are playing fewer sports. Most of Evan's teammates on his All-Star teams of the early 2000s were also playing basketball and baseball. Even as recently as 2010, a healthy number of Griffie's teammates were also involved in baseball, basketball, track, swimming, and water polo. Now, we have year-round soccer, baseball, flag football, basketball, lacrosse, hockey, rugby, crew, water polo, tennis, fencing. It's exhausting.

What's changed?

The money, for one thing. As discussed, there's so much more of it, both to be earned and to be spent trying to earn it. It's an unavoidable presence, with games and highlights viewable day and night, on devices as small as our phones or as large as 80-inch, high-def television screens. Kids have always answered the "what do you want to be when you grow up" question with professional *fill in the sport* player. Now, they spend every waking moment, under the proud eye of their competitive parents, trying to make that happen. Social media and the rise of FOMO (fear of missing out) raise the stakes. *If Charlie's kid is a star on the court, my kid better kick some butt on the field.*

Anxiety, ignorance and fear impel parents toward the precipice. They worry that their children may miss fleeting opportunities to play in prime programs or be passed over altogether, leaving them adrift in less savory activities like skateboarding, video gaming, or chasing the opposite sex.

Despite the threat propagated by coaches and program leaders of being left in athletic perdition, most of the regulating bodies in youth sports agree that the risks of early specialization outweigh the rewards. The American Academy of Pediatrics, for example, advocates against specialization until the age of fifteen or sixteen, if not later.[1] Before then, children are in greater jeopardy of incurring over-use injuries, burn out, anxiety and depression.

Being a multisport athlete can serve a child's changing needs by keeping him challenged, motivated and happy. An article from Velocity Sports[2] lists some of the benefits of multisport participation:

- Playing multiple sports helps athletes avoid burnout.
- Playing multiple sports forces athletes to use different parts of the body and learn new movements.
- Playing multiple sports teaches athletes how to work with different types of people, navigate different team dynamics and learn new perspectives.
- Playing multiple sports gives the body time to physically recover from the demands of the last sport.

---

1 Joel Brenner and Council of Sports Medicine and Fitness, "Sports Specialization and Intensive Training in Young Athletes," *Pediatrics*, the official journal of the American Academy of Pediatrics (September 2016)

2 "Why Being A One-Sport Athlete Is Not A Good Thing," Velocity Sports Performance (January 26, 2017)

- Playing multiple sports gives your mind a break, so that when you return to your sport you are excited, engaged and prepared to give it your all.

In ninth grade, Dori was looking for another sport. She'd been playing soccer almost exclusively since the age of five. She still loved the game, but after ten years, her excitement for it had waned. I suggested swimming. Brentwood had just installed a pool, the coach was eager for recruits, and she could learn at her own pace.

Dori took to the idea. She met with the coach and told him that she'd like to join the team. Her one caveat was that she only wanted to train; she didn't want to compete. Insecure about her inexperience, she figured she could learn best without the stress of competition. The coach nodded in a way Dori couldn't read, but it didn't matter. She was on the team.

The first few practices were demoralizing. "I can barely get across the pool."

Despite her reservations, though, she continued to attend every practice, working hard to improve. Three weeks into the season, I got a phone call from Dori, wailing so hard she was gasping for breath.

"Dad…today's…our…first…meet. Coach…put me in…FOUR EVENTS! WAAAAHH!"

I tried to console her but the persistence of her sobs as she hung up told me my efforts had fallen short.

I arrived at the meet to find that, indeed, Dori was slated for four races. But the coach had wisely placed her in heats with kids of comparable ability. She wasn't tossed in with dolphins; Dori was swimming with the minnows.

By the end of the afternoon, Dori's entire demeanor had changed. She was elated that she hadn't "lost" any of her races, which to her

288

would have been mortifying. Finishing first she couldn't have cared less about; not finishing last was a triumph. She emerged from the pool beaming, and carried this sense of achievement through the rest of the season. Over time, Dori improved. Not dramatically, but that was OK. She loved the overall – the practices, the meets and the bonding.

About six weeks later, I got another lunchtime phone call. Once again, it was Dori, and once again, she was inconsolable.

"Dad," she managed through the tears. "Today…is…the…LAST MEET! WAAAHH!"

To me, the season had been a raging success. Dori never got close to the medal stand. Her times improved imperceptibly. And I still had to endure three-hour meets to watch her in the pool for five minutes. But the glory of the team experience, the confidence she gained from attempting something unfamiliar, and the new friendships she made, sustained her through the next soccer season and the ensuing months until it was time to squeeze her hair into that bathing cap once again.

* * *

Let's be honest. As parents our lives are busy enough. Shedding a few obligations could be a good thing, right? Having our kids specialize in one sport could deliver a consistency of routine, carpool, and experience. And yet, it would be lazy and selfish to ignore the critical benefits of allowing our kids – and ourselves – to explore new challenges. In an article called "Are Kids Specializing in Sports Too Early?"[3] U.S. Youth Soccer observed:

---

3 U.S. Youth Soccer, "Are Kids Specializing in Sports Too Early?", www.usyouthsoccer. org/are_kids_specializing_in_sports_too_early/ (2018)

"If you talk to college coaches . . . whether it's a soccer coach, football coach, basketball coach, doesn't matter – they'll all say, 'We want multiple-sport athletes because those are the ones who perform best at the intercollegiate level.'

"U.S. Youth Soccer surveyed more than 500 college soccer coaches and asked if they prefer an athlete who played multiple sports. Of the 221 Division I coaches who answered, just 16 – 7 percent – said they would prefer a player who played only soccer and was not a multisport athlete."

It's a compelling statistic, one that's supported by a list of superstar athletes who amplified their talents by spreading them around:

- Dave Winfield: basketball, football and baseball
- John Elway: football and baseball
- Jackie Robinson: football, track and baseball
- Bo Jackson: football and baseball
- Babe Didrikson Zaharias: golf, basketball, and track and field
- Jim Thorpe: football, baseball, track and field
- Sam Darnold: karate, football, basketball, baseball and soccer

In high school, Giancarlo Stanton, one of baseball's current crop of sluggers, juggled his schedule so that he could also fit in football and basketball. "I recommend multiple sports for sure. The life experiences and athleticism you get from playing three sports . . . will stick with you and help you progress."[4]

Spencer and his younger brother Justin broke into sports the traditional way, rotating seasonally through soccer, basketball and baseball. Being a California kid, Spencer also took to the waves, spending spare

---

4 Eric Sondheimer, "Slugger Giancarlo Stanton recommends playing multiple sports in high school," *Los Angeles Times* (February 7, 2016)

moments surfing. After his 12U baseball team wrapped up its season with a trip to Cooperstown, Spencer shelved baseball (and basketball) to concentrate on soccer. At thirteen, he towered above his peers, but it was his work ethic that catapulted him forward. Battling through injuries, some attributed to his rapid growth, others to bad luck, his enthusiasm never dimmed and landing on the Northwestern varsity soccer team was the culmination of his efforts.

Justin also showed soccer promise early. As a seven-year-old he guested on the U10 Palaxy team, scoring goals in our Santa Barbara tournament. But baseball exerted an equally strong pull and he pinged between the two into early adolescence. Just as baseball was gaining the upper hand, Justin discovered beach volleyball. That was it. Playing indoors and out, he starred for both high school and club teams, until Ohio State recruited him to spike for them.

Exposure to multiple sports liberated the brothers to discover their true calling at the right time, and being able to incorporate the lessons learned from different disciplines upped their main games considerably.

In sports, as in life, timing is everything. Youth sports researchers Jessica Fraser-Thomas and Jean Côté recommend the following age breakdown for athletes trying to achieve elite status in a specific sport:[5]

- Prior to age 12, 80 percent of time should be spent in deliberate play and in sports *other than* the chosen sport!
- Age 13 to 15: 50-50 split between a chosen sport and other athletic pursuits

---

5 Jessica Fraser-Thomas and Jean Côté, "Youth Sports: Implementing Findings and Moving Forward with Research," *Athletic Insight: The Online Journal of Sport Psychology*, Vol. 8, Issue 3 (September 2006)

- Age 16+: Even when specialization becomes very important, 20 percent of training time should still be in the non-specialized sport and deliberate (free) play.

The idea that encouraging children to play multiple sports will ultimately help them excel in one seems counterintuitive. It's a tough sell to parents, especially as the trend seems to be in the opposite direction. But the facts simply do not support the efficacy of early specialization. In his article "Is It Wise to Specialize?",[6] John O'Sullivan, the founder and CEO of the Changing the Game Project, lays out research-based arguments in favor of multisport participation:

1. ***Better Overall Skills and Ability***: Research shows that early participation in multiple sports leads to better overall motor and athletic development, longer playing careers, increased ability to transfer sports skills to other sports and increased motivation, ownership of the sports experience, and confidence.

2. ***Smarter, More Creative Players***: Multisport participation at the youngest ages yields better decision making and pattern recognition, as well as increased creativity. These are all qualities that coaches of high-level teams look for.

3. ***Most College Athletes Come From a Multisport Background***: A 2013 American Medical Society for Sports Medicine survey found that 88 percent of college athletes surveyed participated in more than one sport as a child.

4. ***10,000 Hours is not a Rule:*** In "The Sports Gene," his survey of the scientific literature regarding sport specific practice,

---

6 John O'Sullivan, "Is It Wise to Specialize?" Changing the Game Project, https://changingthegameproject.com/is-it-wise-to-specialize/ (January 13, 2014)

David Epstein finds that most elite competitors require far less than 10,000 hours of deliberate practice. Specifically, studies have shown that basketball (4,000), field hockey (4,000) and wrestling (6,000) all require far less than 10,000 hours. Even Anders Ericsson, the researcher credited with discovering the 10,000-hour rule, says the misrepresentation of his work, popularized by Malcolm Gladwell in *Outliers*, ignores many of the elements that go into high performance (genetics, coaching, opportunity, luck) and focuses on only one, deliberate practice. That, he says, is wrong.

5. *Free Play Equals More Play*: Early specialization ignores the importance of deliberate play/free play. Researchers found that activities that are intrinsically motivating, maximize fun, and provide enjoyment, are incredibly important. These are termed deliberate play (as opposed to deliberate practice, which are activities motivated by the goal of performance enhancement and not enjoyment). Deliberate play increases motor skills, emotional ability, and creativity. Children allowed deliberate play also tend to spend more time engaged in a sport than athletes in structured training with a coach.

6. *There are Many Paths to Mastery*: A 2003 study on professional ice hockey players found that while most pros had spent 10,000 hours or more involved in sports prior to age 20, only 3,000 of those hours were involved in hockey specific deliberate practice (and only 450 of those hours were prior to age 12).

Still not convinced? O'Sullivan goes on to list five research-based points that demonstrate how early specialization may negatively affect a child:

1. Children who specialize in a single sport account for 50 percent of overuse injuries in young athletes, according to pediatric orthopedic specialists.

2. A study by Ohio State University found that children who specialized early in a single sport had higher rates of adult physical inactivity. Those who commit to one sport at a young age are often the first to quit, and suffer a lifetime of consequences.

3. Children who specialize early are at a far greater risk for burnout due to stress, decreased motivation and lack of enjoyment.

4. In a study of 1,200 youth athletes, Dr. Neeru Jayanthi of Loyola University found that early specialization in a single sport is one of the strongest predictors of injury. Athletes in the study who specialized were 70 to 93 percent more likely to be injured than children who played multiple sports!

Even the most resistant parents soften when confronted with risks to their children's health. Gone are the days of the broken and bleeding athlete, revived with smelling salts, sent back into the game. With fears of future brain damage originating in early and repeated contacts, and concussion protocols fiercely enforced, we are more aware than we were just a few years ago of the dangers inherent in youth sports.

According to Stanford Children's Health,[7] every year 3.5 million children ages fourteen and younger incur injuries playing sports. That's a stunning statistic. Knee injuries, especially ACL tears, occur with alarming frequency for athletes just entering their teens.

---

7 "Sports Injury Statistics," Stanford Children's Health (2019)

Here's O'Sullivan's fifth point:

5. Early sport specialization in female adolescents is associated with increased risk of anterior knee pain disorders including PFP (Osgood Schlatter and Sinding Larsen-Johansson), compared to multisport athletes, and may lead to higher rates of future ACL tears.

Staggeringly, high school female athletes in the United States suffer 20,000-80,000 ACL injuries per year.[8]

A combination of physical and technical factors put girls at four to six times greater risk than boys. An article from the New England Baptist Hospital's Live in Motion Blog "Why Do Female Athletes Suffer More ACL Injuries than Males?"[9] lays out the case.

Physical Differences

* The intercondylar notch, the groove in the femur through which the ACL passes, is naturally smaller in women than in men. Accordingly, the ACL itself is smaller in women, which makes it more prone to injury.
* Women more commonly have "knock-knee" alignment, meaning that their knees bend inward when they land from jumps. When a knee buckles, it puts a strain on the ACL to maintain the knee's stability.

---

8 Cynthia R. LaBella, MD; Michael R. Huxford, MEd, ATC; Joe Grissom, MPP; et al., "Effect of Neuromuscular Warm-up on Injuries in Female Soccer and Basketball Athletes in Urban Public High Schools," *JAMA Pediatrics* (November 2011)

9 "Why Do Female Athletes Suffer More ACL Injuries than Males?" Life in Motion, New England Baptist Hospital (January 18, 2016)

Technique Differences

- Women often land flat-footed, instead of on the balls of their feet, after a jump. This improper landing puts pressure on the knee when the calf muscles should be absorbing the force.
- Women tend to have an imbalanced quadriceps/hamstring ratio. A female athlete is more likely to rely on her quadriceps muscles to decelerate or change speed, putting more pressure on the knee.
- Women run in a more upright position than men, adding stress to the ACL and resulting in less control over rotation of the knee joint.

So how do we protect our children, girls and boys, from injury, whether they specialize early or not?

Velocity Sports Performance website[10] talks about tips that are essential to include in a comprehensive preventive conditioning program:

Proper Warm-Up: A proper warm-up is key for preparing the body for activity. By warming up your muscles first, you greatly reduce your risk of injury during competition or practice.

Strength Training: Strengthening of the hamstrings, quads, core and gluteus musculature can help to maintain upper and lower leg alignment, thus reducing stress and excessive rotation at the knee.

Improve Balance: Single-leg exercises and drills can help to eliminate imbalance differences between the right and left leg.

Controlled Plyometrics: Vertical jumps and plyometric exercises should be included but must be controlled, not allowing the knees to collapse together. This inward movement (valgus collapse) of the

---

10 "How to Protect Against ACL Injuries," Velocity Sports Performance, https://velocityspusa.com/category/general-blog/sports-medicine/ (January 31, 2017)

knees is a predictor of ACL injuries. Start by using both legs and progress to single-leg lateral jumps.

Injury Prevention Screening: Screenings can be a key to possibly identifying individual needs, thus further reducing the risk of injury. Mobility (range of motion) and/or stability (strength-related motor control) asymmetries must be addressed. The *Functional Movement Screen* and similar objective standardized measures can be used to assess for possible impairment of proper functional movement.

In his decade plus of coaching boys and girls at the recreational, club and high school level, Coach Christian can point to a formidable won-loss record that has included championships, medals and promotions. What he is just as proud of is the sustained orthopedic health of his players. During his tenure, *not one* of them incurred a knee injury. Christian has been an enthusiastic advocate of the Prevent Injury and Enhance Performance (PEP) program, a series of warm-up exercises designed by Dr. Bert Mandelbaum and his Santa Monica Orthopaedic and Sports Medicine Research Foundation.

Dr. Mandelbaum, the longtime head orthopedist for the U.S. Men's National Soccer team, was alarmed by the number of teenage athletes – especially girls – with blown-out knees crowding his waiting room. He supervised comprehensive research and devised the PEP Program, a fifteen- to twenty-minute exercise routine done at least three times per week. Consisting of warm-ups, stretching, strengthening exercises, plyometrics, and sports-specific agilities, the program addresses specific weaknesses and builds on strengths in an athletes' preparation.

Mandelbaum's protocol dramatically diminished the number of injuries, particularly critical knee injuries, for players who utilized his techniques. But whether the coaches in your program use this protocol or some other, the information needs to be out there. Injury prevention drills, exercises, stretches and warm-ups before games and practices are a must. If the specialization trend is going to continue, and our kids are going to be exposed to rigorous drills, multiple practices and tougher competition at younger and younger ages, we must do all we can to prevent non-impact injuries.

The real question, though, is: do our children need such intensive workouts in the first place? What do we seek to gain from specialization that couldn't be gained over time through patience, practice and exploration? Mostly lost in the surge of specialization, but staging a comeback, is the concept of Free or Deliberate Play. Letting the kids control the game, the practice, the moment, without coaching, correction or interference. It's a return to recess in the schoolyard, or pickup games in the gym, where having fun is both the journey and the destination. We often say that the game itself is its own best teacher. Kids learn by playing. Absent the pressure of performance or results, and without the worry of adult judgment or censure, they are free to experiment, express themselves, problem solve, manage relationships, and experience the purity of sports.

Let's assume, though, that you've gotten this far in the story and you're still convinced you have a future college or professional athlete sitting next to you at the dinner table. What can you do to make sure he or she realizes this destiny? A parental pedigree in college or professional sports does confer an edge; athletic DNA cannot be denied. Short of that, is there anything that you, the parent, can do?

Sorry.

You can outfit your child with all the latest gear. You can book private lessons with all the best coaches. You can enroll your future superstar in the most exclusive academies and development programs.

But if your kid's heart isn't in it, you can watch all that time and money circle the drain.

Before club soccer was the behemoth it is now, when it was a bastion for the tippy-top tier of players, parents asked, "How do I know if my kid is club-worthy?" The answer my mentor Jeff offered, which I've tweaked and amplified over the years, is this:

If your kid comes home from school and races outside to bang a ball against the garage... If she does her homework while kicking a ball under the desk... If he has a ball at his feet at all times, dribbling up and down the hallway... If her preferred TV (or any screen) viewing is professional or college soccer... Then you have a child with the proper disposition for club. If his skills match his commitment, there will be a spot for him on a team.

The pattern translates to any sport. If she's sleeping with that basketball she dribbles to school, shoots for hours in the driveway, and bounces deafeningly all through the house, she could be ready. If he's wearing his mitt to bed, pitching against the garage door every afternoon, and studying not just the players but how they play the game, travel baseball could be for him.

If, however, your child thinks of his sport only when it's time to go to practice or when she can't find her cleats... If, when the season is over, the equipment is stashed in the closet gathering dust for nine months until the next season begins... And if every sport he or she plays is *the best one*, perhaps specialization is not the answer.

It doesn't matter how hard you try, push, discuss, cajole, leverage, bargain, or, god forbid, threaten, it's not going to happen. And please, there's no reason for you to feel bad about this. Just realize and accept that . . .

. . . it's not about you.

If it isn't coming from deep inside your child; if playing at a higher, more competitive level is not his burning desire or the object of her drive and hard work, it won't happen.

And that's the secret. The road to the highest level is long and hard, filled with the random and the unpredictable, and desire can't be imposed from the outside. (Not without consequences that are beyond the scope of this volume, though happy to refer you to the appropriate resources and practitioners.) But then, what's so bad? If our kids have a ball playing ball and the joy of sports keeps them engaged – at any level – throughout their lives, then we have succeeded in the most profound fashion.

CHAPTER NINETEEN

The Name Game

"Float like a butterfly, sting like a bee;
his hands can't hit what his eyes can't see."
— Muhammad Ali, before the "Rumble in the Jungle," 1974

The Greatest didn't invent trash talking but he elevated it to an art form. For him it wasn't boasting; he was stating facts, or as he put it: "It's not bragging if you can back it up." With a career record of 56-5, and battling opponents like Joe Frazier, George Foreman and the U.S. Government, Ali more than "backed it up."

Trash talking in sports has a long and storied tradition. At the first Olympic Games in 700 BC, a decathlete from Thebes was teased about the size of his javelin. After that it was "game on." Several millennia later, baseball immortal Babe Ruth replied to a query about making more money than the President of the United States: "I had a better year than he did." During the 2010 NBA playoffs, when President

Barack Obama teased Kobe Bryant that the Bulls' "Derrick Rose may have your number," Kobe shot back: "If he calls that number, I'll be sure to pick up after the fifth ring," an allusion to the four championships he'd already won and the fifth he was shooting for.

Trash talking is a way for players to puff out their chests and beef up the ante. It adds bluster to the bravado. The language can be funny or boastful or gritty, but it's always got an edge. As a lockdown defender, Dori had no problem throwing a hip into an attacker, finishing her with a *"You're kidding, right?"*

Griffie's take on trash talk was novel and insidious. Eschewing bravado, he presented as affable and unassuming. Idling next to an opposing forward at midfield, both momentary observers as the action played out elsewhere, Griffie would engage his rival in collegial repartee about math facts, video games, or anything completely unrelated to soccer. If the forward was antsy, fluttering around to get open, Griffie would loudly continue the conversation with a nearby teammate – David Michael, Christopher, Cameron, Noah, Cooper, or anyone in the same zip code. The upshot was identical. The opponent would be sufficiently lulled or distracted as to be easily outmaneuvered when the ball eventually rolled his way. Advantage Griffie.

Should trash talk tilt toward the profane, we must do our best to squelch it. Swearing, an automatic red card infraction, casts an ugly pall over a beautiful game. A seat on the bench to cogitate on the virtues of anger management and sportsmanship is an applicable remedy. *Words matter*, we tell our players. *So be careful how you use them.*

The same goes for names. From the relatively benign preschool Poopoohead, delivered with cackling glee, to the more caustic S**thead (and worse), cresting with the hormones of adolescence, names can be cudgels delivered to wound or intimidate.

Simply for identification, though, names are important, and every coach should know those of his players. That's Coaching 101. It communicates caring and commitment, while fortifying a child's self-esteem and confidence. I knew a U14 coach who never managed to master his players' names. He had no "Henrys," "Willies" or "Sams" on his team. Everyone was "Guy," "Son" or "Young Man." How dispiriting for the fifteen boys who felt anonymous and insignificant in this coach's company. Granted, some people struggle to remember names. But after three and a half months of twice-weekly interaction? Take photos and study them at home or slap on "Hello, My Name Is" stickers, but learn the damn names. It's not hard to understand why this coach's teams struggled on the field.

It was an article of faith in Region 69 that we preached using players' names as frequently as possible. From breaking the ice to building the team, familiarity facilitated a cohesive experience. Who wants to respond to *"Hey you!"*

Again, this coach may have suffered from a porous memory, more likely a lack of effort. What it certainly reflected, though, was a failure of imagination. Even with his amnesia for official names, could he have looked at his players and devised nicknames? Speedy, Mr. Clutch, Bigfoot, to offer just a few that could have been inspired by game-time exploits.

Nicknames can be funny, or descriptive, alliterative or just off-the-wall. When employed thoughtfully, they bolster, humanize, and lighten, emphasizing the fun and whimsicality of our common enterprise. Forget about science; at their best, nicknames are high art.

In sports, nicknames are not only common, they're de rigueur. Every athlete worthy of a shout-out on SportsCenter has one. Any fan can readily recall the alter egos of The Great Bambino (or the

Sultan of Swat, same guy), Shoeless Joe, Dr. J, Magic, Air Jordan, Big Papi, Broadway Joe, Sugar Ray… Through time, and loving use, the athletes and their nicknames have merged to burnish their legend.

Let's get interactive. See if you can match these athletes with his/her nickname:[1]

1. Eldrick Woods	a. The Great One
2. Lionel Messi	b. Yogi
3. Shaun White	c. Charlie Hustle
4. Charles Barkley	d. The Refrigerator
5. Dominique Wilkins	e. Tiger
6. Mildred Didrikson Zaharias	f. The Bus
7. Wayne Gretzky	g. Beast Mode
8. Pete Rose	h. Flo-Jo
9. William Perry	i. The Flea
10. Randy Johnson	j. The Human Highlight Reel
11. Florence Griffith Joyner	k. The Big Unit
12. Marshawn Lynch	l. The Round Mound of Rebound
13. Lawrence Berra	m. The Flying Tomato
14. Jerome Bettis	n. Babe

Everyone I know gets a nickname. Peter becomes Petie, Paul Pablo, Robin is Robbo. Growing up on Long Island, every Gary, Larry, Barry or Harry became Ga, La, Ba or Ha (pronounced with the flat "a" of hat). Laurie was Law.

Early on, Morris was shortened to "Mo" and to a sizable portion of my friends, that's who I still am. It never bothered me; on the

---

1 Answers: 1 (e), 2 (i), 3 (m), 4 (l), 5 (j), 6 (n), 7 (a), 8 (c), 9 (d), 10 (k), 11 (h), 12 (g), 13 (b), 14 (f)

contrary I've answered to it proudly. Maybe it began my own career of nicknaming friends, campers, players, and even my own kids, who possess an ever-evolving collection of crazy monikers.

Even in utero Evan had a nickname. Marcy and I jokingly referred to her expanding belly as Horace or Doris Morris. There was palpable relief expressed in some quarters that we didn't saddle our baby boy with that antique appellation, Horace. Toddler Evan became Evalito, then Evalico and Evarico, which morphed into Rico and Rico Taco. Dori into Dori Dor was a simple, if obvious twist. From there it became Dori Dog, then Dog Leg, then Leg, finally alighting on Leggie. Griffie's moniker followed no traditional etymological pathway. One day I looked at him and he became Crumbo Joe, a far cry from Griffin, Griff and Griffie. But Crumbo Joe had its own evolution with Crummy, Joey and CJ all referring back to young Griff. A former colleague of mine somehow whipped up Freddie Cheese, which every now and then works its way into the rotation.

My brother Alan has gone through life as Fraido. I'll bet all the residuals from this book (with some actual money on top) that you can't figure that one out. When we were young, there was a fairly pedestrian late-career John Wayne exercise called Circus World. The trapeze act was the Flying Alfredos. From Alan it was a short leap to Alfredo. Fraido was the logical next step, even if the spelling had no real antecedent.

Camp Baco, my summer home away from home, was a mecca of nicknames. Owning one was a badge of honor, one proudly worn to this day. Adz, Ammie, Bean, Boog, Creamy, Dart, Dean (for John), Dobie, Draiz, Freedie, Fru, Germ, Hefty, Namor, Poochie, Reese, Schnitzel, Slevy, Stitch, Tez, The Wrapper, Vi and Zez are just a small sampling of colorful monikers from my decade at camp. Each one summons smiles from a distant lifetime.

Some are obvious – Coopie or Coopuh for Cooper, Jordo for Jordan, Morgo for Morgan, Steenie for Christine or Christie. Meedo for Hamid? Why not. You can probably guess where Nato and Claydo began. Adding an "a," "e," "i," "o," "u," and more than sometimes "y" can do the trick for almost any name, proving that vowels can be fun. But some, rather than emerging from a person's actual name, sprout from character traits.

Ari was a beast, a force of nature on Evan's U12 Pythons. The first time I saw him, two years earlier at All-Star tryouts, packing Thor's hammer inside his shoe, he pounded the ball the length of the field, high over the heads of all the boys, and landed it just in front of the other goal. In that moment, Ari the Boot was born. Over time, The Boot has been sanded down to Booto.

Pali-Cat Dani was also a monster. Already at ten, she played with pluck and determination, outworking opponents, and scoring buckets of goals with an authoritative right leg. She was also effervescent, her enthusiasm occasionally overflowing. She became The Monster, almost immediately shortened to Monster. Monster became the Long-Island-inflected Monsta. Monsta became Monstie, then Monstro, and the abbreviated Stro, beefing slightly back up to Strollie, a more mellifluous variation. From Monster to Strollie? No matter. Dani basks in the singularity her name confers.

How Noah became Caveman? Or Andrew Mailman? Take one little boy with a Mohawk for whom talking over others was his preferred mode of communication. And another who insisted on flinging whiffle balls over the fence into the post office parking lot. One's boorish behavior suggested a prehistoric moniker. Watching the balls roll around under the mail delivery trucks gave birth to the other.

Some nicknames are clunky and clamor to be changed. The Pali-Cat years saw two Mackenzies on the squad. One became Mac G, the other Mac H, differentiating them by the initials of their last names. Compromised from conception, they were awkward to cheer for (Go Mac HHHHH! Nice shot, Mac GEEEE! Nah). It was Dori and her teammates who ultimately and organically converted to Howie (Mac H's last name being Howe) and G for Mac G. Short sweet, easy. Go Howie! Go G! Makes sense.

A nickname can serve a higher calling. It can be transformative, liberating inner forces to roam free. On Evan's White Tigers, Alex was most definitely not a Secret Weapon. As Alex, he exhibited intermittent skill and occasional interest, but as the stealthy and lethal Secret Weapon, he had a mission, and that mission was to kick the ball in the goal. You could read in Clay's eyes that there was something he wanted to say. But when questioned, he'd retreat, silently swallow the thought, and quickly look away. As The General, Clay met your gaze with a knowing smile before charging off with his friends. Could a nickname confer that much power? Ask the General. He'd be happy to give you an answer.

Sophomore year of college I took American Diplomatic History with Professor Gaddis Smith. I loved the course, a one-semester jaunt from the XYZ Affair through the Treaty of Versailles. Weekly five-page papers were a nuisance but I acquitted myself fairly well, receiving anodyne comments like "Nice job" and "Well argued." And then I got a paper back with a veritable screed scrawled across the title page.

"The NUBILE American Republic??? A nation cannot be nubile. Invest in a dictionary if you're unsure of your terms!"

I sheepishly snatched my lightly-used Merriam-Webster from the bookshelf...

> nubile *adjective*
>
> : of marriageable condition or age
>
> //nubile young women

Then it hit me. I was referring to our country in its infancy. The word I wanted to use, should have used, was "nascent."

> nascent *adjective*
>
> : coming or having recently come into existence
>
> // a nascent middle class

After my embarrassment-induced nausea subsided, I filed the paper where much of my work went – on the floor. Later that week, with friends over, one happened to pick up the paper and glance at the front page.

"The nubile American republic??? *Nubile?*" Our other pal burst out laughing. "Nubile?" They obviously didn't need the dictionary. In that moment a new nickname was born. Nubile, often shortened to Nubes, followed me around for years. At least the speaker always had a chuckle in his voice when he called to me.

Within reason – and the bounds of good taste – *almost* anything goes when conferring nicknames. Maybe not Shorty or Chubbs, even if employed ironically for tall or skinny athletes. Kids' sensitivities are difficult to predict. Maybe the towering ten-year-old feels insecure about his elevation and that super-slight thirteen-year-old, despite being on a milkshake diet, simply cannot gain weight. If we're trying to motivate, empower or charm the young athlete, staying away from physical characteristics in awarding nicknames would be a wise idea.

But for the most part, when bestowed with affection, humor and understanding, kids love nicknames. They make them feel bigger than themselves. Appreciated. Seen. What could be more important than that?

CHAPTER TWENTY

Bringin' It All Back Home

And you thought it was as easy as buying a pair of sneakers and showing up at the field. In the good old days of taking off on your bike, choosing sides for a pickup game and racing in the door just before the dinner plates hit the table, it was. These days, with a cornucopia of sports and leagues, each requiring specific skills, equipment, time commitments and cash, and all of them hyped or trashed by coaches, friends and neighbors, even selecting the appropriate athletic shoe (sneakers are gone) can trigger a migraine. (Might be time to add a sports psychologist to your speed dial.)

There's no guarantee that the long and winding road of youth sports opens onto a billowing horizon. Even the smoothest of rides can suddenly careen off course, as any athlete who has gone from starter to the bench, fit to injured, or thriving to flailing, can attest. As the engines of our child's experience for so many years, we are doomed to make mistakes. But on balance – the key word – if we center our

311

attention on the little voice in our head, odds are good that we'll navigate a happier path. That inner voice is the real road map, the key to keeping our kids and our family heading in a positive direction.

It's an endless – at times, positively Sisyphean – quest to correlate our child's stage of development with his level of athletic acumen. The focus changes through the years. Early on, we have to monitor the value of his programs. As he gets older, our job is to step back and encourage him to take the initiative. We want him to fall in love with sports – all sports, any sport – and to follow that path wherever it leads him. (If it leads him, however, from soccer in the morning to basketball sixty miles away after lunch to flag football and another long ride before dinner – and repeats that every week – maybe we need to call a timeout. Not sure this road to excess is going to lead to wisdom. More like injury and burnout, for him and for you.)

Key to making these decisions is being attuned to your child's mode of communication. Is she a drama queen or a brooder? Does she go all rock-star-destroying-Vegas-hotel-room or does she retreat to her bed frowning, shoulders slumped? On practice days, is she kicking up sparks of resistance as you drag her toward the car, only to have her fly into her circle of friends at the field? Maybe her protestations reveal anxiety, rather than disenchantment or activity fatigue. Or maybe she's donning a brave face to save face and knowing how much you want her to participate, she feels boxed in, forced to surrender. How can we know which it is?

"Talk less. Smile more." To this advice, given by *Hamilton*'s Aaron Burr, I'd add "…and listen always." We can glean more from supportive silence than we can by questioning and probing, which can slide into badgering and nagging, and provoke grunts and grudges from the other side.

You might show up at his door, car keys in hand, and find him lying on his bed. "Can I not go tonight? I need a break."

"Are you feeling okay?"

"I'm kinda tired."

"Does anything hurt?" (Now you're giving him an opening, probably should skip that question…unless he offers…)

"No. I just need a break tonight."

If you haven't noticed any larger stirrings, trouble on the team or with the coach, you could stop here, and, depending on junior's age, one of you contact the coach. The parenting adage "better to end a playdate five minutes too early than five minutes too late" acknowledges that an excess of a good thing often ends in screaming and tears. Same with this conversation. If you can disengage with "OK, honey, you'll go next time, right?" and leave on his gratefully nodding head, bravo. However, if you insist on adding five more minutes to this "playdate," welcome to hell…

"…But you made a commitment to the team. What if everyone else suddenly decided to take the night off?"

"It's one night. And lots of kids don't show up for practice. It's no big deal!"

Here's a preview of your unfortunate next missteps: "I don't believe other kids aren't showing up for practice," or worse, "I don't care what other parents are letting their kids do. You made a commitment," or the final, nonsensical version of sez who, sez me, "And it *is* a big deal."

As this spins round and round, with tensions rising and positions hardening, a wall rises out of the floor between you. You're translating his resistance as criticism of your parenting. He's lashing out, protecting himself with his limited arsenal. This battle of wills congeals into a stalemate.

As parents, we've invested an ungodly amount of time, energy, and emotion into our kid's journey, but that's just what it is: *his* journey. We surely know what's best for him, or at least we think we do. But the sooner we accept that on this ride we're the passengers, not behind the wheel, the happier all of us will be. Rather than battle to a grudging standoff, wiser would be to grant the one-night pass and stay tuned to see if this is a one-off or the beginning of a trend.

Empower your child to make certain decisions on his own terms. It might be devastating when your twelve-year-old star striker announces at the dinner table, "I'm over soccer. I want to try lacrosse." Your brain may scream, "Quit? Now? After all we've invested in this?" But, honestly, beyond the shock, what's so bad? He explores another interest that takes him in a different direction, maybe even to something – or many things – he enjoys even more? If he can't explore now, when can he?

Childhood is defined by change. From the molecular to the structural to the intellectual, our kids are growing at an exponential, if imperceptible, rate. Line up their school photos from kindergarten to senior year. Early on the changes are subtle, mostly marked by haircuts and missing teeth. Around adolescence, hormones ignite like rocket fuel, triggering physical and emotional explosions that overnight transform your sweet baby into an unrecognizable intruder living just down the hall. By the graduation shot, the skin is smooth again, the features all seem to fit on the same face, and the upward gaze of future promise completes this arc of maturation.

Growing up, Evan flitted between soccer and lacrosse, with a pit stop on the football field. Concurrently, he was mad for shells, then tropical fish, and on the cusp of puberty, he tried out airsoft and paintball. As his artistic sensibility blossomed, graffiti painting became his rage. (Thankfully we had a bare concrete wall he could use as his canvas.) During college, he arrived at music, which claims his attention to this day.

As parents, we need to resist the expectation (that word again!) that the activity of the moment will inform the rest of our kid's life. Rare is the child whose passion at five roars on undiminished into adulthood. Sudden lane changes and screeching stops are not just lurches we get over when they're learning to drive; this is life's highway. We need to buckle up and forge ahead.

Just as the best coaches encourage their players to experiment and learn from their mistakes, we shouldn't shrink from messing up a few times either. Perfection is not an option; "OK" is the bar we need to reach. I can remember a few instances when I've either pushed a little too hard or stepped back a little too far. But over the course of my involvement with youth sports, I'm satisfied that I've scored more than I've whiffed.

My ten-year window of experiencing sports with my kids has closed. Their "careers" in youth sports now consist of drawers full of medals, team pictures hanging on the wall, and friends and memories they will carry with them always. I am happy to report that all three are happy, constantly-adjusting, working-toward-thriving young adults. Evan entertained the notion of college lacrosse, but showed up for tryouts unfocused and out of shape. He lasted through a few cuts before putting his stick away for good. Ultimately, that same crazy energy he brought to soccer he devoted to music, with more control and less volatility as maturity sanded down some of the rough edges.

Dori's club soccer career ended when Jillian quit for her. She continued to play through high school and competed on coed intra-mural teams through college. What she loved about the recreational side was its lack of coaching and stretching, never her forte. The game was the thing, and it's what drew her and her teammates to the field each week.

Griffie stuck with club the longest, aging out after the U19 season. For a few years, he'd been itching to retire but Evan's "Stay gold, Ponyboy" pep talk, emphasizing Griffie's dwindling chances to play organized sports, resonated. Griffie stayed in and went out on a high note.

I believe that, ultimately, all of my kids played for the love of the game, bonding with friends and family, and the exhilaration of exercise. None of them felt the urge to play competitively beyond high school, yet I think they all would consider their experiences to have been complete and regret-free.

I've tried to follow the advice that I give to the coaches I instruct and my team parents: keep it light, keep it moving, and keep it in perspective. Focus on fun and fulfillment; the rest will come. After experiencing the good, the bad and the ugly of youth sports, I have a greater appreciation for the simple.

For my family, my friends, and the thousands of kids that I've had the honor of working with through the years, it has been a joy. I miss it now that it's over. I now understand what my friends whose kids wrapped up before mine were saying when they lamented their weekends devoid of driving, bad food, and emotion-packed games. It's more bittersweet than you might imagine. People joke that I'm going to have to adopt a crop of young kids to keep my Saturdays and Sundays alive.

The lessons we learn in youth sports are life lessons. One by one, bit by bit, we come to know our essential selves. It's difficult to see when our kid is struggling to make the team, or his team isn't winning, or he's not growing as quickly as his friends, or…or…or a million other things that cloud our vision. But each of these scenarios has the capacity to show us how to be more patient and balanced, more accepting of disappointment and more able to handle growth and success. The values that guide us through the rough patches will see us through the rest of our lives, and help our children become the happy, healthy adults we want them to be.

The Epiphany

It began with a ball and a boy and a desire to do what his siblings were doing – playing soccer. Flash forward to the moment baby Griffie, then eighteen, was about to hang up his cleats. Beginning in U6, his career stretched through AYSO, club and school, and in three days, the long and winding road that had defined much of his youth would come to an end. His club team was headed to Las Vegas for a last tournament hurrah.

Comprised primarily of boys from the Westside, teammates also hailed from the Valley, East LA, and Torrance. What they had in common was a deep commitment to the sport and to each other. Most of these boys had played together for the better part of a decade. They'd experienced victory and defeat, endured capricious refs and rowdy parents, and watched injuries and retirements ravage the squad. They went to Vegas with no expectations. Winning was unimportant, losing mattered even less. Their sole goal was to have fun.

Four games and forty-eight hours later, they'd had so much more than that. Exuding unalloyed joy, and unburdened by the pressure to succeed, they performed with a giddy abandon that produced their most inspired play in years. Goalies played forward, forwards played defense, everyone got a chance to play where he wanted. The bench, customarily a seat of gnawing anxiety and festering frustrations, was a sea of smiles and conviviality. The other teams, hunkered and serious, were shaken by the boys' jocularity and creative flair.

When the last whistle blew, the boys lingered on the field. They wanted the game, the weekend, the moment, to stretch into forever. Right then, a truth that had eluded me during two decades of coaching and managing and living for the sport finally revealed itself...

As little kids, they couldn't wait to play sports. Any sport. Every sport. Yet from the moment they landed on a team, with a coach, and the expectation to learn and perform, and, if good, to be better, and if better, to be great... From the moment parents began coming to games and cheering too loudly or critiquing in the car... From the moment they had to choose between a game and a birthday party, or a trip, or a vacation... From the moment they had to go to practice when they were tired, or had homework, or just didn't feel like it... From the moment winning became a thing, and the game turned into a job, a responsibility, an obligation... From the accumulation of all these moments, little by little, year after year, the boys found themselves further and further away from the joy that sparked their entry into the game.

Here, for a magical time warp of a weekend, all of that was gone. There were no expectations, no demands, and no pressure. The freedom to play for no one but themselves and their teammates allowed them to rediscover the wonder and innocence of sports. The irony that they had tasted this bliss at the end of their run only added to its power and poignancy.

The boys hugged and high-fived and headed home, transformed and grateful. What Griffie and his teammates expressed, what they wished for those just starting out, or for those further along in their journey, was to have the opportunity of a moment like this. What I wished for was a way to dial back the stakes and the gravity that diminish youth sports, and to reclaim the pure and easy joy of kids with a ball and a love of the game.

CHAPTER TWENTY-ONE

A Lagniappe for the Survivors

lagniappe [lan yap]
Noun *North American*
something given as a bonus or extra gift

You've made it this far, hopefully buoyed by this distillation of my twenty years in the trenches of youth sports. One of my joys throughout was crafting recaps of games and tournaments. This started as lengthy Sunday night emails to the Pali Xtreme families. It wasn't until Dori and her Pali-Cats first took the field in Santa Ynez that I formalized these memos into "The Kitty Litter." I'd sometimes put double-digit hours into writing and shaping them, making sure each player got a shout-out for her contribution. I loved doing it, and my audience eagerly gobbled up these posts, but after three years, with the pressure of making them unique and compelling, I hit the wall. (How many different ways can a shot on goal be described? After about thirty, I was tapped out.) Somehow I continued the tradition through Griffie's All-Star years and with diminishing frequency, through all three kids' careers in high school.

Besides a recitation of the facts (who scored, who assisted, who made the game-saving stops on defense), the challenge was to replicate the emotions that drove the players and thrilled the parents in the stands. I composed this "lagniappe" detailing the CIF quarterfinal game Griffie's senior year at Brentwood. It commemorates the most exciting moment I experienced in my years as part of the game. Definitely in the top five.

Traffic on the 10 crept along at such a petty pace that had we not given ourselves two hours for what should have been a forty-minute drive, our stress level would have been through the sunroof. Last year the drive out to Diamond Ranch for the first-round playoff game was similarly excruciating, and with the team bus missing the exit, the boys arrived ten minutes before game time. Butts sore from hours of sitting, and legs cramped from an insufficient warm-up encountered a loose and limber opponent that ran Griffie and his teammates off the field, and all the way back to Brentwood.

This year promised a different outcome. With a new, hugely respected coach and an upper-class-heavy lineup, optimism ran high as the squad headed out to Wilson High School for the quarterfinals. Parents who'd cut the drive a little close were still getting settled at kickoff, but despite the long slog, it was a confident corps gathered to see the Eagles advance to the semifinals for the first time since Evan's senior campaign, seven years before. Regret from that contest lingers to this day, as Brentwood missed two completely wide open nets in the first five minutes of the game and ended up losing 1-0 in overtime. But the current version of the team was riding a high of invincibility and Wilson was going to be another notch on their belt on the way to a championship ring.

Unfortunately, no one had sent Wilson the script. They burst out of the gate and nicked the Brentwood side for a goal in the first two minutes of play. Quickly surrendering two more, the Brentwood boys were rescued from total collapse by the halftime whistle. The faithful in the stands were shaken. Parents, siblings, grandparents, even school officials who, only an hour before were soaring with possibility, were now reeling, crushed. We ached for our kids, and yes, for ourselves, as well. Losing, ever-present in any contest, had been banished to the periphery of possibility. It came roaring back and hovered in the cold, overcast February evening, taunting us. The next forty minutes would provide ample opportunity to fish for soothing, if hollow, words of comfort for our sons.

Strange thing, though; there was a different look to the same boys who lined up for the second half kickoff. It began slowly, a double team tackling away the ball, a tightening midfield forcing a turnover, a settling of the defense as they crisply pinged the ball around. And then Andy came up with the ball and kicked into gear. Fending off defenders as he raced downfield, he scorched a pass to Andrew, who cut it back to his left foot and unleashed a seeing-eye missile deep into the top left corner of the goal.

The boys suddenly grew a few inches taller; a measure of respect had been reclaimed. And moments later, a Scott corner found a Nyman head and it was now 2-3. The home side of the stadium stopped breathing as if they knew what was coming. Our Eagles didn't disappoint. Another Scott corner, this time to Dylan, and it was a whole new ball game, 3-3. Brentwood was back and surging. A fourth goal was imminent.

And then disaster struck. The second half, which had become a festival of yellow cards, suddenly caught Ryan in its sights. His second yellow sent him to the stands with fifteen minutes remaining. Wilson smelled blood, but Brentwood closed ranks and took the game to them. We had chances, far more than they, but both teams' goals seemed to be closed to business for the duration. The whistle blew. An amazing game was about to become legendary...

The first overtime period continued the Brentwood advance. Yet after ten minutes, no golden goal. The start of the second OT nearly settled the deal. Nyman put the game on his back and sliced into the Wildcats' viscera, first veering to his left, then changing fields and lunging right. Sheer will got him to the edge of the box where he uncorked a blinder that whistled through the night and forced the keeper to the limits of his athleticism to pop it out.

More excitement, more thrills, more almosts . . . but moments later it was kicks from the mark, the most painful and unforgiving method of resolving what one hundred minutes of hard-fought, will-testing, lung-bursting battle couldn't. From the stands, Calahan the Elder screamed to the boys, "You've already won, there's no pressure boys, you've already won!" We all wished that CIF would take that cry for the official outcome.

Drew bounced in the mouth of the goal and slapped the crossbar defiantly. He dove to his right, guessing perfectly, but the Wilson shooter angled the ball just beyond his reach.

Noah marched up, stared at the ball, and with ice in his veins, slotted it home.

From the stands, it looked as if Drew stole the read from the second Wilson player's eyes before confidently dropping down to cradle the ball. Yes!

With a lilt in his step and a smile on his face, Scott stepped up. He had no doubt and neither did we.

Down 2-1, the next Wilson shooter set the ball on the spot. Drew was ready again, but no one saw this rocket as the back of the net fielded the ball.

Steven, who had played most of the game on one leg, his other awkwardly arced like it had been riding a horse for the past two hours, hobbled up to the mark. Anxiety roiled the Brentwood faithful. But Steven knew himself and never wavered. Brentwood 3-Wilson 2.

The next two shots had the crowd on both sides screaming. The Wilson shooter caught the crossbar and the ball bounced out. But the ref on the goal line signaled that it had gone over the line before the backspin sent it back onto the field. Dylan hit a near copycat shot but it was signaled, no go. 3-3.

The last Wilson shooter took his place. Drew had him the whole way, pushing his ball to safety.

When Nyman stepped up with the season on the line, it was almost too much to believe . . .

. . . and seconds later!@#$#@!!#$!#!!!! Wow.

As the ball whistled into the back of the net, the sea of Brentwood warriors and coaches streamed from midfield toward the corner where they dogpiled the delirious Nyman and Drew. In the stands, crushing hugs and whoops of joy were shared by the disbelieving believers, whose smiles were so wide, faces nearly split in half. Tommy Goldstein, frozen like an icicle, instantly thawed. Mark Calahan, still in his sunglasses, came roaring down the bleacher walkway and clapped a high-five on me that had my hand throbbing like a cartoon character who'd just caught a falling anvil. If the most precise GPS had directed us to this intersection of the improbable and the illogical, we would surely have missed the exit.

The emotional G forces we pulled left us dazzled and dazed . . . and hungry for more. Everyone on our sideline squished into a room at a Chinese restaurant in Monterey Park for a celebratory dinner. The heart-stopping, adrenaline-surging, larynx-shredding power of the victory, its validation of every sports cliché in the canon, and the shared realization that no one wanted this moment to end, impelled us to tempt fate and have our victory party two games early. Spirits were sky high, even as a layer of disbelief and what-the-hell-just-happened hovered above the room.

Before the toasts and the pats on the back, though, we had to leave the field. Our feet barely touching the ground as we approached the gate, we saw the Wilson team's parents lined up, a gauntlet we had to pass through. Each of them, through their tears and shattered dreams, congratulated our contingent on a tremendous game. This display of sportsmanship at such a heartbreaking moment was both unexpected and inspirational.

Two truths from that evening remain as vivid to me today as they were that night: sports have the power to exalt, and heartfelt sportsmanship ennobles us all.

It's Another Corona Sunrise

"This Corona virus has affected me by not only
canceling school, and keeping me from my friends,
but also taking away what I love most, sports."
– *Andrew, 11*

Marcy and I were late. It shouldn't have been a big deal, Coach Bryan was helming today, but I was holding the player ID cards needed to check in the team. Without the cards, the team faced a forfeit. As Marcy pulled into the lot, I exploded out of the car and flew toward the field. I saw the teams in position, somehow ready to go, so I slowed down to watch. On the kickoff, the other team pounded a high looping ball down the field. Goalie Jordan raced off his line to snare it but he misjudged its flight. The ball bounced at his feet, leapfrogged over his head and skipped into the goal. Three seconds in and we were already trailing, 1-0.

I always hated 8 a.m. games.

An inauspicious opening, to be sure. But moments later, Evan left-footed a rocket past the other team's keeper. That tied the score, but . . . wait a second . . . why was Evan even playing? Coach Bryan didn't coach Evan. He coached Griffie and Jordan, both six years younger. But Jordan wasn't on that team either. He and Griffie didn't become teammates until club, years later. Something wasn't right.

Then it hit me. You know that moment in the middle of a dream when you realize that's where you are?

In the weeks since the sporting world had turned off the lights and gone home in mid-March, I've had this dream over and over. I now recognize where I am pretty quickly and I don't stress about the player cards. I'm happy that Evan is playing with Jordan and Griffie. If only I could wake up in that world.

It wasn't until the NBA floated playing games in empty arenas that the seriousness of the Corona pandemic cracked the national indifference. Public health officials had been shouting into an unplugged microphone since late January, yet all through February, while politicians and the media argued the legitimacy and imminence of the threat, the rest of us went about our business.

In Kid Land that meant carpool, school, practice, dinner, homework, get up and do it all over again. Spring, the season of renewal and endless possibility, was knocking on the door and baseball, softball, lacrosse, track, and swimming were primed to answer the call. March Madness was a fluttering heartbeat away. It was the best time to be playing and an even better time to be a fan.

Talk about an emotional afternoon. In three hectic hours, Ryan, a senior on the baseball team at Crossroads School in Santa Monica, learned that his school was closing, the NBA was shutting down, and Tom Hanks had the Covid-19 virus. Peering out the window on the bus ride to crosstown rival Campbell Hall, he could see long lines stretching out the door and into the parking lots of supermarkets he passed. *This must be what the Apocalypse looks like,* Ryan thought. But the worst was yet to come.

The empty stadium gambit didn't gain much traction and it wasn't because LeBron James announced his resistance. European soccer stars were testing positive and then two members of the New Orleans Pelicans revealed their diagnosis. The rest of the dominoes rapidly tumbled. Professional soccer, then Major League Baseball and the National Hockey League suspended their seasons. Once the NCAA canceled March Madness, there was no pretending anymore.

By the end of March, virtually the entire U.S. was shuttered, sports and all. Schools had sent their kids home, originally for an extended Spring Break, but when April dawned, students were ordered to stay there, with their classes resumed remotely.

Technology to the Rescue

Kids logged on from their dining room tables to teachers who were standing in their breakfast nooks. Both sides were unnerved, interacting with a screen that resembled *The Brady Bunch* theme song on steroids. Some schools maintained a rigorous routine of classwork and testing while others offered the equivalent of online study hall. Parents who fretted over the amount of time their kids were perched in front of a screen now fought to make sure their kids showed up for "class."

The desire to normalize the abnormal was an all hands on deck operation and every department was pressed into service. Math and history transitioned easily, but squeezing much more out of Physical Education than jumping jacks and burpees for kids stranded in their living rooms tested the creativity of coaches. Coach Rio characterized it this way: "Trying to teach PE on Zoom is like trying to paddle a canoe with a tennis racket. You can go through the motions but it's going to take you a lot longer to get to the same place."

As difficult as it was to focus on school while sheltering at home, for many kids the absence of sports was a harsher reality. Once the pros shut down, youth sports fizzled faster than a drop of water on a New York City sidewalk in summer. There was little warning and no goodbyes. An email saying "we're suspending activities effective immediately" circulated, and in an instant, fields, gyms, parks and pools popped an Ambien and descended into a deep doze.

The shock decimated the players.

Eleven-year-old Oren tells it this way: "Lacrosse practice had been canceled all week because of cold, rainy weather. My brother Andrew and I were looking forward to our game on Saturday. Thursday, it all went away."

Twin brother Andrew continues: "When I received the news, my heart sank to my stomach. Sports were my favorite moments of life. I felt furious and depressed. I was losing everything that I loved."

The sense of loss was compounded by the sudden separation from teammates. Relationships that were forged over time, and bonded by hard work and goofing around, were suddenly put on hold. Ashley, a high school junior playing up a year in club soccer, lamented that she would no longer get to play with her graduating teammates.

While rehabbing his pitching arm after elbow surgery in the fall, Ryan still saw game time as a designated hitter. He was having his best season, in nine games batting over .400. Still, on this day in March, his world seemed to be shrinking around him. Best friend Jeremy, with whom he'd played ball since they were four, seemed oblivious to the ramifications of the Covid-19 closures. He couldn't foresee a

Zoom-conference Senior Day or a backyard Signing Ceremony. No final team party? Was that even a possibility? In the seventh inning, as they were waiting on deck, Ryan turned to Jeremy.

"Ya know, we've been on the same teams for fourteen years. This is probably our last game together ever." That got Jeremy's attention.

For younger kids, years away from Ryan and Jeremy's final curtain, the sudden separation from their teammates proved difficult to process. Mom Amy relates the feelings of Griffin, 10, and Molly, 7. "What they have missed most, without a doubt, is the camaraderie of being on a team. Nothing can compare to the feeling of being in the dugout, chanting their songs and stuffing handfuls of Big League chew in their mouths. Not having the face-to-face contact and being with the team has been challenging."

The indefinite demise of personal interaction wore on parents as well, even those who initially cheered the return of scheduling sanity to their lives.

Melissa, a mom of three club-soccer-playing sons, noted, "We're now having dinner every night as a family. If this was a normal weekend, we'd be off in different directions. But I miss the community of the teams."

Baseball parent Heather adds, "Since Henry plays year-round, we have never had a break for this long. He misses his teammates, and I miss the parent camaraderie. The upside is not having to wake up at the crack of dawn on weekends, but we wander around the house wishing for a game!"

Few sports celebrate a rite of passage as uniquely as baseball. Every summer, more than 1,300 teams of twelve-year-olds – that's over 17,000 kids – descend on the sleepy hamlet of Cooperstown, New York, home of the Major League Baseball Hall of Fame, for a week-long tournament. For many, this marks the end of their baseball careers. For all, it's a highlight of their childhood. This year, the tournament was canceled.

Leagues and clubs were ambushed by the sudden suspension of sports, but after a moment of stomach-clenching free fall, they mobilized to care for their constituents and ensure their own survival.

For Coach Corinne, my successor as Region 69 Coach Administrator, mid-March was prime time. The EXTRA and All-Star tournament season was in full swing, with teams training twice a week and tournaments beckoning every weekend. Spring League, a leisurely, closer-to-home enterprise, stoked the enthusiasm of the pre-tournament set.

Determined not to let the Covid-19 blackout turn into an extinction event, Corinne and her coaches launched a weekly schedule of group interactions filled with YouTube skills videos, relay races, footwork and juggling contests, remote get-togethers, and a Video of the Week. The older players received tactical sessions to enhance their game IQ, while the Spring League juniors sprinkled frivolity into their conferences. What U8 girls team wouldn't be giggling uncontrollably as each member took turns adding a word to a lengthening hypothetical handle like "The Diamond Sparkler Dream Team That Likes Spicy Waffles"? Keeping it light meant keeping it fun.

"The delivery system has changed but it doesn't mean the principles are different." Corinne nailed it.

With competitions mothballed, and everything from tryouts to college recruiting put on ice, club and travel coaches, like their colleagues in every interrupted sport, tacked to technology. Zoom, Band, V Loop, Huddle and an expanding host of group conferencing apps became the sinew that held entire programs together.

Tim, Evan and Griffie's former coach, and the LA Breakers' Director of Coaching for Boys, always pined for the opportunity to do film sessions. But in seasons wall-to-wall with training and competitions, there was little opportunity. Here was his opening. He steered his younger boys to a Barcelona match, assigning them the task of counting and analyzing Lionel Messi's touches. His older players found much to dissect in videos of their own performances, too.

Across town at Santa Monica United, Christian convened weekly chats with each of his players, then customized practice plans for them based on their field position and skill needs. He described it as "doing private lessons with every kid on the team." It was no less work than he was used to in normal times, but the commute was a whole lot better.

Additionally, he delved into a conversation that is too frequently glossed over in the hectic pace of an ongoing season – preparation. Sleep, diet, warm-up and recovery. Christian directed his team to compile a weekly food log, correlating what they consumed with how they felt later or the next day. Same thing with sleep. How many hours did they get and how alert were they afterward. Always a stickler for a sound warm-up, Christian appended his knee-saving exercises onto every session, while educating the players on proper post-training and game-day icing, plus the use of a foam roller to knead out knots and spasms. He calculated that getting the players acclimated to these habits now would serve them well once play resumed.

Some kids ardently adapted to this mode of connection. They looked forward to the meetings, the extra skill challenges and the personalized programs. Others didn't see the point of training with no games at the end of the rainbow. This at-home version of team life effectively separated those who were passionate from those whose commitment was more casual. This was hardly a bad thing – sports are for everyone regardless of why they play. But for the more competitive parents with the less driven kids, Corona Valley was an even unhappier place to live.

The Billion-Dollar Questions

It's difficult to see the light at the end of the tunnel when that tunnel is sealed up with concrete. That's what it feels like when attempting to predict a return to sports and project what that return will look like. Until there is a vaccine or the no-gain-without-unconscionable-pain herd immunity, there will always be a measure of risk in resuming team activities. Masks, gloves, thermometers, and on-site rapid testing, will become as commonplace as bats and balls. The timetable will be determined more by science than politics, as schools, leagues and parents will be moved first and foremost by the safety of their players.

Even in the fog, though, we can see the landscape changing. In mid-April, U.S. Soccer's Development Academy, considered the pinnacle for competitive youth soccer, with hundreds of elite teams across the country, permanently closed its doors. The ensuing frenzy of marquee teams suddenly without a league sparked a top-down reshuffling of the pay-to-play soccer world, the ramifications of which will be revealed over time.

No organizations or clubs saw this coming, so there were few contingency plans in place. Many are secure enough to ride this out, albeit with some discomfort. Others, with budgets that barely limp to the finish line of the fiscal year, look to the future through a hazy lens. With cash flow constricted or evaporated entirely, many are straining to pay their coaches, who in turn are dealing with their own financial deprivation.

Some are sneaking off to do lessons in backyards or empty parks. Others utilize the conferencing apps to connect with kids whose parents will pay a premium to keep them off the couch an hour longer. Tennis, golf and baseball instructors report record bookings, as their trades can be plied with only mild adjustments. But for the majority of coaches, the longer this lasts, the more they will be hustling to find other options. Will they or their teams still be around when the ban is lifted? How many organizations, recreational or club, will survive this period? Casualties are a certainty.

There is one incontrovertible fact: youth sports will survive.

Some sports lend themselves more readily to the new world order. An argument can be made for tennis, golf, and swimming emerging first. As they're focused on the individual, the elements of the game that involve closer contact with opponents, staff or equipment can be modified without losing the essence of the activity.

With adjustments, baseball could also foresee a timely return. Soccer, basketball, football, wrestling, volleyball and water polo will be more problematical as we won't be banging bodies or dripping sweat on each other any time soon.

For AYSO, Corinne foresees a hybrid with a gradual rollout. Small groups working on dribbling, passing, shooting, moving without the ball and positional play. When it comes to games, small-sided contests – 3 v 3, 5 v 5 – with distancing and amended rules for contact may be the baby steps toward a complete comeback.

The availability of field space, a critical issue for many programs in the best of times, will loom even larger when the "all clear" is sounded. Practice fields churning with teams shoehorned into tight spaces? Gone the way of the high five. Each time slot will feature fewer teams spread across more real estate, something coaches have been coveting for years. That is, if the programs can provide it. A not inconsiderable "if."

Crowded conditions at soccer tournament fields will also have to be reconsidered. One of the quirks of the Riverside Locomotion tournament was the claustrophobic proximity of the side-by-side fields, where parents standing next to each other are yelling at referees in two different games.

Once sports are allowed to come back, though, more than their technical aspects will be altered. Pre-hiatus, the family unit was stretched to its limit with competing schedules, meals on the run, and texting replacing conversation as the main mode of communication. Parents have now reassumed primacy in their children's day-to-day world. How will this play out when the restrictions are lifted?

In "Reimagining Youth Sports in a Post-COVID-19 World,"[1] Changing the Game Project's John O'Sullivan details the factors that parents will consider when the youth sports universe opens back up:

1. We just had family dinners night after night for the first time in years. I want my kids to go back to playing sports, but do we really want to be running around with our heads cut off 7 nights a week?

2. My child is feeling healthy and well rested for the first time in years because he/she had some time off. Perhaps we should cut back a bit on the number of sports practices and training load.

---

1 John O'Sullivan, "Reimagining Youth Sports in a Post-COVID-19 World," Changing the Game Project (April 14, 2020)

3. My child is enjoying the time off and pursuing other passions. He/she is also getting better practicing on his/her own for the first time, or playing unorganized sports with siblings.

4. This has been a tough hit financially for our family. Perhaps there is a better, less expensive local sports option.

5. We already live in an area with millions of people, why do we need to travel by bus and plane to get games when we can get plenty of games close by?

6. The virus has settled down in our area, but not in other places. I am not sending my child to play games against teams where the virus is not under control.

Scheduling, finances, and travel are just some of the variables we took for granted. Perspective and sanity barely made the list. Might we see a renaissance of thoughtfulness and reflection in the rendering of post-Covid youth sports?

A healthy cohort of parents may be reluctant to relinquish slower-paced evenings centered on the dinner table to leap back into the sports rat race. Questioned will be the trade-off of driving an hour each way for a game when there's an option at a field five minutes away. And after draining financial reserves or living close to the edge for so many months, will shelling out $3,000+ dollars for club programs seem like a good idea? Everything will be on the table: length of seasons, numbers of practices and games, composition of rosters, you name it.

Just as the past few years have witnessed a migration of families from local recreational programs to the more competitive club and travel variety, will we see the tide wash back the other way? It's a distinct possibility. Whether it can be sustained will depend on the YMCAs and recreation centers, the atrophied former foundations of the youth sports universe, proving themselves viable and worthy.

During these Corona days, we've sacrificed the thrill of competition, the adventure of travel and the supportive comfort of friends. What we've received in return is time. Time to slow down, time to appreciate, time to do other things, time to reassess, even time to be bored. And what modern kid has the tools to deal with that?

In recreational terms, there's been another tangible benefit:

"One of the positive, unintended consequences of this pandemic may be the return of free play, which had essentially died in America. But now, without the hectic schedule of organized sports, we're anecdotally hearing of more kids and families enjoying outside play on their own terms."[2] Taking a step back to move forward? Wouldn't that be nice?

This virus has wrought dislocation and suffering in our daily lives and in the world at large. What it has proved unsuccessful in fracturing or obliterating are the friendships among teammates and the abiding bonds of community. Those have only grown stronger, deeper and more resilient. When we're finally released from this nightmare, what will we rush back to and reclaim first? Our friends.

Here's my hope: The fog of pandemic clears, we head back to our lives, and once again the chirping of kids on fields becomes the soundtrack of our weekends. In this rebirth, we find a new appreciation for what we've missed. And maybe, while we're still reflecting on the blessing that we've come out of these unsettling days in one piece, we can approach our roles as parents and coaches with renewed wonder and fewer expectations – and just be happy our kids are outside playing again.

---

2 Jon Solomon, Editorial Director, Sports & Society Program, The Aspen Institute's Project Play, Webinar, April 29, 2020

Acknowledgments

This book has been banging around inside my head for years. Freeing it to live on its own required the assistance and encouragement of a host of believers to whom I owe a debt of gratitude. Attempting to name them all would take another volume, but let this be a start.

My light, my partner, my wife, Marcy, captured my heart seventeen years before either of us knew it, and has been holding it dear ever since. My miraculous children, Evan, Dori and Griffie, gifted me with their love and graciously allowed me to grow up with them. Brady and Reggie, canines supreme, were at my side for every word. Family, this is all your fault.

Abby Adams, sensing a book in the Coach Steve kiddie classes, contributed the ball-curious title. David Rotman, the Johnny Appleseed of karma, embraced the idea so passionately, he directed me to Kuwana Haulsey, who patiently extracted all the strands. Christian Williams, the catcher in the wry, steered me through the gauntlet of publishing. Betsy Spier, Heather Duffy Boylston, Christophe Galland, and Ben Hellwarth helped carry me over the finish line.

Christian Chambers, Tim Pierce and Julio Castillo may have thought they were killing time between practices, not realizing that those endless hours of conversation about soccer and life bound me tighter to the game.

Debbie and Dick Held, Jeff "Coachie" Melvoin, Judi and Richard Firth, Janet Anderson, Bob Ortwin, the late great George Wolfberg, and all the commissioners, coaches, referees, parents and players who joined me on a Region 69 field filled me with purpose and a lifetime of stories.

My coaching colleagues Hadi Morshed, Bryan King, Dan James, Bill Barnum, Sergio Vasquez, David Howard, and Dan Forman fed my hope that the weekends of car rides, forgettable food and match-less matches would never end.

The community of Pythons, Pali/Devil-Cats, Gatorators, Palaxy, Pal Real, B98s, Moms Club, and all the other teams I helmed, managed and cheered for, provided me with spiritual sustenance and cherished friends.

My parents, Betty and Paul Morris, were proud of every television commercial, unproduced screenplay, and soccer weekend I was a part of. They buckled up and came along for the ride. My brother Alan, whose talent I've always been in awe of, delivered a brilliant concept for this cover.

And Jackson Senator, Dylan David, Tommy Mark, and Jack Aronzon, who gave as much as they had for as long as they could, inspire me every day to give nothing less.

About the Author

Steve Morris took a circuitous path to discover his life's mission. After studying history at Yale, producing television commercials around the world, and writing screenplays that adorn his shelf, it was in youth sports that "Coach Steve" became the living, breathing embodiment of falling into something you love. He founded Coast Sports in 1997, and has been operating his successful summer camp for the past twenty years. He resides in Southern California, where he raised three kids with his wife, Marcy.

Join the Conversation Online with Coach Steve

Parents and Coaches,

We invite you to our online community, dedicated to making our kids' years in sports as happy and productive as they can be. Keep the conversation going through our latest blog posts and information about sports parenting, coaching, high school and college athletics, health, fitness, nutrition – frankly, anything youth-sports-related. Sprinkle with humor; we're ready to serve.

Join our mailing list to keep up with events, and arrange for Coach Steve to speak to your team or your school. Contact us through our website **www.whatsizeballs.com** or email **coachstevela@gmail.com**.

We know that youth sports can be a minefield for parents to navigate, and we are here to help you safely and sanely make it through. It's definitely an adventure. Let the fun begin!

Coach Steve